ROBOTS and DRONES

Past, Present, and Future

written by

Mairghread Scott

illustrated by

Jacob Chabot

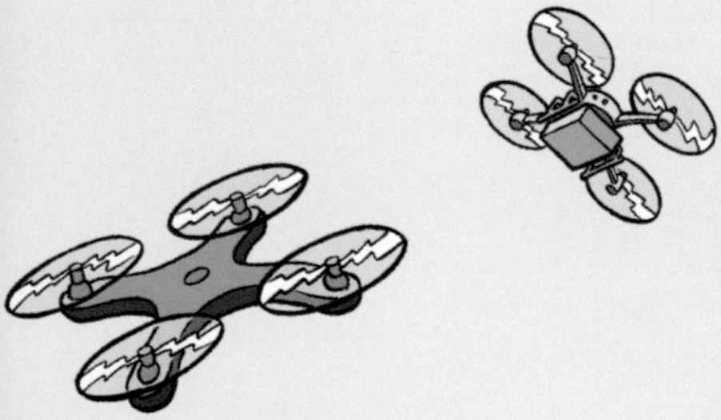

First Second
New York

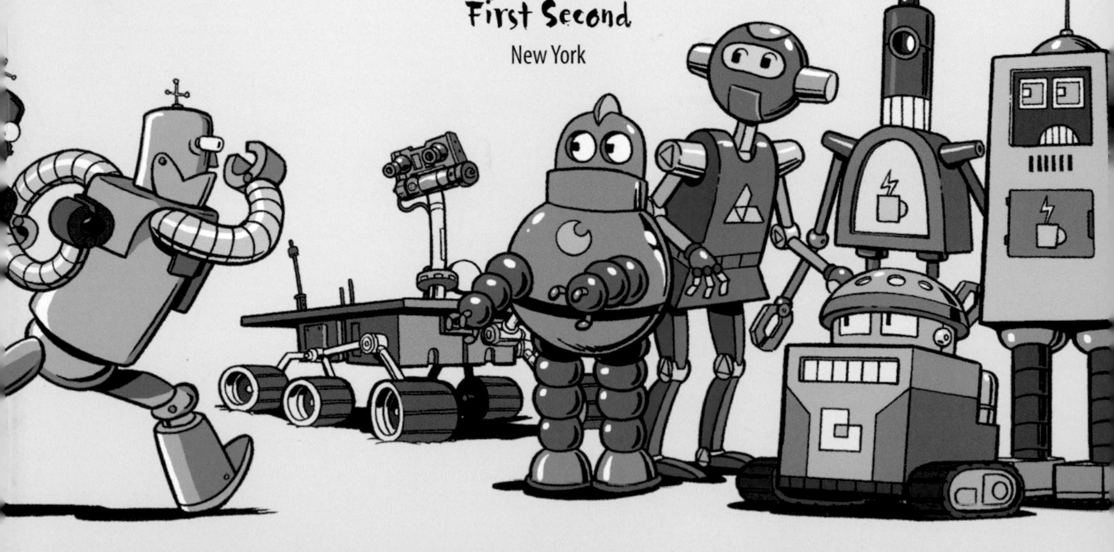

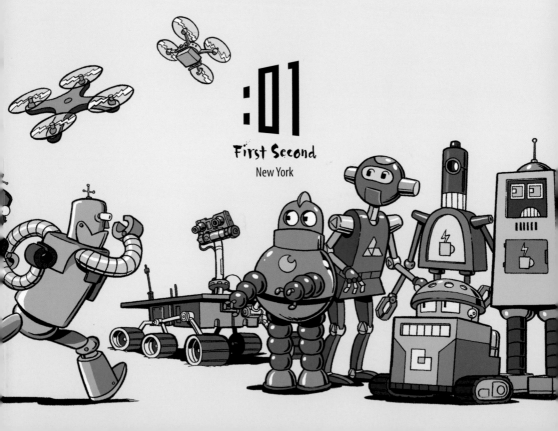

To Jason and Corran. Always.
—M.S.

To all the hardworking robots out there.
—J.C.

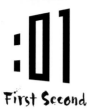

First Second

Text copyright © 2018 by Mairghread Scott
Illustrations copyright © 2018 by Jacob Chabot

Drawn with a 0.5 mm HB lead mechanical pencil and inked with a variety of pens and brushes on Strathmore 100 lb. Smooth Bristol. Colored in Adobe PhotoShop and lettered using Comicrazy font from Comicraft.

Published by First Second
First Second is an imprint of Roaring Brook Press,
a division of Holtzbrinck Publishing Holdings Limited Partnership
120 Broadway, New York, NY 10271
All rights reserved

Library of Congress Control Number: 2017941168

Paperback ISBN: 978-1-62672-792-2
Hardcover ISBN: 978-1-62672-793-9

Our books may be purchased in bulk for promotional, educational, or business use. Please contact your local bookseller or the Macmillan Corporate and Premium Sales Department at (800) 221-7945 ext. 5442 or by email at MacmillanSpecialMarkets@macmillan.com.

First edition, 2018
Series editor: Dave Roman
Book design by Rob Steen and John Green
Color assists by Stephen Mayer
Robotics consultant: James Smith

Printed in China by Toppan Leefung Printing Ltd., Dongguan City, Guangdong Province
Paperback: 20 19 18 17 16 15 14 13 12
Hardcover: 10 9 8 7 6

The book *Robots and Drones: Past, Present, and Future* brings us on a journey from the history of robotics to the very tools that will allow you to build your own robot helpers.

Robots are not new. We've been making simple ones for a long, long time. Just yesterday, I saw a mechanical monk at the Science Museum in London. It was nearly 500 years old! And we've all read about robots or seen them in science fiction stories and movies. They are a big part of our popular culture. My favorite robot movies are *WALL-E*, *Big Hero 6*, and *Robot & Frank*.

Robots are finally becoming a part of our everyday reality and are increasingly useful to society! Robots have the potential to improve the way we work, live, and explore new frontiers. In fact, there are already robots busily exploring Mars!

And there are plenty of tasks that we need help with. In the future, robots could help farmers grow enough food to feed the planet and carebots could help us as we grow old. And right now, smart prosthetics and exoskeletons are helping disabled people walk, and doctors are now using robots to perform surgeries. Let's face it, robots are also just really fun. Have you ever watched a robot soccer match?

As prevalent as they may be, building advanced robots still involves a lot of work. It takes time and effort from designers, engineers, and programmers to align the right components to make a robot that is good at doing even a single simple task. A robot might be good at vacuuming or taking pictures from the sky or driving, but it can't do all these things at once, like us humans. It's still "early days," but robots are getting better and better. Some robots can even learn on their own using machine learning!

Advances in robotics have also led to questions about how we can make sure robots are really helping us. Some people are worried that robots can't be trusted or that they will outperform us. That's why teams around the world—including those made up of ethicists, roboticists, governments, and everyday citizens—are asking questions today about what we want robots to do and not do. This is important because, in the end, we want robots and humans to work together as a team. Robots should be helpers so we can lead better lives.

And we need kids from all backgrounds to join forces so that together we can build the robots of tomorrow. The key is to think about where you would want a robot helper and go from there to design it. Do you want to be a doctor, a firefighter, or a teacher? You could put together a team to build just the right helper for your profession. Do you want to be a programmer, a designer, or an expert in human-robot interactions? You could be part of that exciting team.

Teamwork is actually what got me into robotics! It all started when I joined a robot soccer team at Carnegie Mellon University. It was so exciting to see the little robot dogs we'd spent the year programming score goal after goal on the field. Our team went on to win the RoboCup U.S. Open that year! I really encourage everyone to join a local robot club or competition; it's a great way to get into robotics. This motivated me to do a PhD designing swarms of flying robots

at EPFL in Switzerland. I then went on to MIT to study how nanobots could be used to treat cancer. Throughout the years, I've worked with computer scientists, mechanical engineers, bioengineers, chemists, and doctors! And, through my nonprofit Robohub.org, I've spoken to hundreds more, including designers, artists, lawyers, social scientists, and philosophers. It turns out, anyone can be involved in robotics! And we need these diverse teams to build the robots of the future. Working in robotics is a wonderful way to explore many different disciplines and be creative.

I've now built my own cross-disciplinary team at the Bristol Robotics Laboratory, where we design robots that work together, a bit like ants work together to create a trail to your picnic table or how birds work together to create beautiful flocking patterns in the sky. We call this swarm engineering. I hope our robots can one day work together to help in rescue scenarios, explore and monitor environments, and navigate bodies to fight cancer. We've still got a long way to go, but it's so exciting to be building a future where robots can help us even more effectively.

What do you want a robot to help you with?

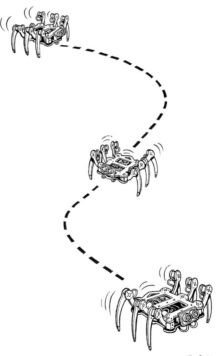

—Sabine Hauert
Bristol Robotics Laboratory, cofounder and
president of Robohub.org

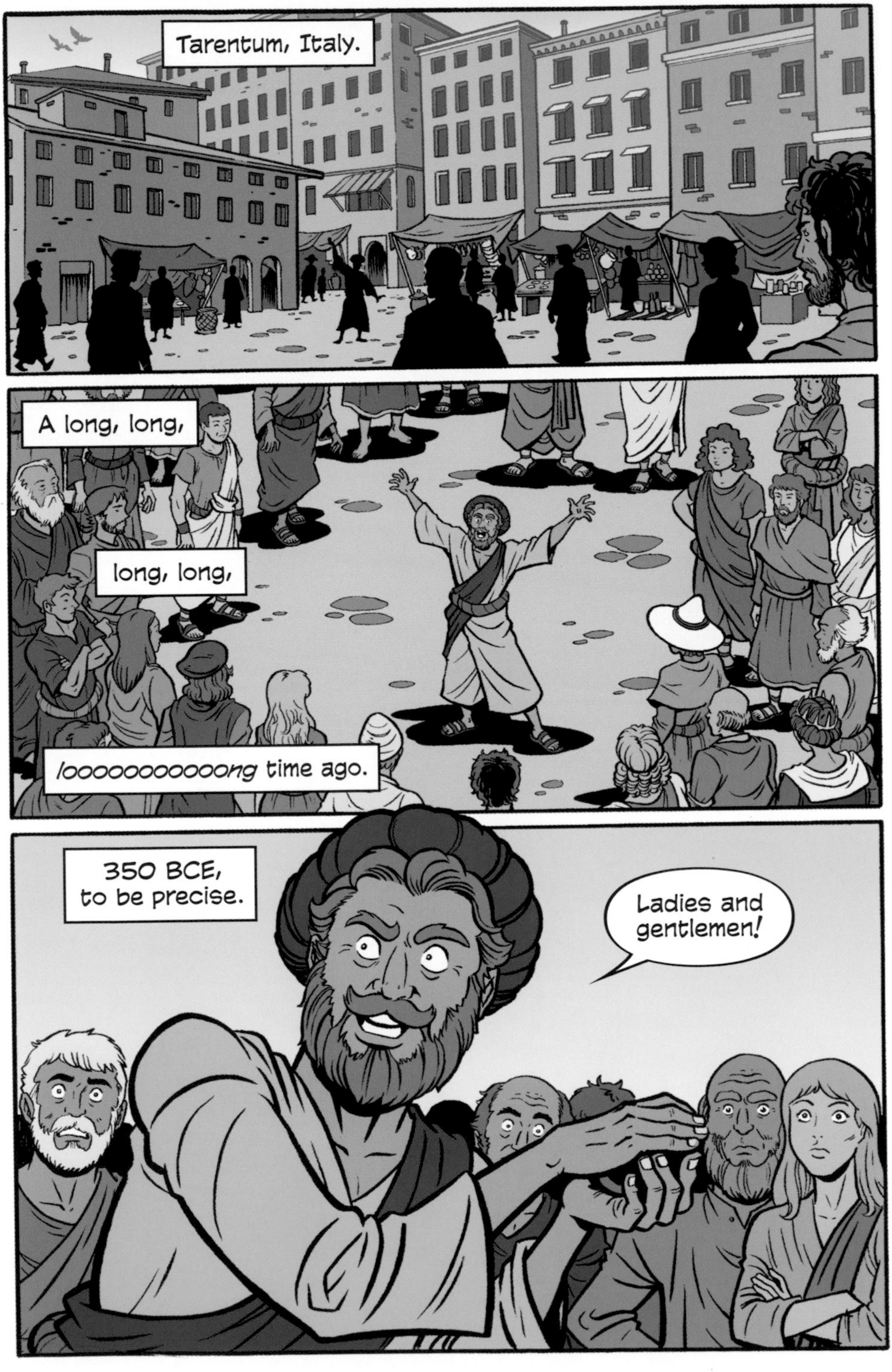
Tarentum, Italy.
A long, long,
long, long,
loooooooooooong time ago.
350 BCE, to be precise.
Ladies and gentlemen!

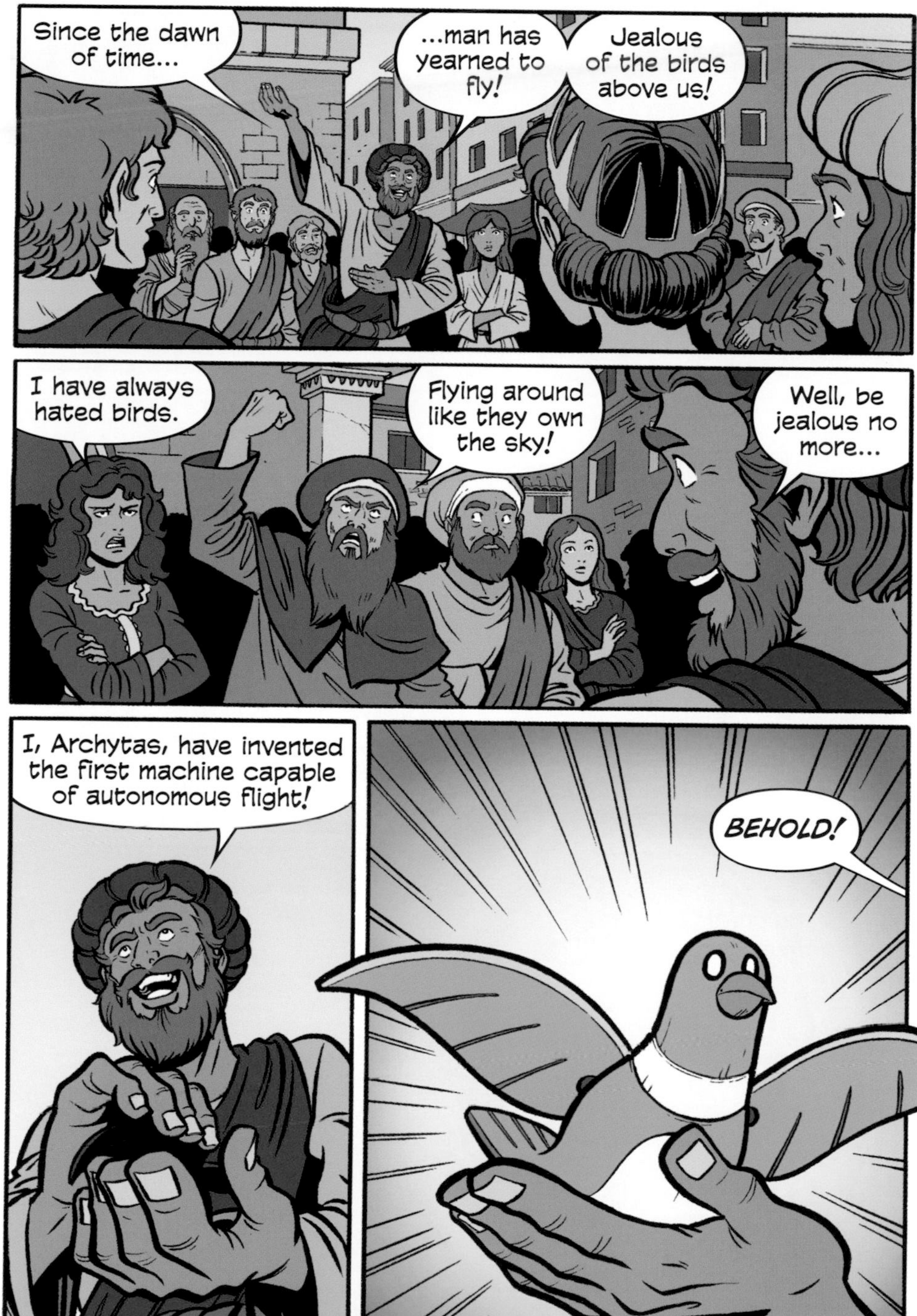
Since the dawn of time...
...man has yearned to fly!
Jealous of the birds above us!
I have always hated birds.
Flying around like they own the sky!
Well, be jealous no more...
I, Archytas, have invented the first machine capable of autonomous flight!
BEHOLD!

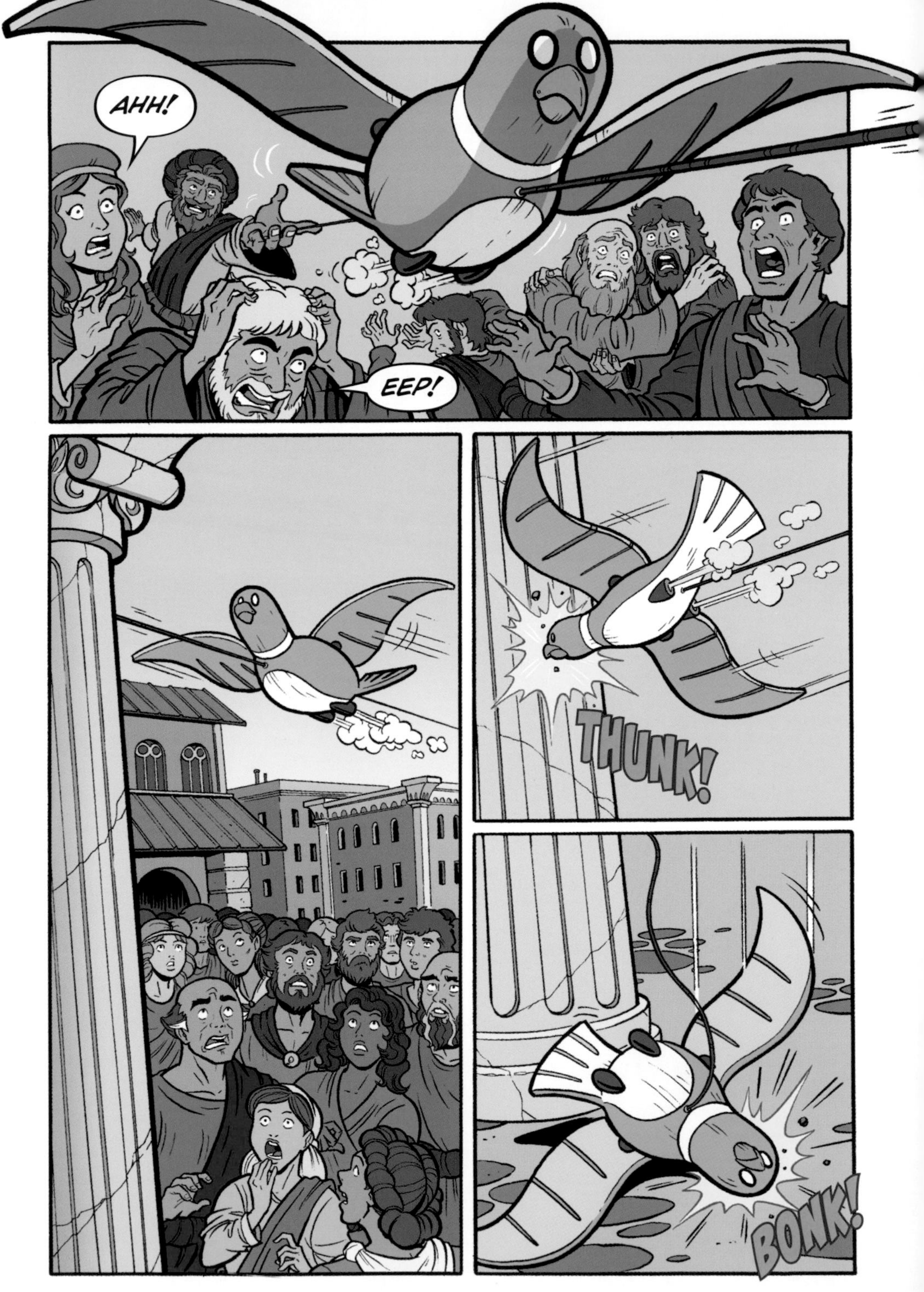
AHH!
EEP!
THUNK!
BONK!

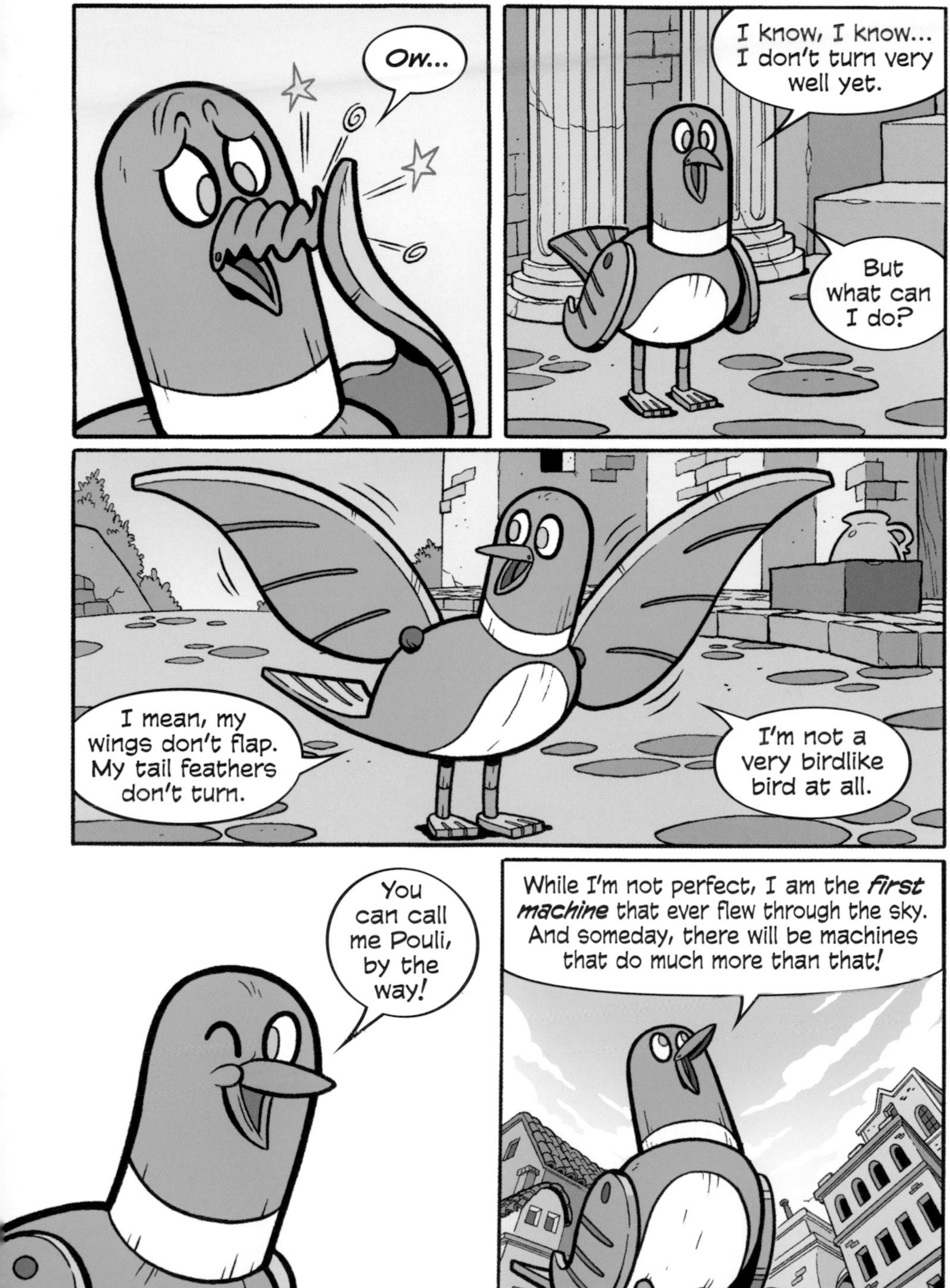
Ow...
I know, I know... I don't turn very well yet.
But what can I do?
I mean, my wings don't flap. My tail feathers don't turn.
I'm not a very birdlike bird at all.
You can call me Pouli, by the way!
While I'm not perfect, I am the *first machine* that ever flew through the sky. And someday, there will be machines that do much more than that!

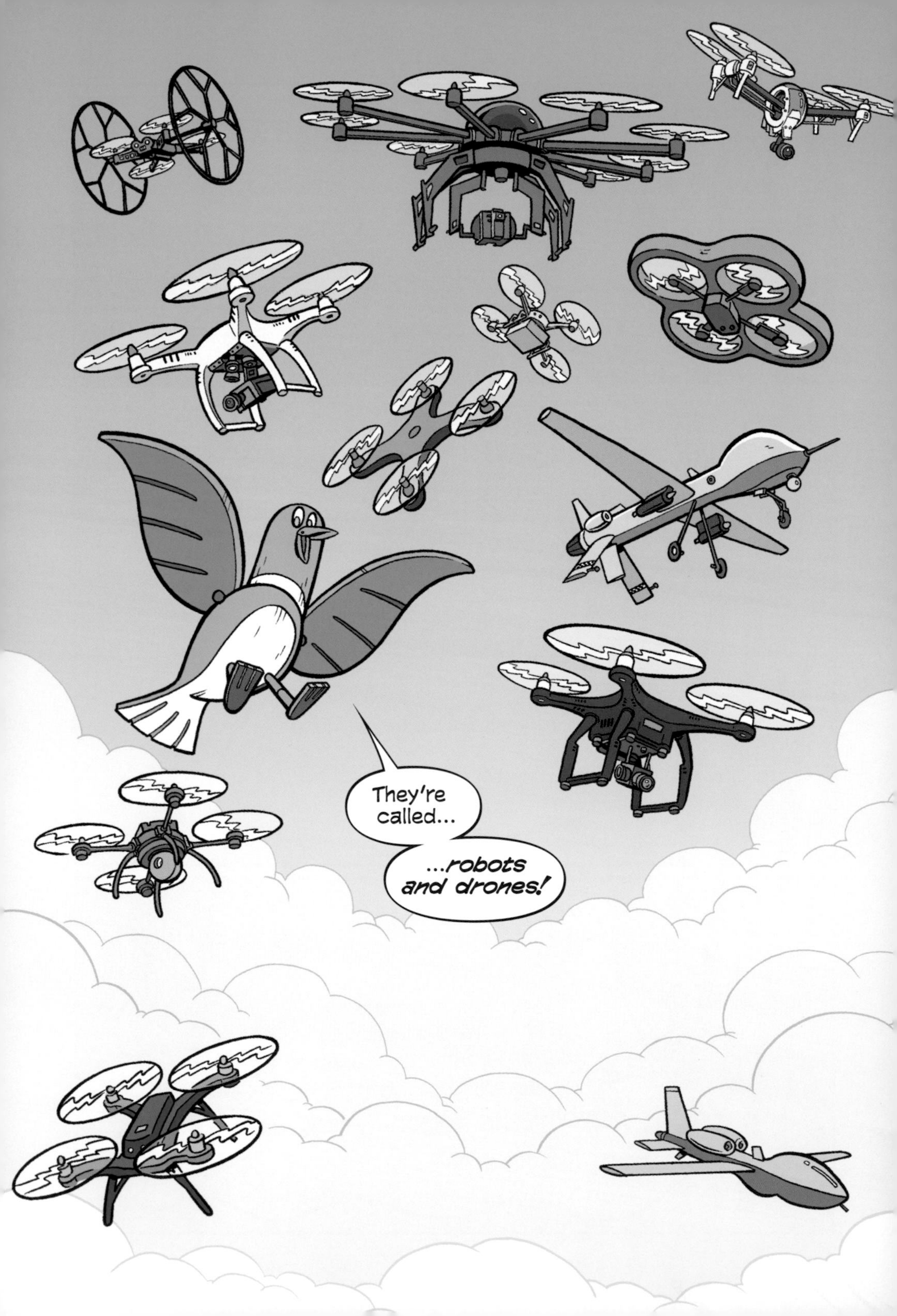
They're called...
...robots and drones!

So what exactly is a robot, anyway? Or a drone?
Like a lot of things, some people disagree.
It's *PEE-tah.*
It's *pee-TAH,* you uncultured swine!
Merriam-Webster says a robot is "a machine that can do the work of a person and that works automatically or is controlled by a computer."
The Encyclopedia Britannica calls it "any automatically operated machine that replaces human effort..."
But *we'll* say...
A robot is a machine that senses something in its environment, makes a choice about what it senses, and performs an action in response.

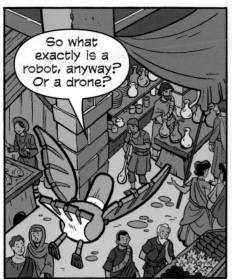

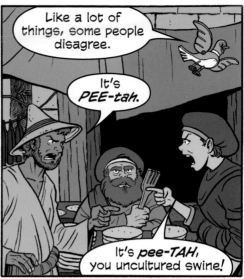

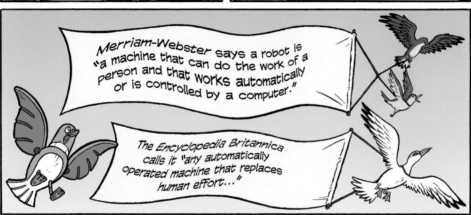

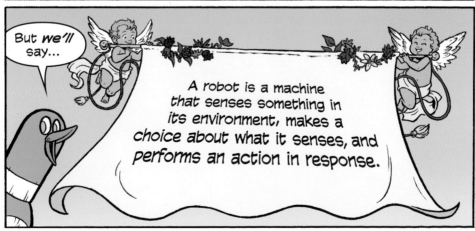

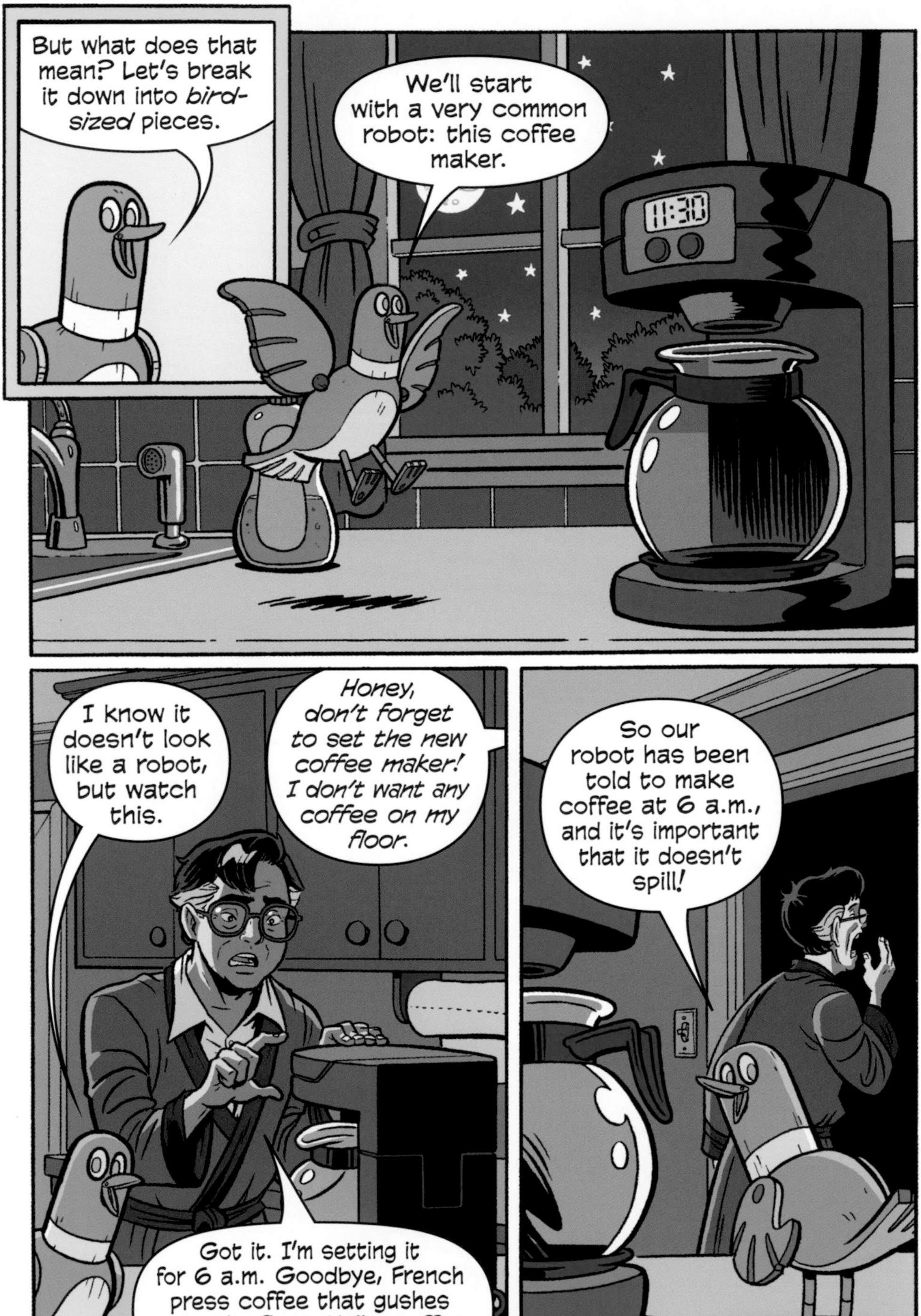
But what does that mean? Let's break it down into *bird-sized* pieces.
We'll start with a very common robot: this coffee maker.
11:30
I know it doesn't look like a robot, but watch this.
Honey, don't forget to set the new coffee maker! I don't want any coffee on my floor.
Got it. I'm setting it for 6 a.m. Goodbye, French press coffee that gushes onto the floor. Hello, coffee that stays in the pot.
So our robot has been told to make coffee at 6 a.m., and it's important that it doesn't spill!

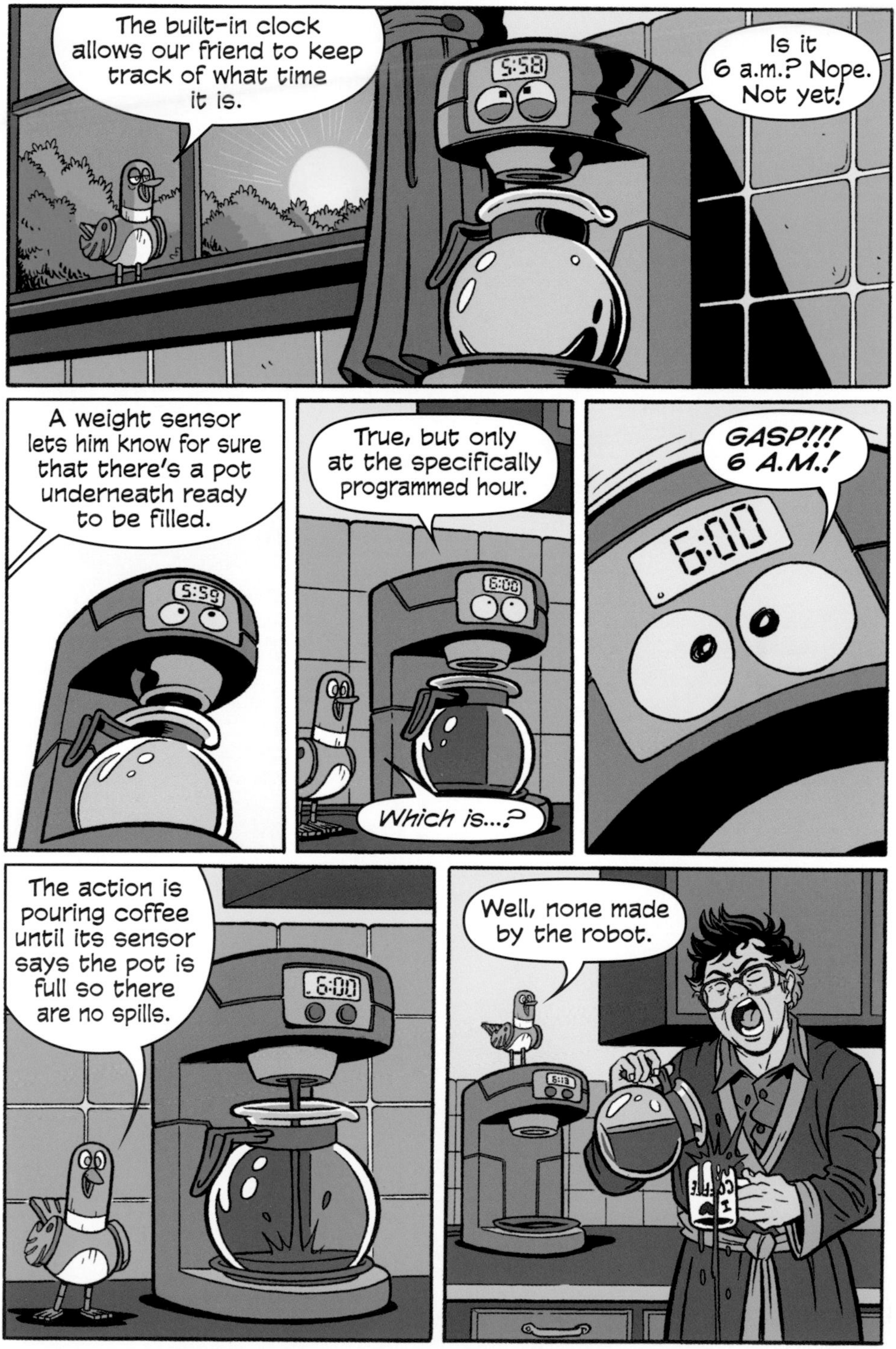
The built-in clock allows our friend to keep track of what time it is.
5:58
Is it 6 a.m.? Nope. Not yet!
A weight sensor lets him know for sure that there's a pot underneath ready to be filled.
5:59
True, but only at the specifically programmed hour.
6:00
Which is...?
GASP!!! 6 A.M.!
6:00
The action is pouring coffee until its sensor says the pot is full so there are no spills.
6:00
Well, none made by the robot.
5:13

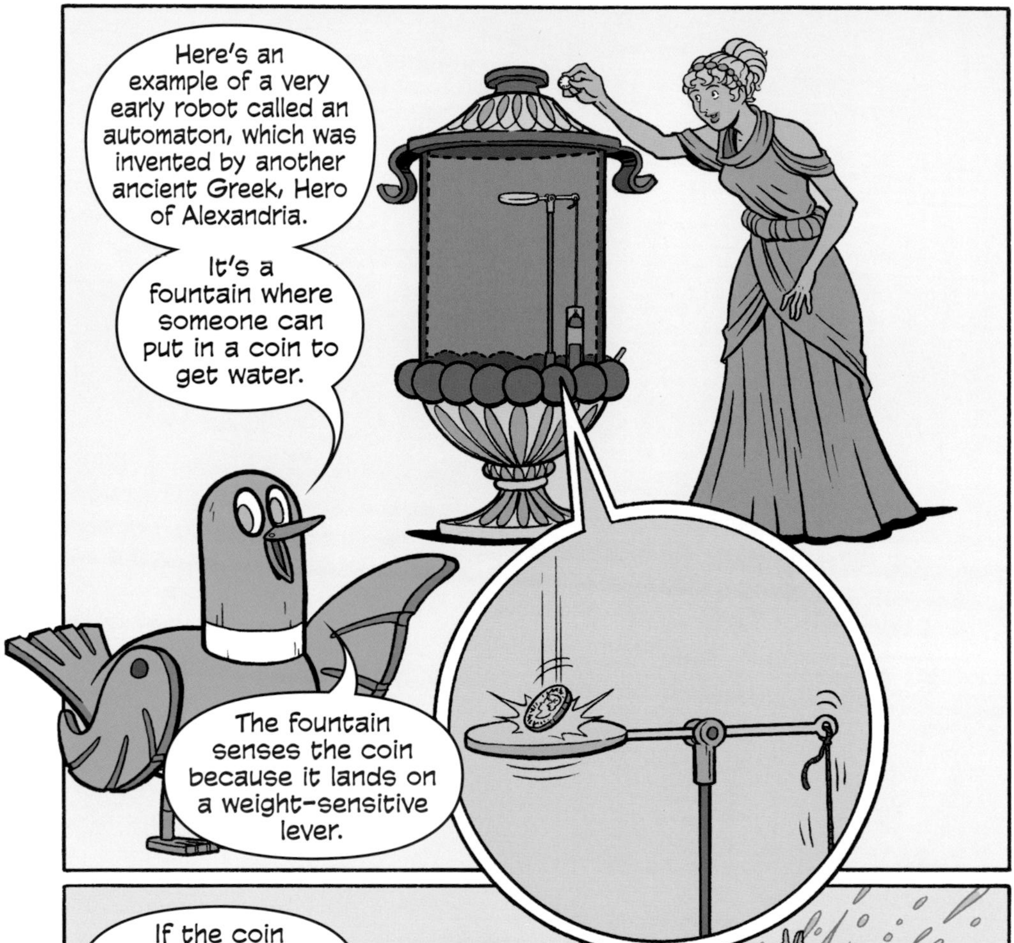
Here's an example of a very early robot called an automaton, which was invented by another ancient Greek, Hero of Alexandria.
It's a fountain where someone can put in a coin to get water.
The fountain senses the coin because it lands on a weight-sensitive lever.

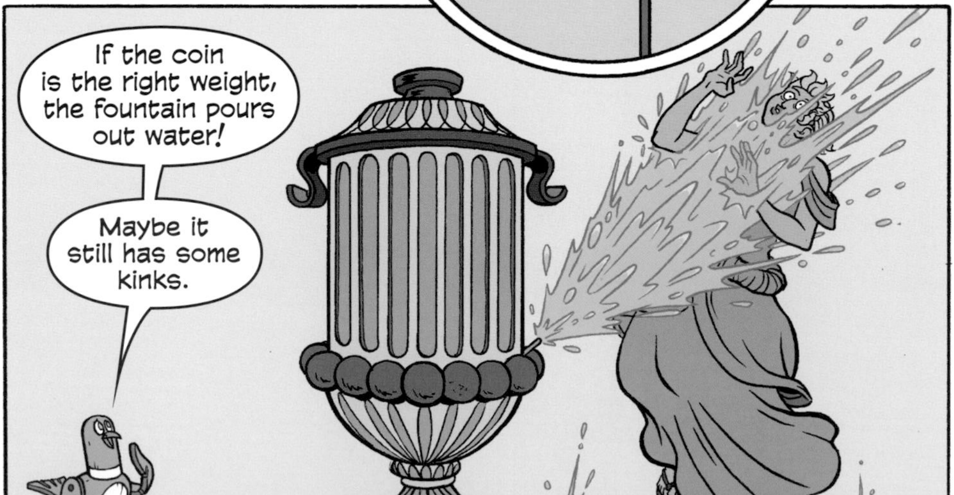
If the coin is the right weight, the fountain pours out water!
Maybe it still has some kinks.

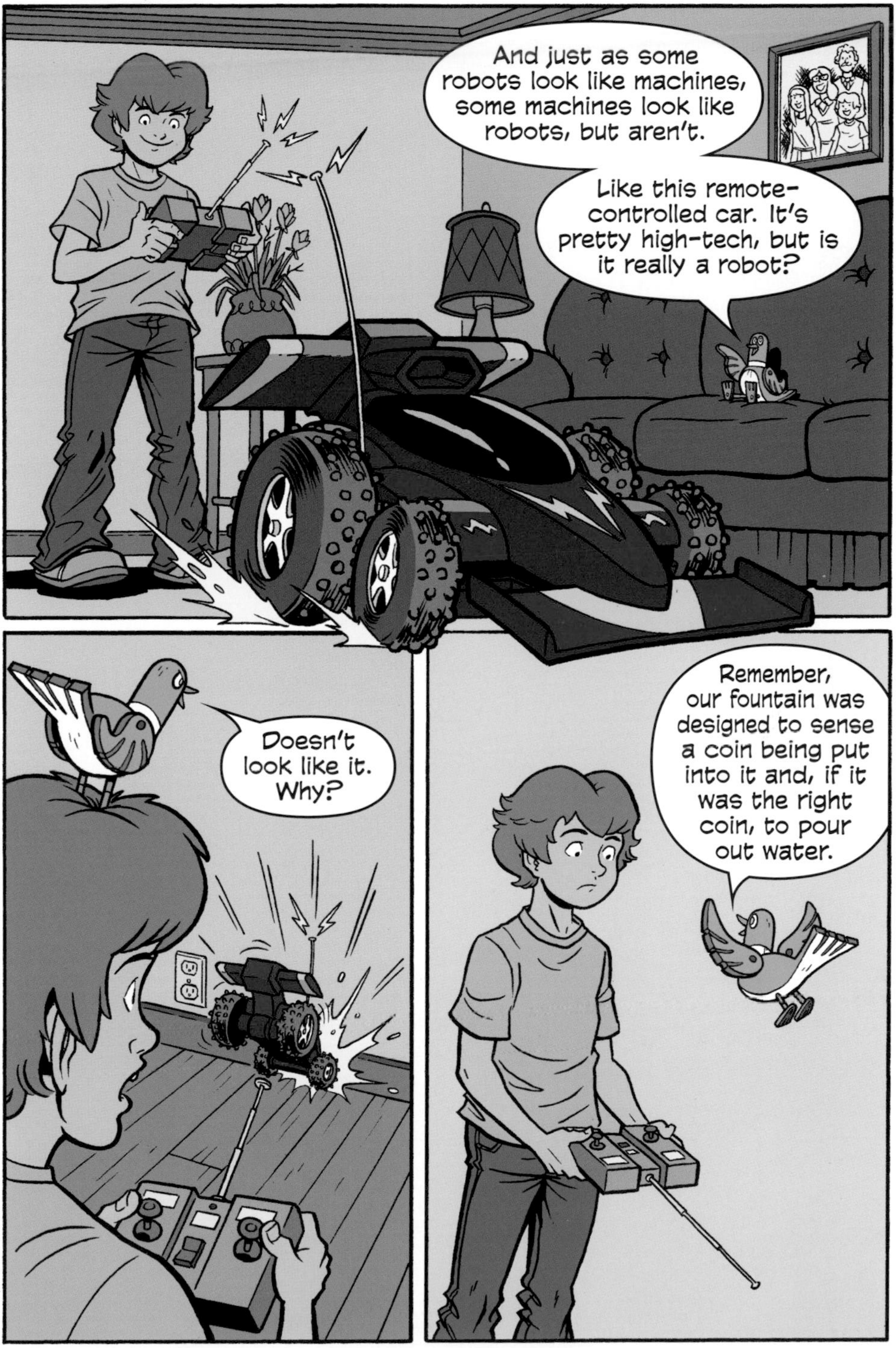
And just as some robots look like machines, some machines look like robots, but aren't.
Like this remote-controlled car. It's pretty high-tech, but is it really a robot?
Doesn't look like it. Why?
Remember, our fountain was designed to sense a coin being put into it and, if it was the right coin, to pour out water.

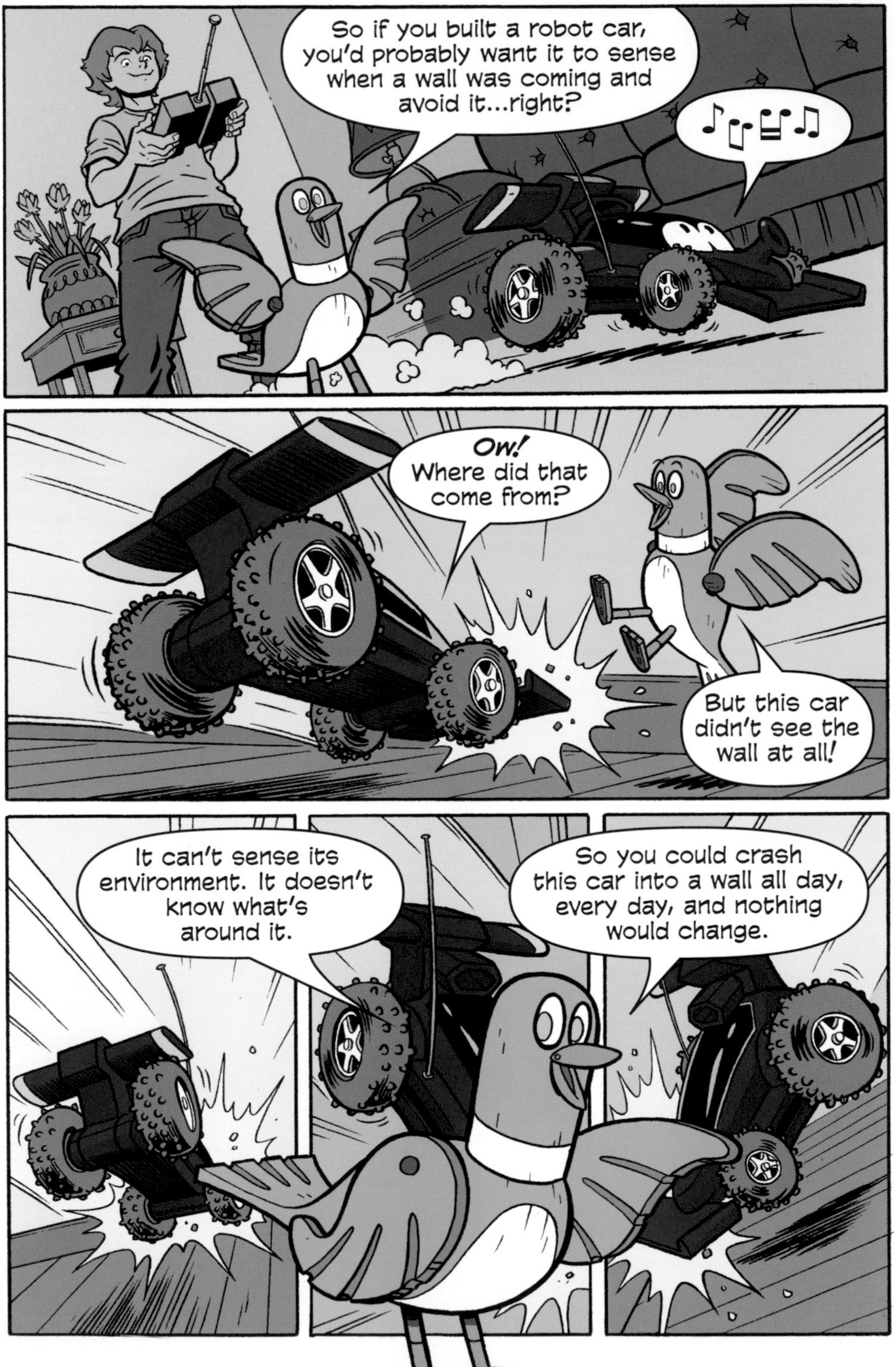
So if you built a robot car, you'd probably want it to sense when a wall was coming and avoid it...right?
♪♫♫♫
Ow! Where did that come from?
But this car didn't see the wall at all!
It can't sense its environment. It doesn't know what's around it.
So you could crash this car into a wall all day, every day, and nothing would change.

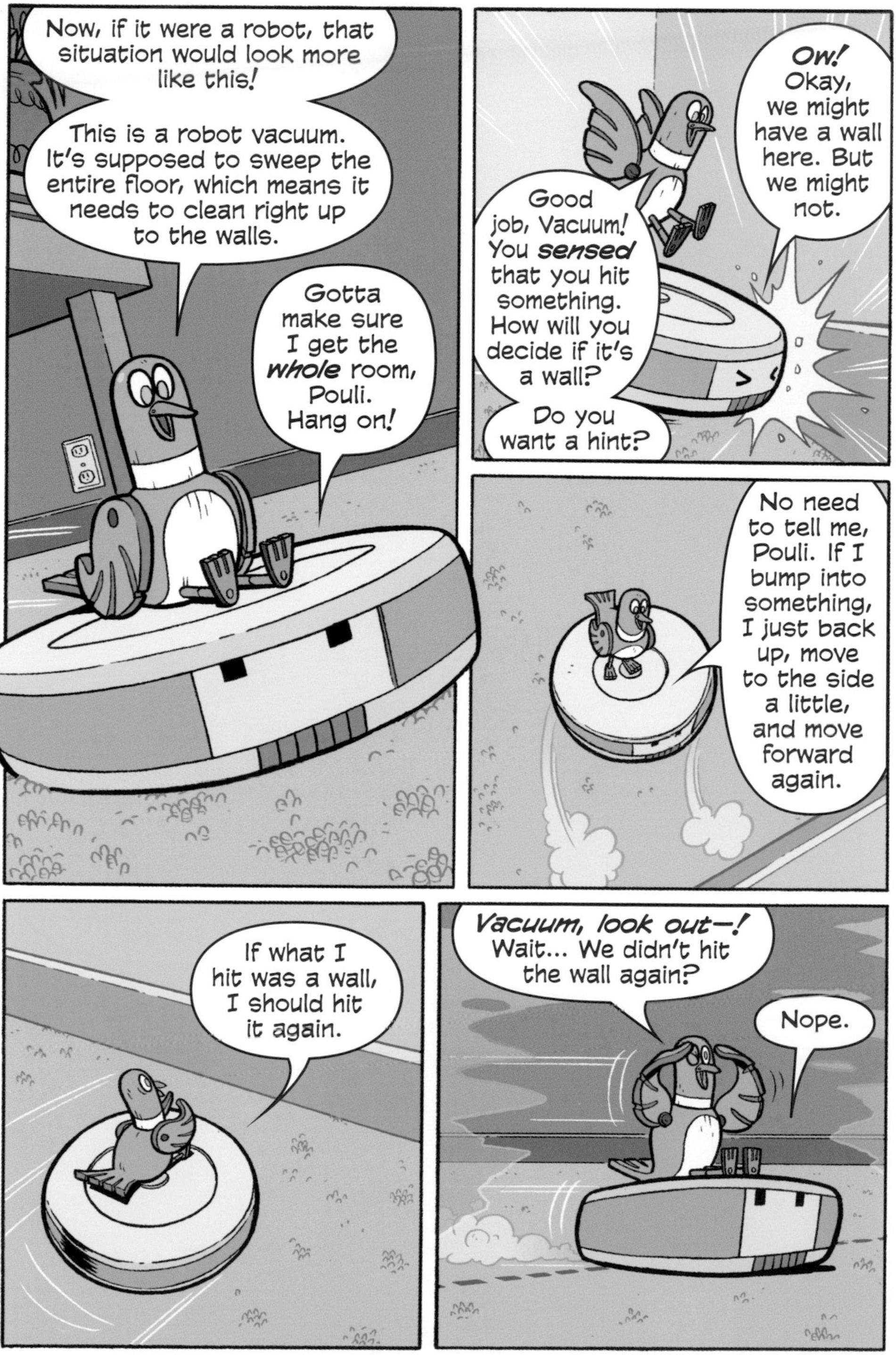
Now, if it were a robot, that situation would look more like this!
This is a robot vacuum. It's supposed to sweep the entire floor, which means it needs to clean right up to the walls.
Gotta make sure I get the *whole* room, Pouli. Hang on!
Ow! Okay, we might have a wall here. But we might not.
Good job, Vacuum! You *sensed* that you hit something. How will you decide if it's a wall?
Do you want a hint?
No need to tell me, Pouli. If I bump into something, I just back up, move to the side a little, and move forward again.
If what I hit was a wall, I should hit it again.
Vacuum, look out—! Wait... We didn't hit the wall again?
Nope.

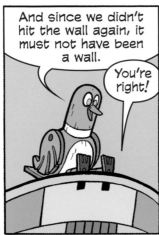

And since we didn't hit the wall again, it must not have been a wall.

You're right!

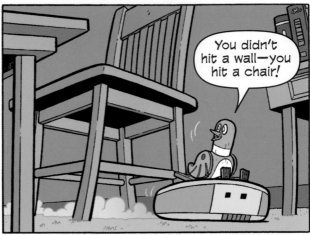

You didn't hit a wall—you hit a chair!

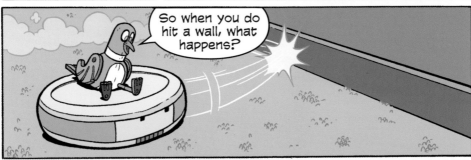

So when you do hit a wall, what happens?

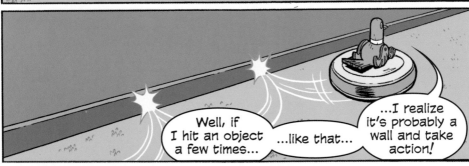

Well, if I hit an object a few times...

...like that...

...I realize it's probably a wall and take action!

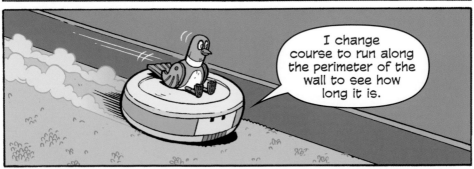

I change course to run along the perimeter of the wall to see how long it is.

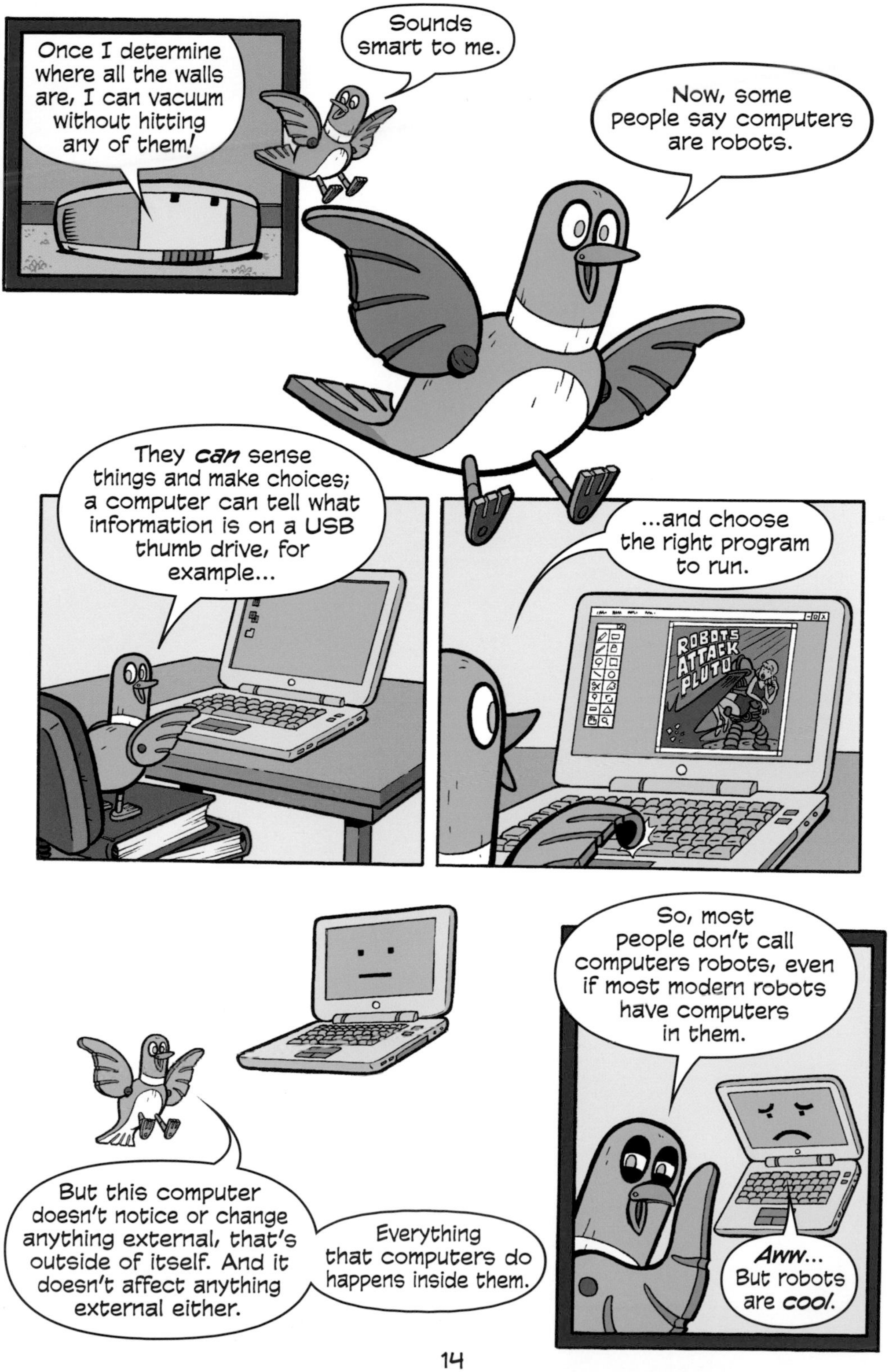
Once I determine where all the walls are, I can vacuum without hitting any of them!
Sounds smart to me.
Now, some people say computers are robots.
They *can* sense things and make choices; a computer can tell what information is on a USB thumb drive, for example...
...and choose the right program to run.
ROBOTS ATTACK PLUTO
But this computer doesn't notice or change anything external, that's outside of itself. And it doesn't affect anything external either.
Everything that computers do happens inside them.
So, most people don't call computers robots, even if most modern robots have computers in them.
Aww... But robots are *cool*.

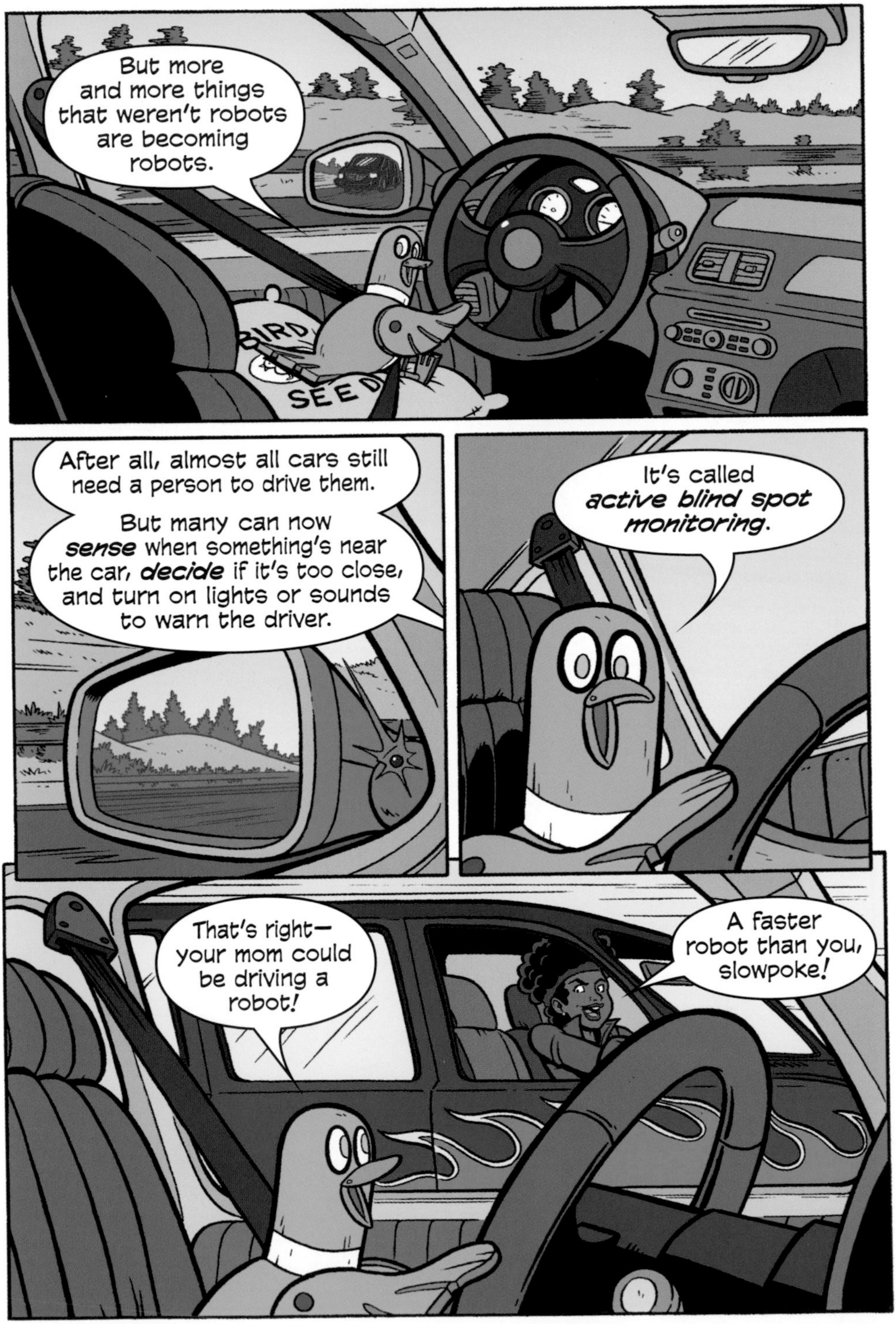
But more and more things that weren't robots are becoming robots.
BIRD SEED
After all, almost all cars still need a person to drive them.
But many can now *sense* when something's near the car, *decide* if it's too close, and turn on lights or sounds to warn the driver.
It's called ***active blind spot monitoring***.
That's right—your mom could be driving a robot!
A faster robot than you, slowpoke!

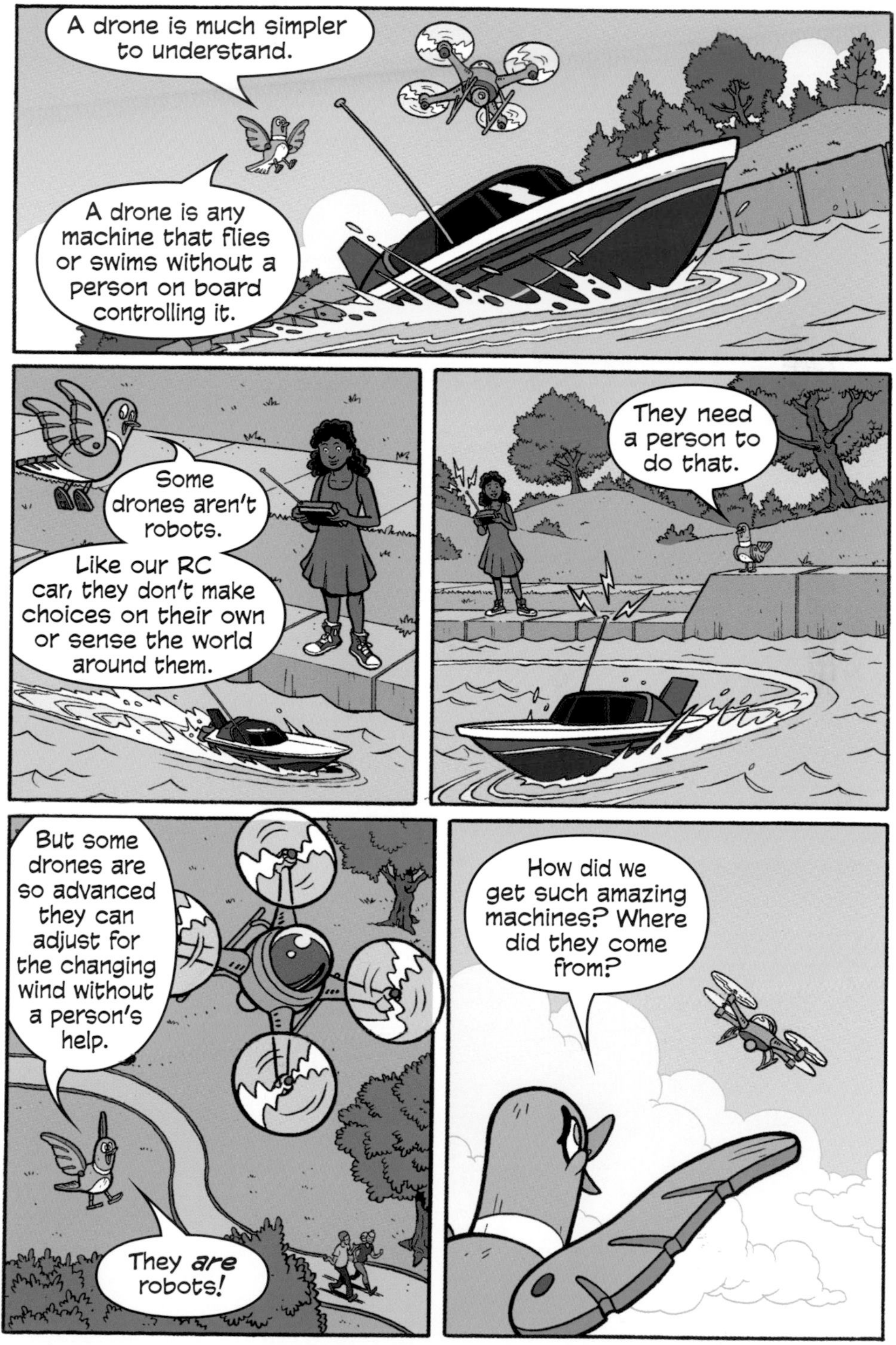
A drone is much simpler to understand.
A drone is any machine that flies or swims without a person on board controlling it.
Some drones aren't robots.
Like our RC car, they don't make choices on their own or sense the world around them.
They need a person to do that.
But some drones are so advanced they can adjust for the changing wind without a person's help.
They *are* robots!
How did we get such amazing machines? Where did they come from?

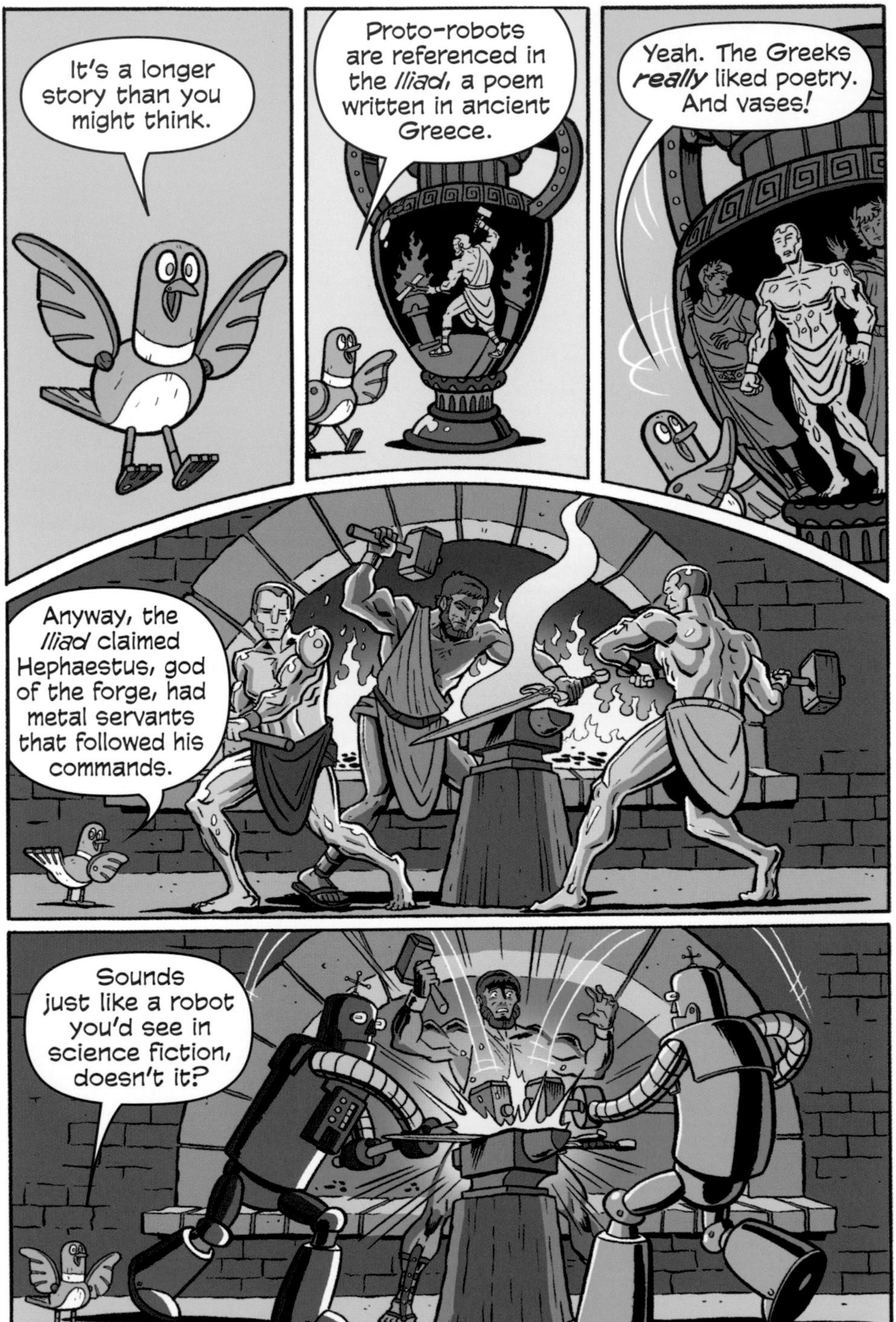
It's a longer story than you might think.
Proto-robots are referenced in the *Iliad*, a poem written in ancient Greece.
Yeah. The Greeks ***really*** liked poetry. And vases!
Anyway, the *Iliad* claimed Hephaestus, god of the forge, had metal servants that followed his commands.
Sounds just like a robot you'd see in science fiction, doesn't it?

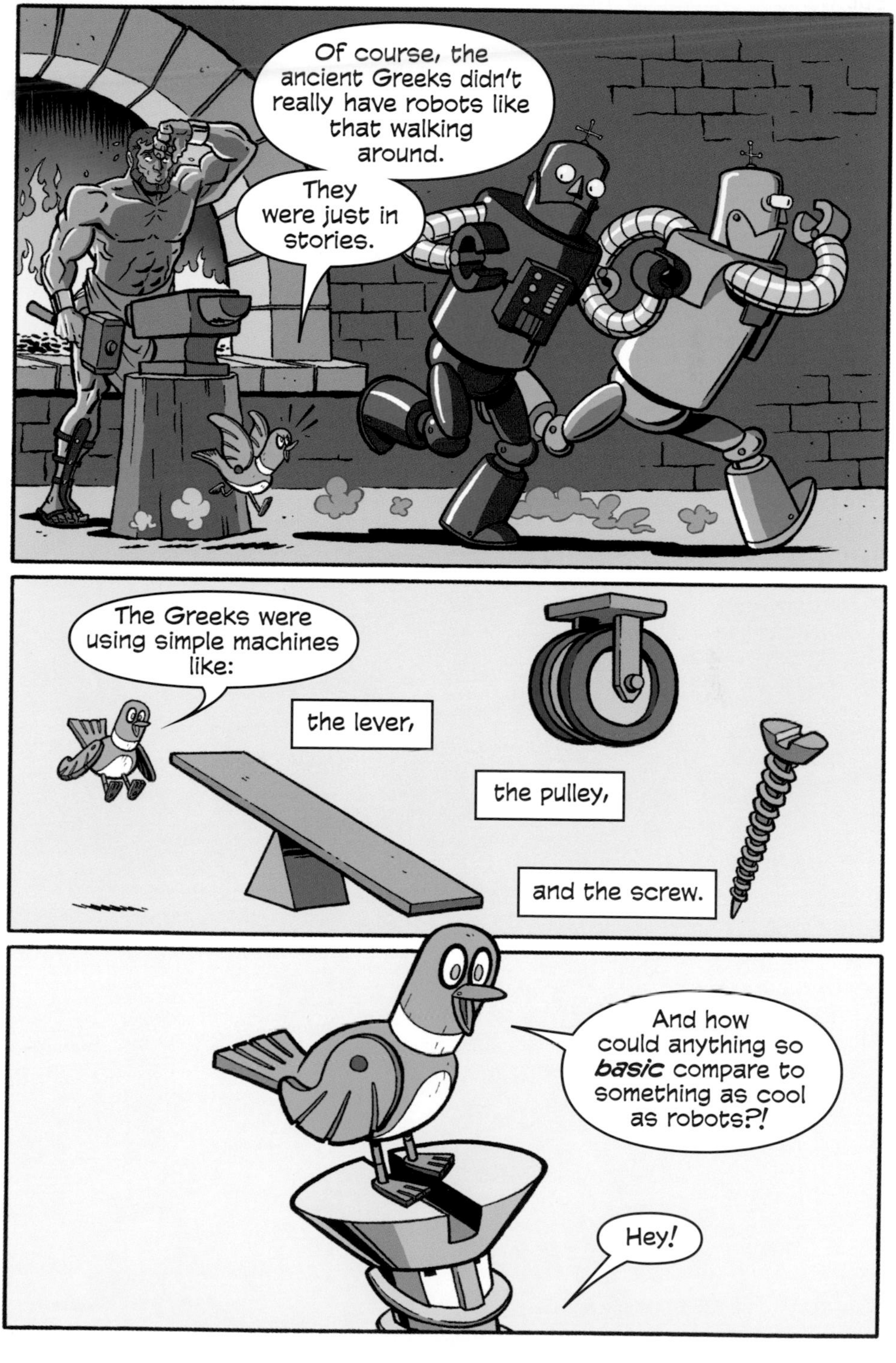
Of course, the ancient Greeks didn't really have robots like that walking around.
They were just in stories.
The Greeks were using simple machines like:
the lever,
the pulley,
and the screw.
And how could anything so *basic* compare to something as cool as robots?!
Hey!

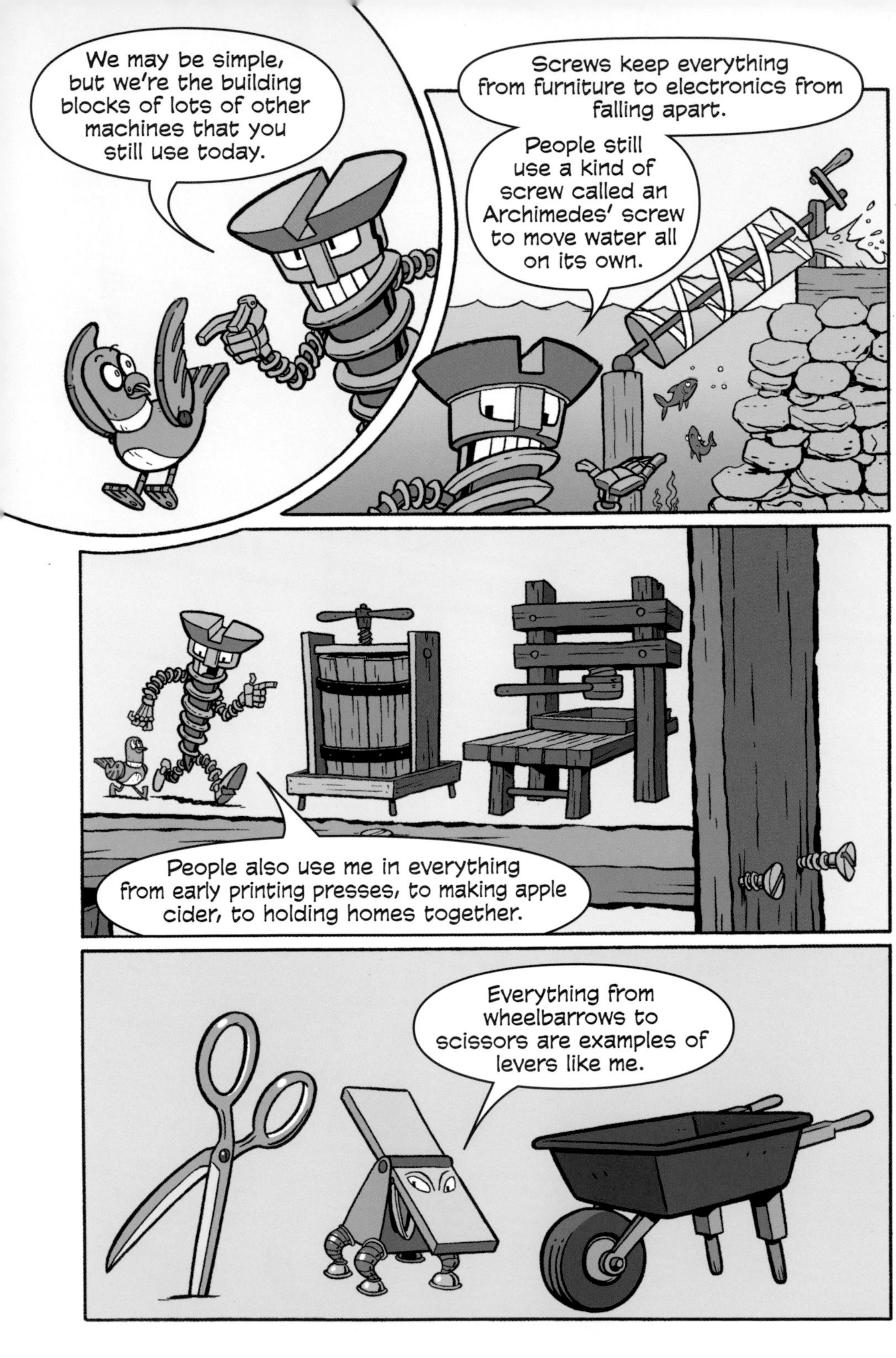
We may be simple, but we're the building blocks of lots of other machines that you still use today.
Screws keep everything from furniture to electronics from falling apart.
People still use a kind of screw called an Archimedes' screw to move water all on its own.
People also use me in everything from early printing presses, to making apple cider, to holding homes together.
Everything from wheelbarrows to scissors are examples of levers like me.

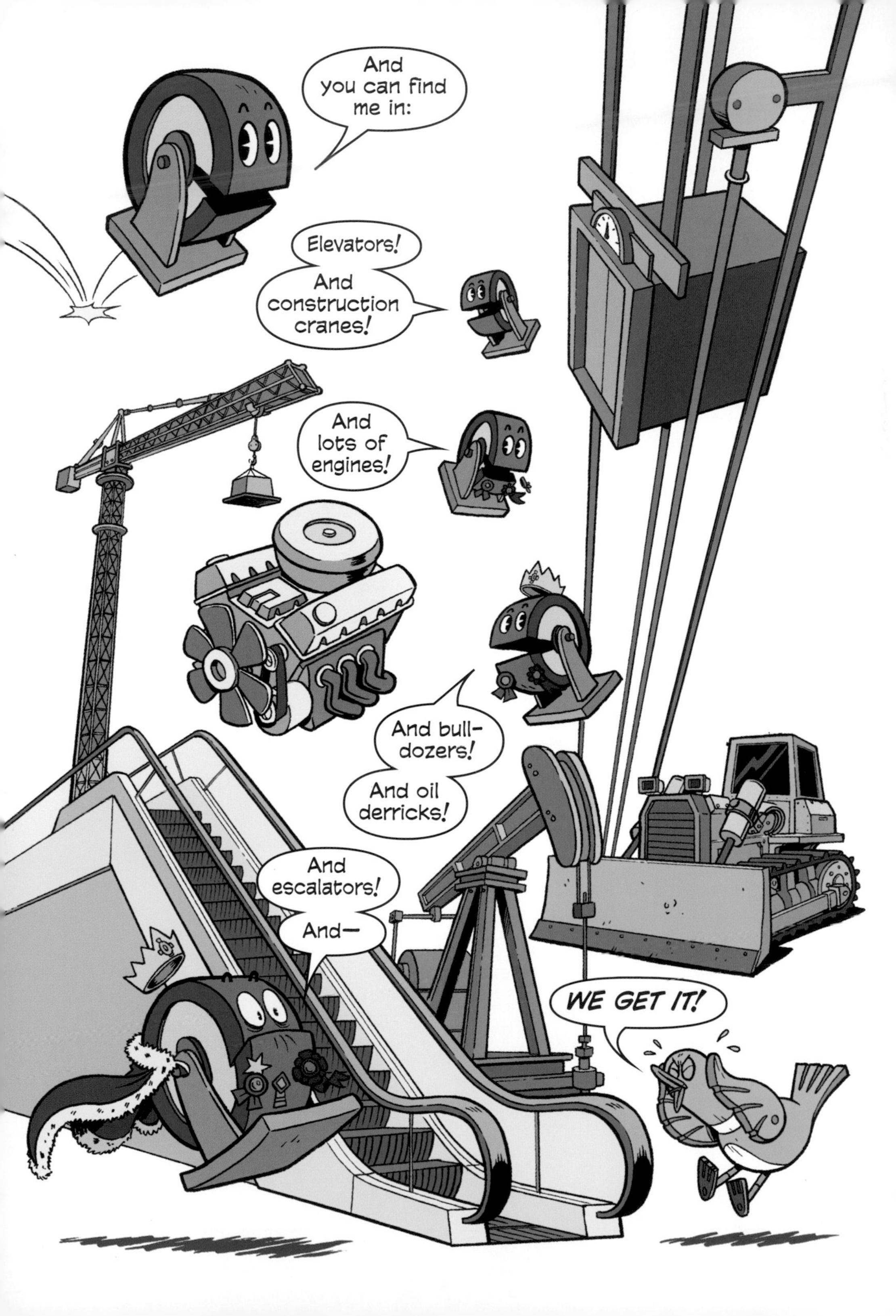
And you can find me in:
Elevators!
And construction cranes!
And lots of engines!
And bull-dozers!
And oil derricks!
And escalators!
And—
WE GET IT!

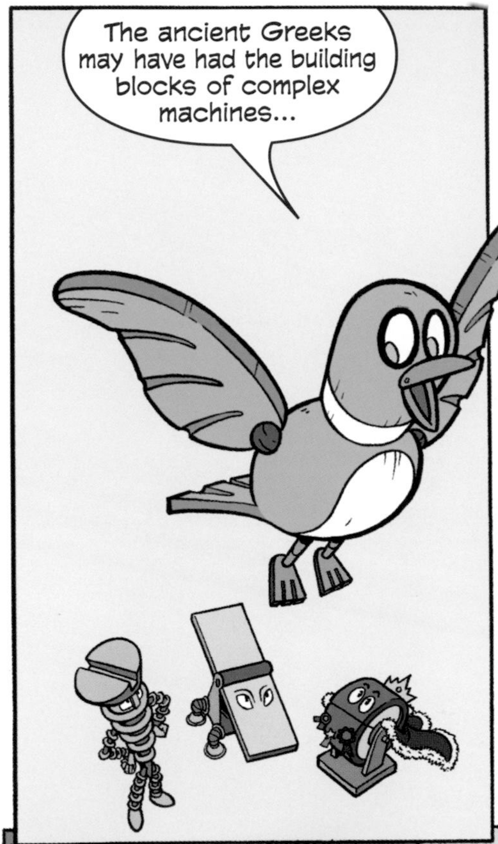
The ancient Greeks may have had the building blocks of complex machines...

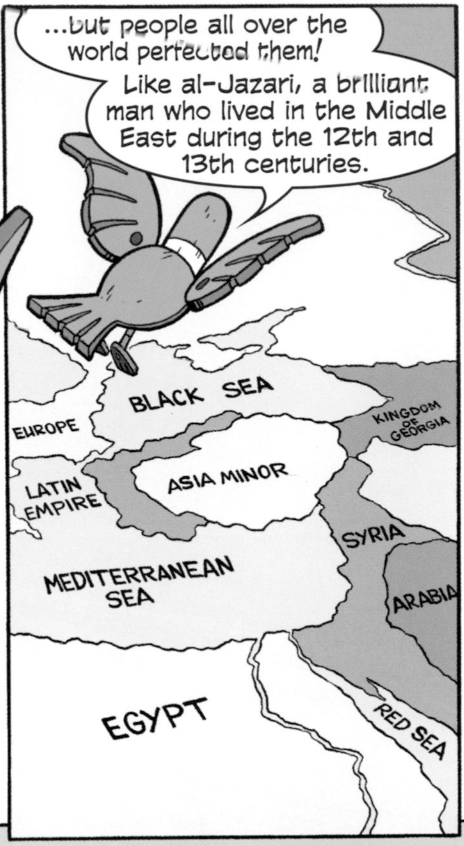
...but people all over the world perfected them!
Like al-Jazari, a brilliant man who lived in the Middle East during the 12th and 13th centuries.
BLACK SEA
EUROPE
KINGDOM OF GEORGIA
LATIN EMPIRE
ASIA MINOR
SYRIA
MEDITERRANEAN SEA
ARABIA
EGYPT
RED SEA

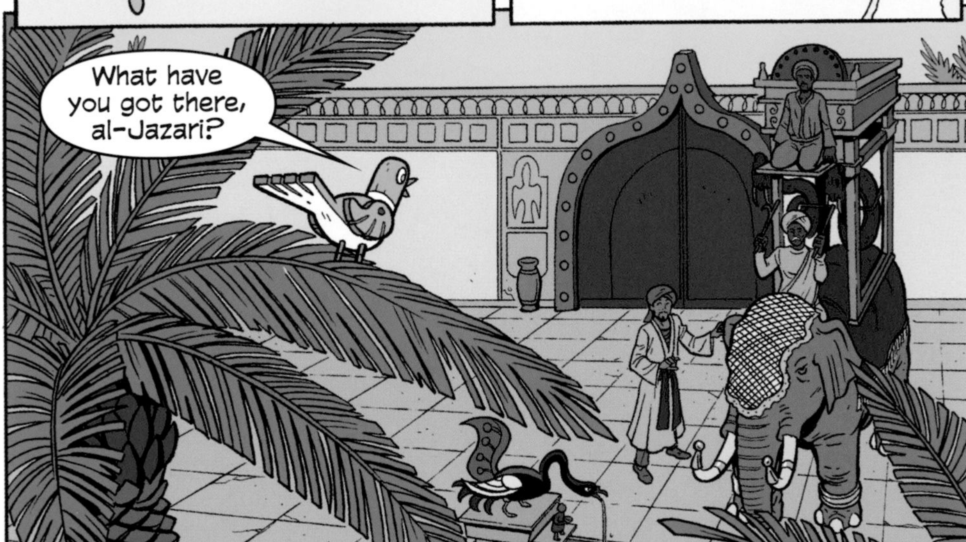
What have you got there, al-Jazari?

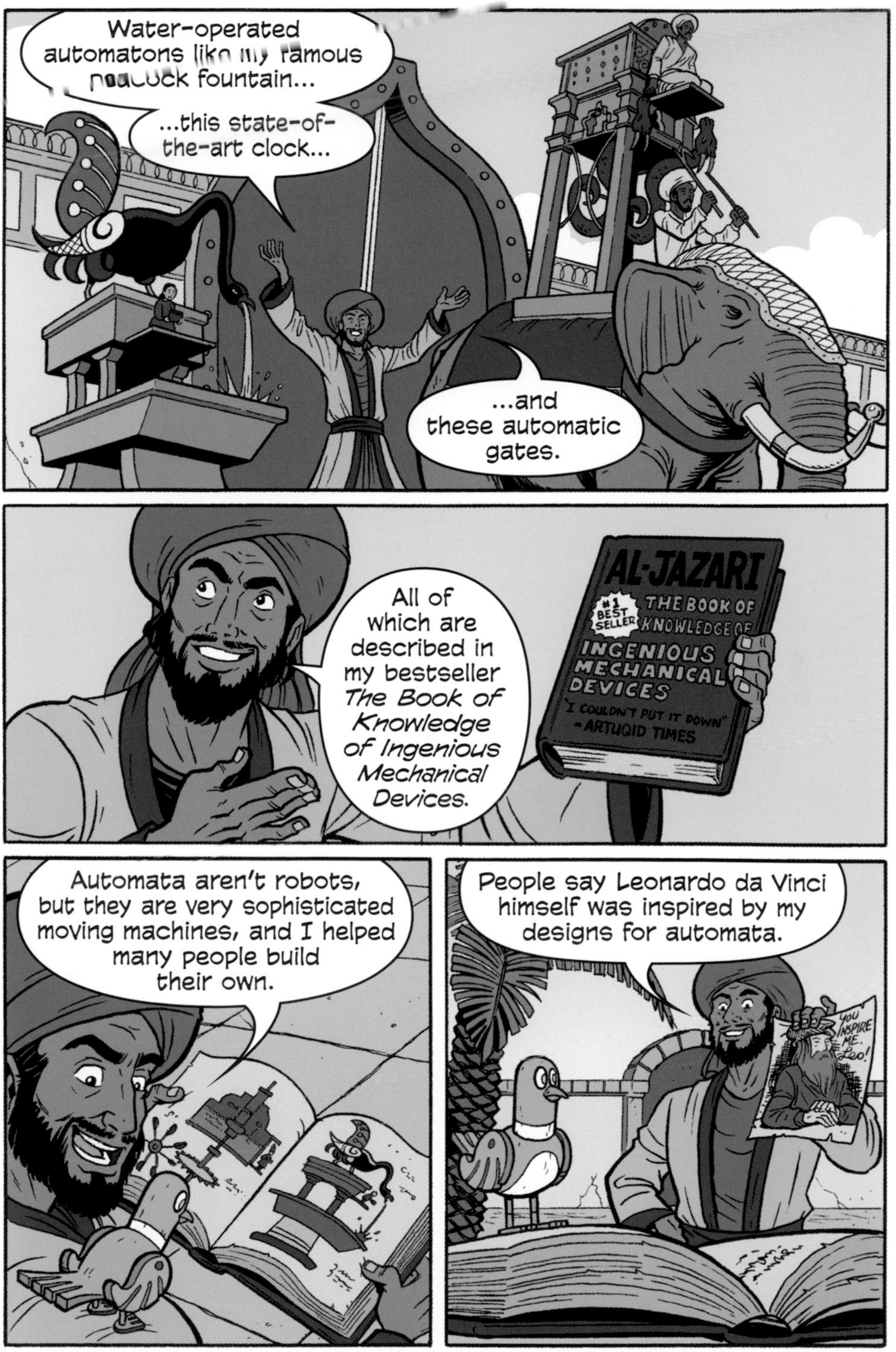
Water-operated automatons like my famous peacock fountain...
...this state-of-the-art clock...
...and these automatic gates.
All of which are described in my bestseller *The Book of Knowledge of Ingenious Mechanical Devices.*
AL-JAZARI
#1 BEST SELLER
THE BOOK OF KNOWLEDGE OF INGENIOUS MECHANICAL DEVICES
"I COULDN'T PUT IT DOWN" —ARTUQID TIMES
Automata aren't robots, but they are very sophisticated moving machines, and I helped many people build their own.
People say Leonardo da Vinci himself was inspired by my designs for automata.
YOU INSPIRE ME. Leo!

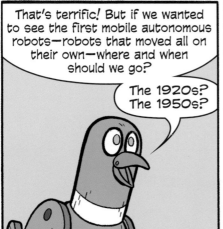

That's terrific! But if we wanted to see the first mobile autonomous robots—robots that moved all on their own—where and when should we go?

The 1920s? The 1950s?

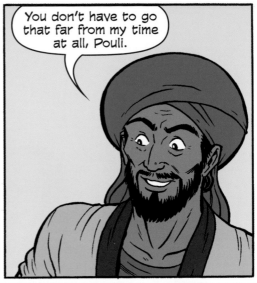

You don't have to go that far from my time at all, Pouli.

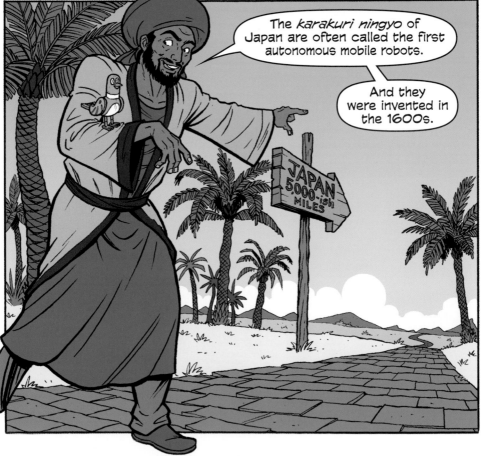

The *karakuri ningyo* of Japan are often called the first autonomous mobile robots.

And they were invented in the 1600s.

JAPAN 5000-ish MILES

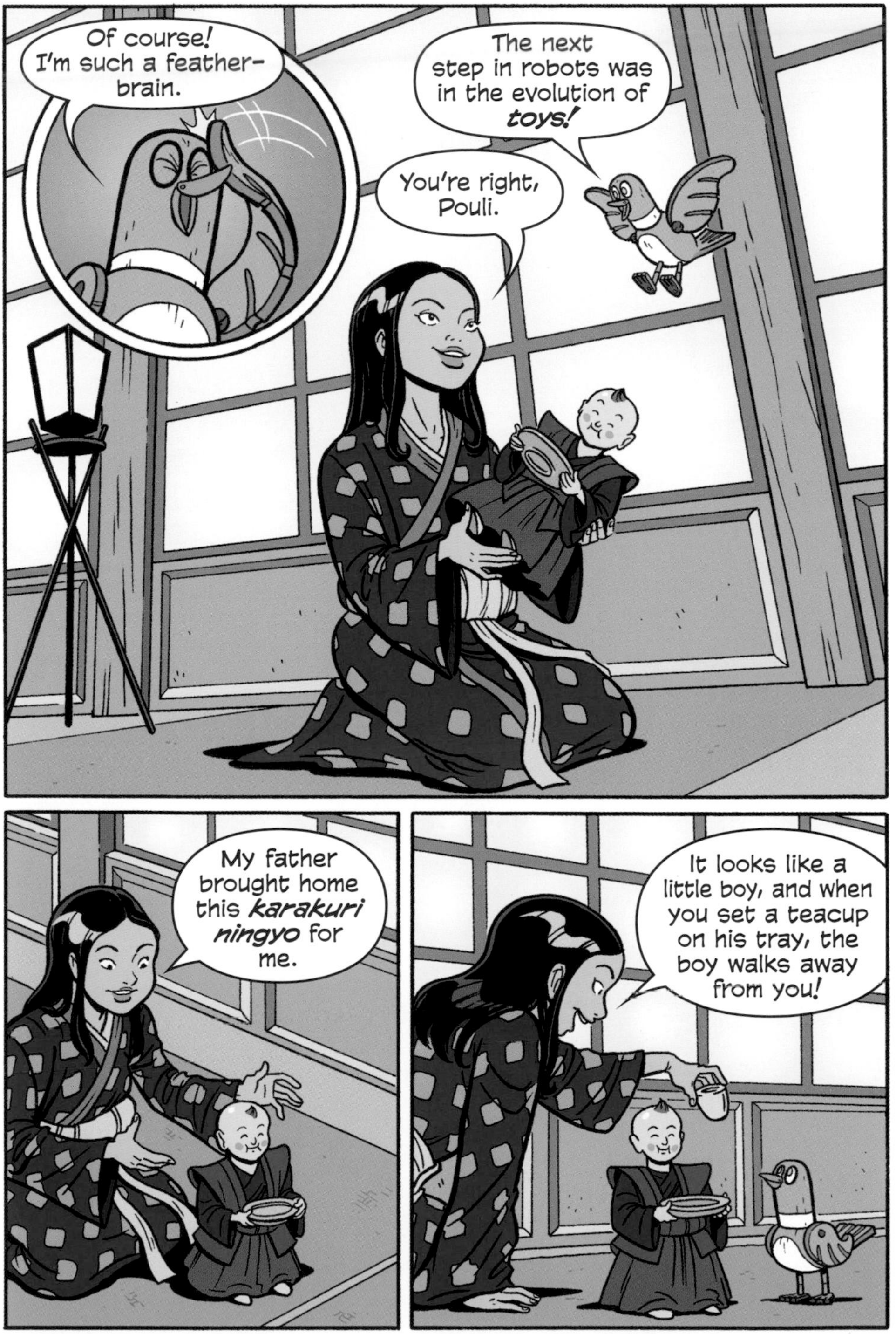

Of course! I'm such a feather-brain.
The next step in robots was in the evolution of *toys!*
You're right, Pouli.
My father brought home this *karakuri ningyo* for me.
It looks like a little boy, and when you set a teacup on his tray, the boy walks away from you!

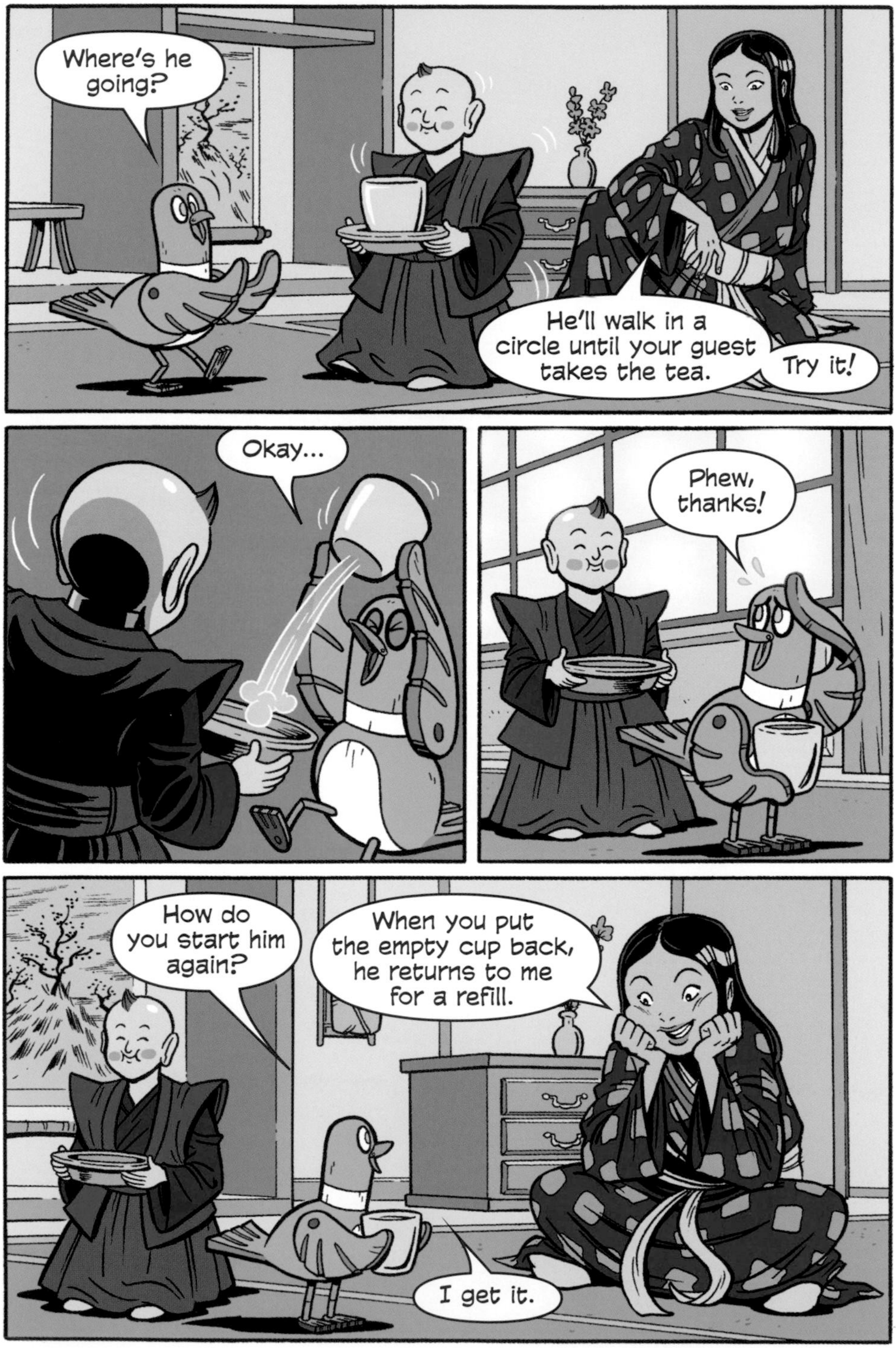
Where's he going?
He'll walk in a circle until your guest takes the tea.
Try it!
Okay...
Phew, thanks!
How do you start him again?
When you put the empty cup back, he returns to me for a refill.
I get it.

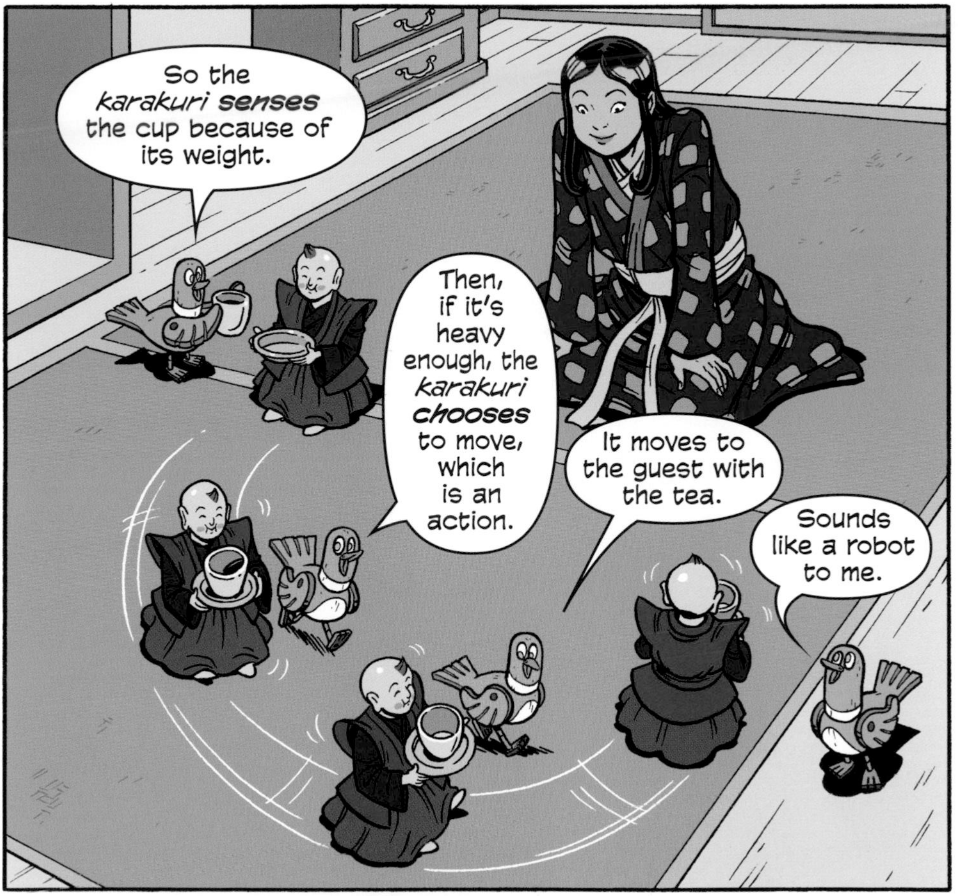
So the *karakuri* **senses** the cup because of its weight.
Then, if it's heavy enough, the *karakuri* **chooses** to move, which is an action.
It moves to the guest with the tea.
Sounds like a robot to me.

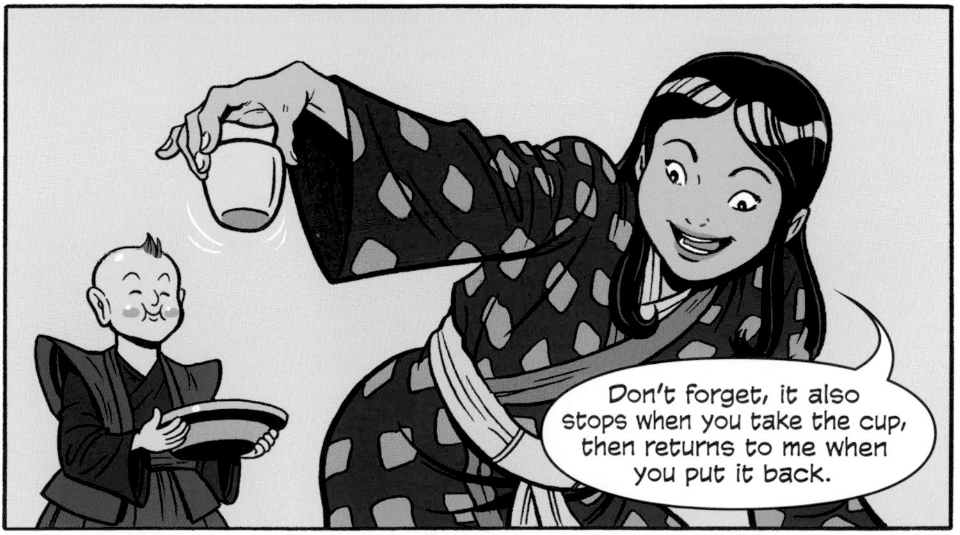
Don't forget, it also stops when you take the cup, then returns to me when you put it back.

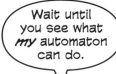

Wait until you see what *my* automaton can do.

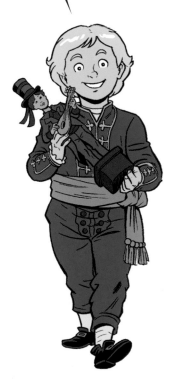

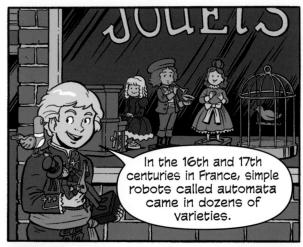

In the 16th and 17th centuries in France, simple robots called automata came in dozens of varieties.

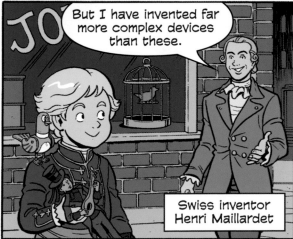

But I have invented far more complex devices than these.

Swiss inventor Henri Maillardet

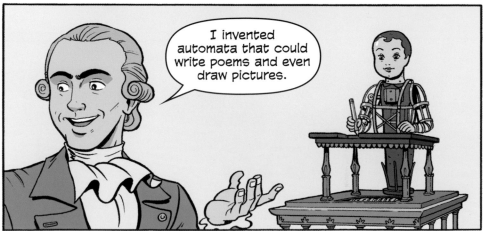

I invented automata that could write poems and even draw pictures.

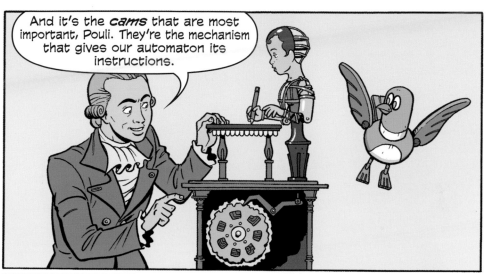

And it's the *cams* that are most important, Pouli. They're the mechanism that gives our automaton its instructions.

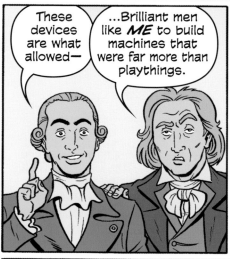

These devices are what allowed—

...Brilliant men like *ME* to build machines that were far more than playthings.

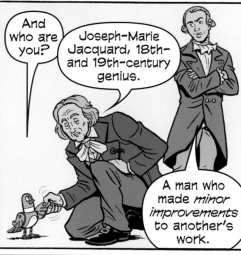

And who are you?

Joseph-Marie Jacquard, 18th- and 19th-century genius.

A man who made *minor improvements* to another's work.

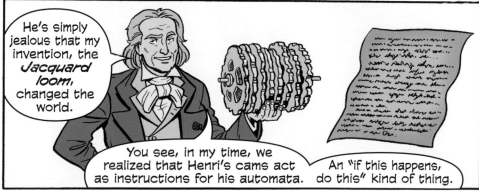

He's simply jealous that my invention, the *Jacquard loom*, changed the world.

You see, in my time, we realized that Henri's cams act as instructions for his automata.

An "if this happens, do this" kind of thing.

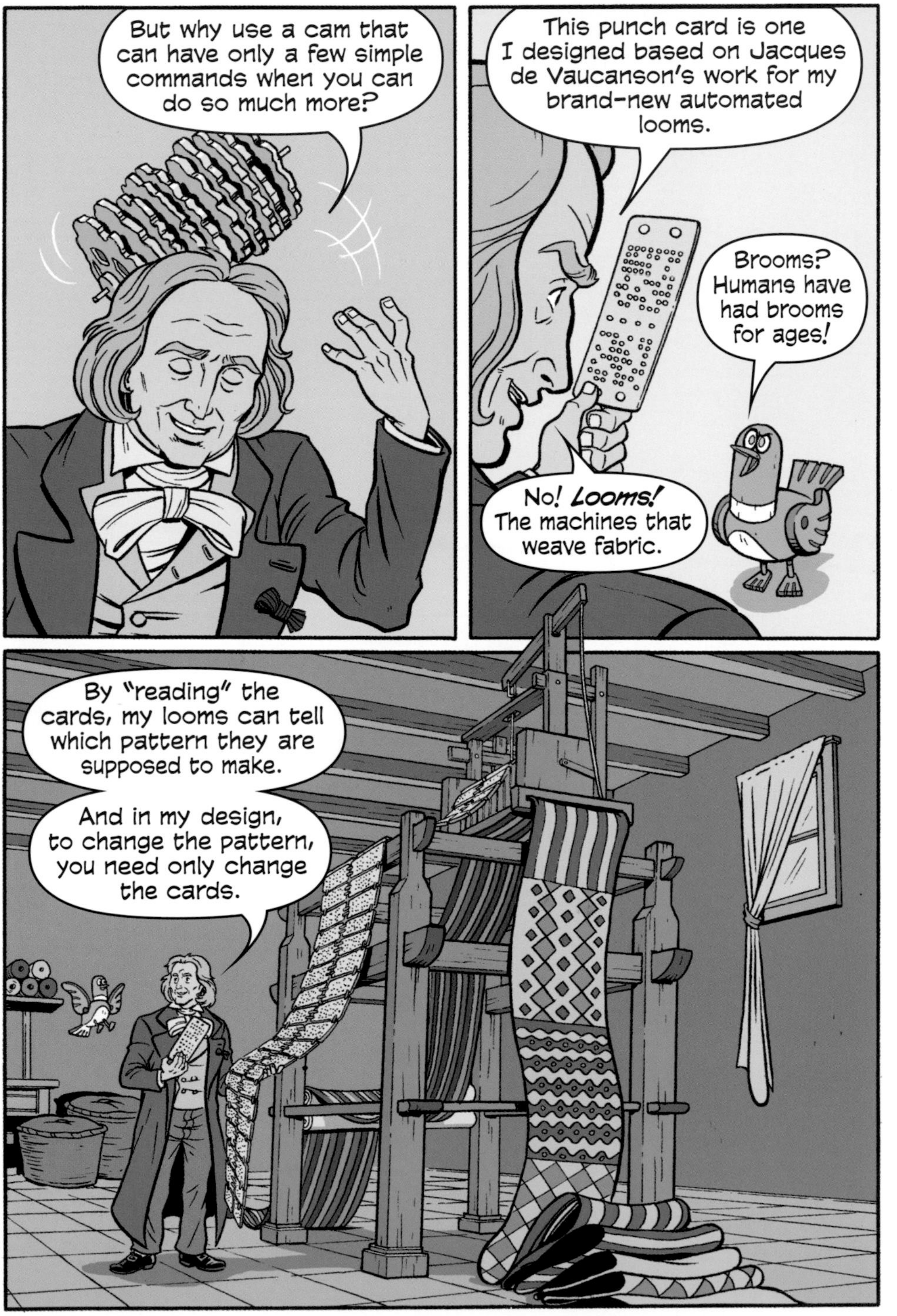

But why use a cam that can have only a few simple commands when you can do so much more?
This punch card is one I designed based on Jacques de Vaucanson's work for my brand-new automated looms.
Brooms? Humans have had brooms for ages!
No! *Looms!* The machines that weave fabric.
By "reading" the cards, my looms can tell which pattern they are supposed to make.
And in my design, to change the pattern, you need only change the cards.

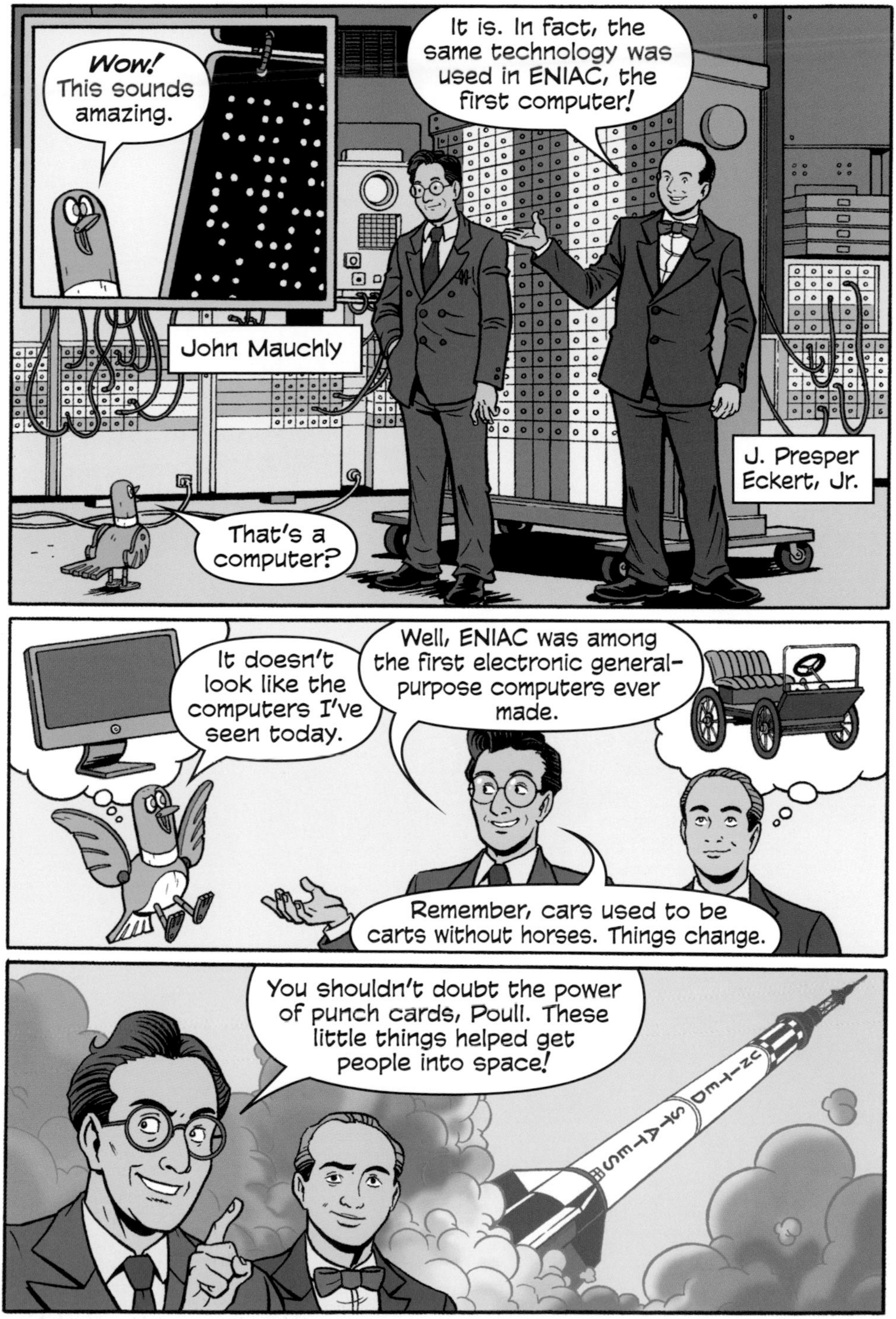
Wow! This sounds amazing.
It is. In fact, the same technology was used in ENIAC, the first computer!
John Mauchly
J. Presper Eckert, Jr.
That's a computer?
It doesn't look like the computers I've seen today.
Well, ENIAC was among the first electronic general-purpose computers ever made.
Remember, cars used to be carts without horses. Things change.
You shouldn't doubt the power of punch cards, Poull. These little things helped get people into space!
UNITED STATES

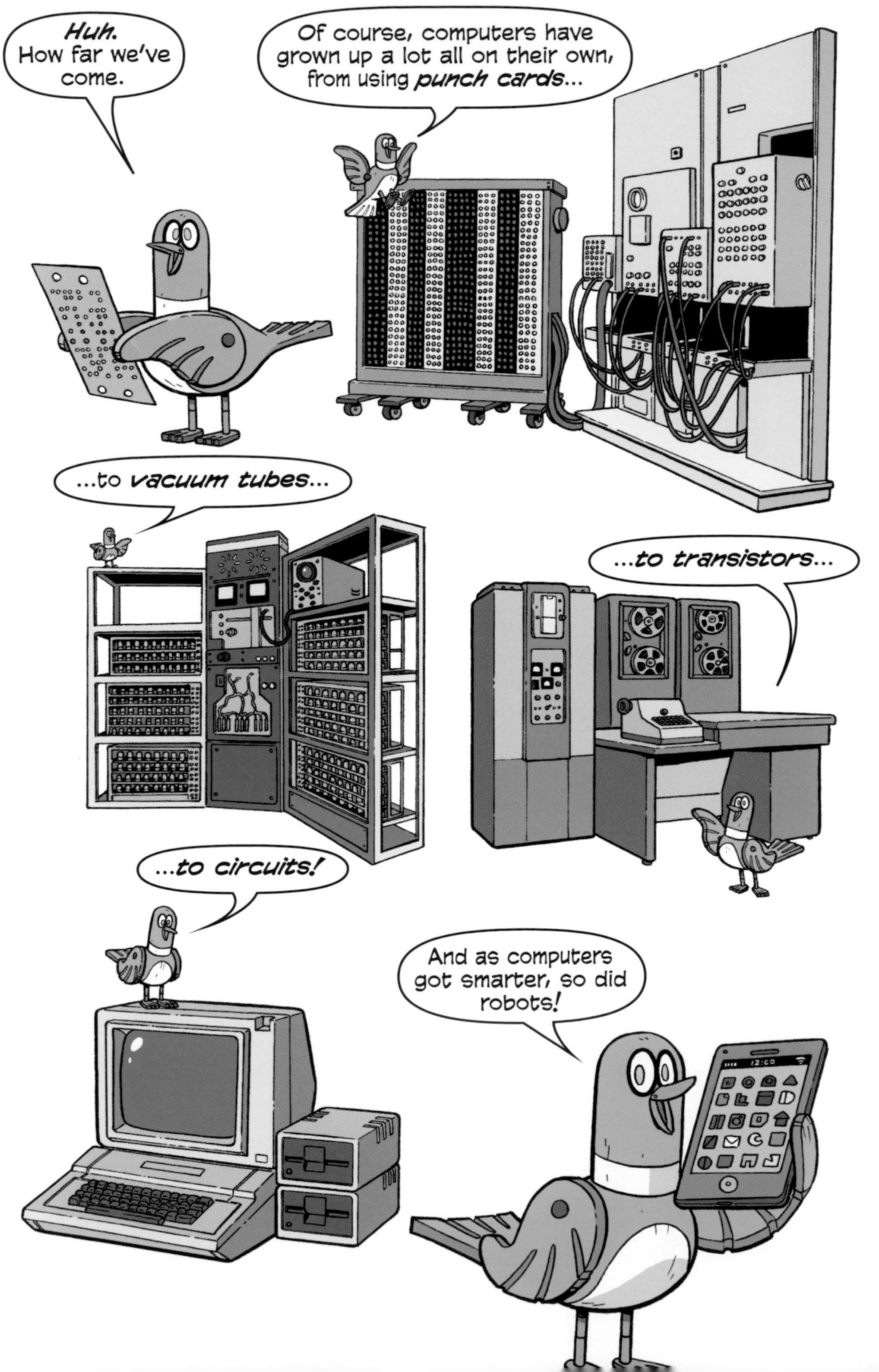
Huh. How far we've come.
Of course, computers have grown up a lot all on their own, from using punch cards...
...to vacuum tubes...
...to transistors...
...to circuits!
And as computers got smarter, so did robots!

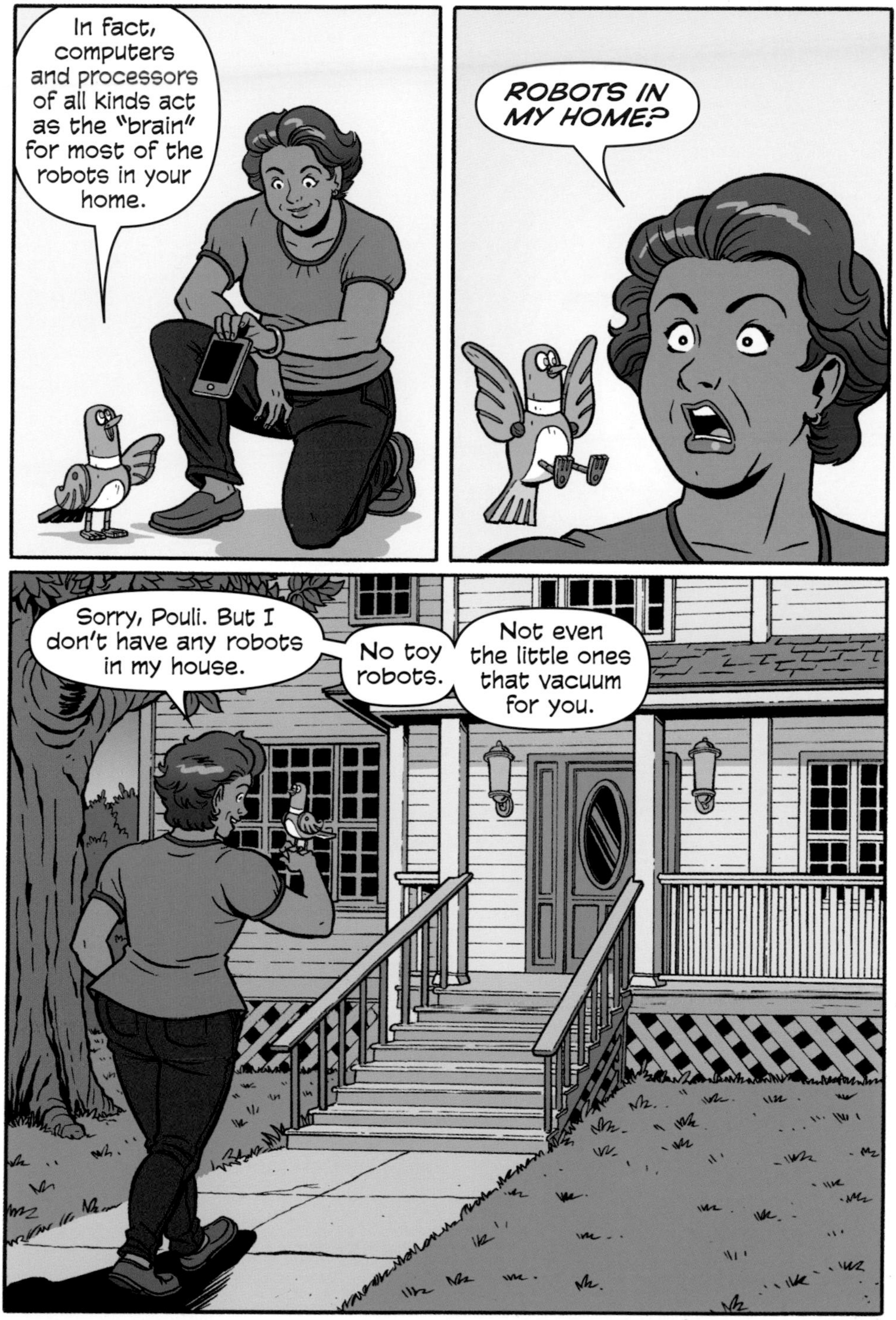
In fact, computers and processors of all kinds act as the "brain" for most of the robots in your home.
ROBOTS IN MY HOME?
Sorry, Pouli. But I don't have any robots in my house.
No toy robots.
Not even the little ones that vacuum for you.

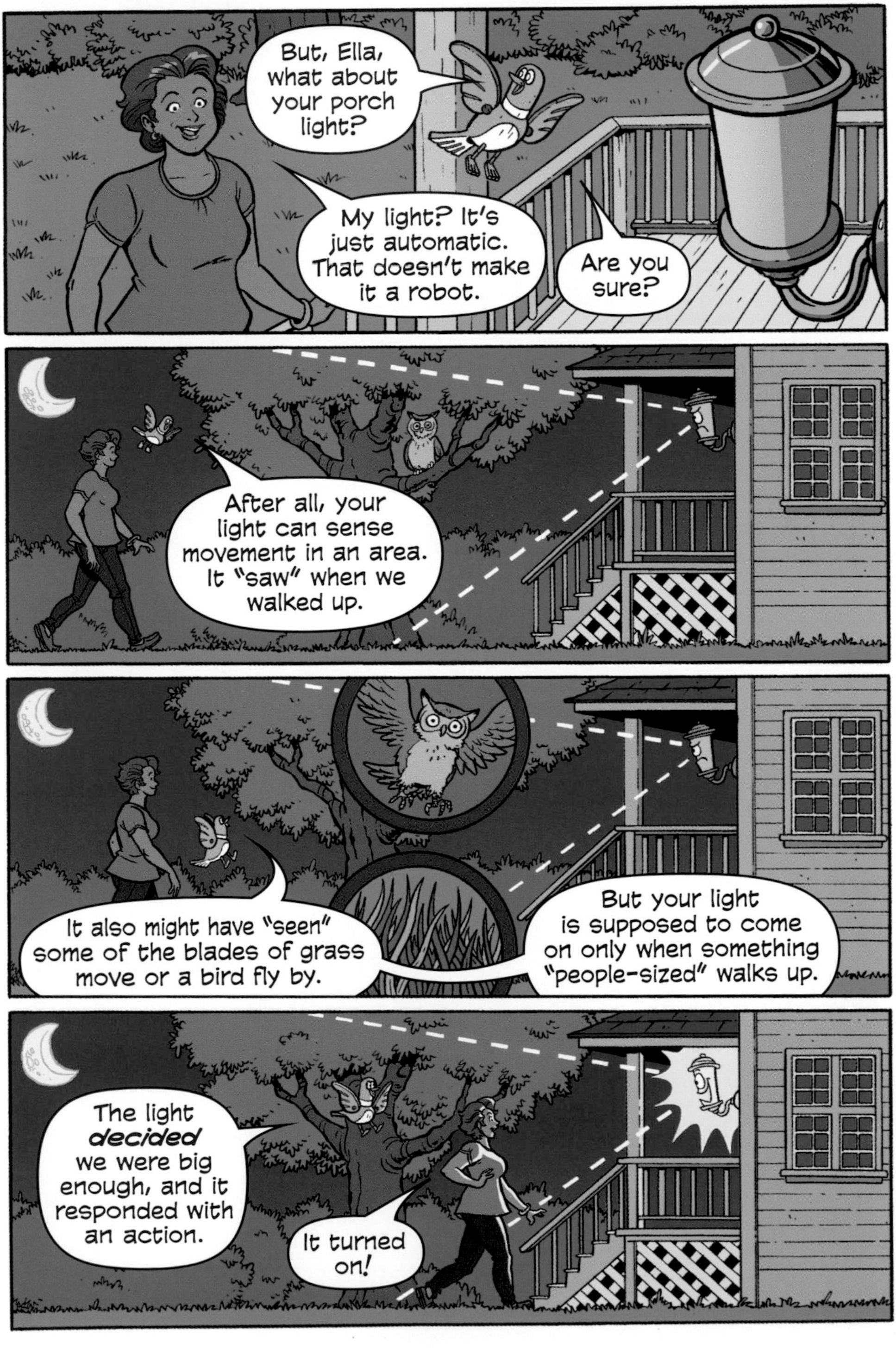
But, Ella, what about your porch light?
My light? It's just automatic. That doesn't make it a robot.
Are you sure?
After all, your light can sense movement in an area. It "saw" when we walked up.
It also might have "seen" some of the blades of grass move or a bird fly by.
But your light is supposed to come on only when something "people-sized" walks up.
The light *decided* we were big enough, and it responded with an action.
It turned on!

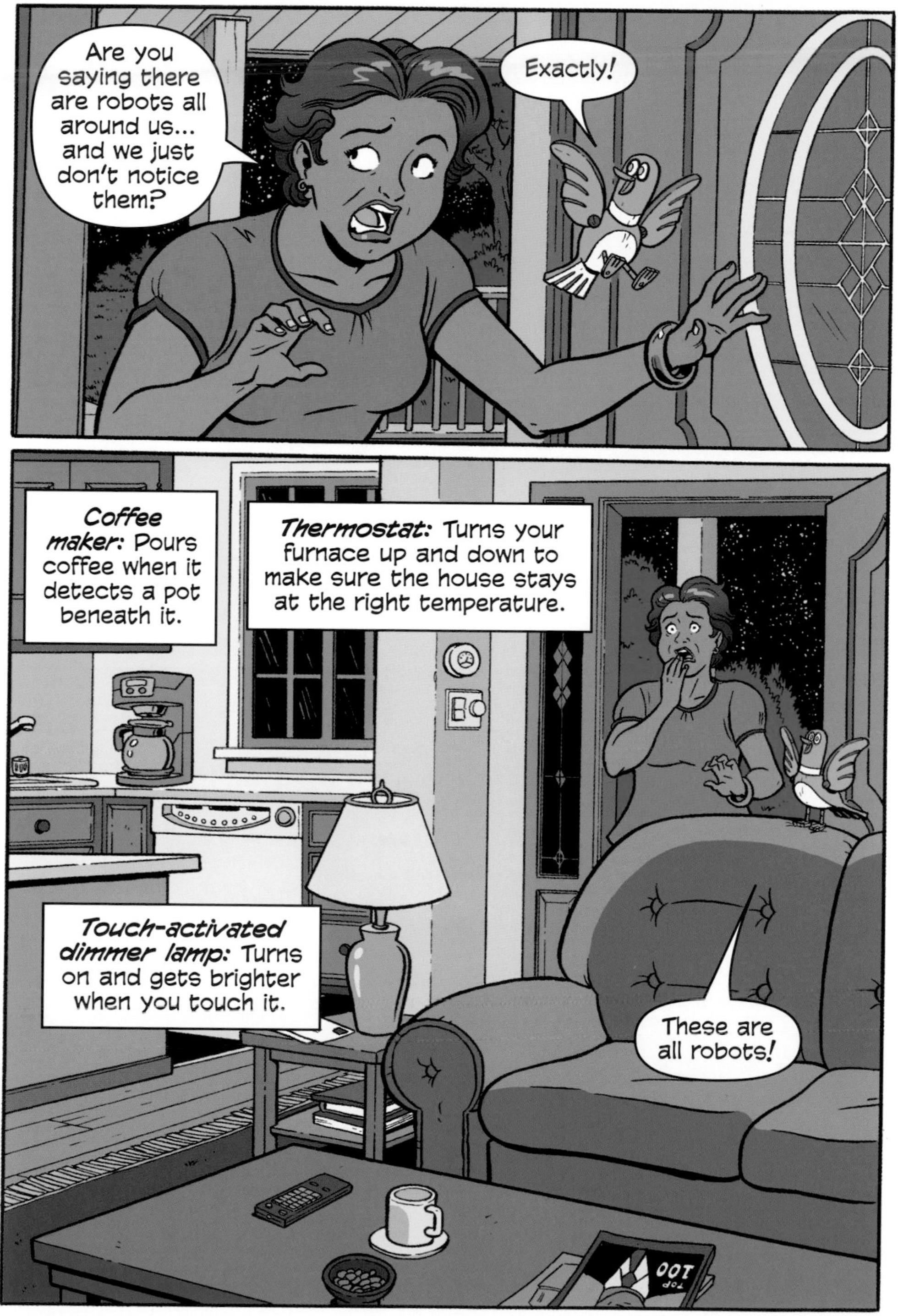
Are you saying there are robots all around us... and we just don't notice them?
Exactly!
Coffee maker: Pours coffee when it detects a pot beneath it.
Thermostat: Turns your furnace up and down to make sure the house stays at the right temperature.
Touch-activated dimmer lamp: Turns on and gets brighter when you touch it.
These are all robots!

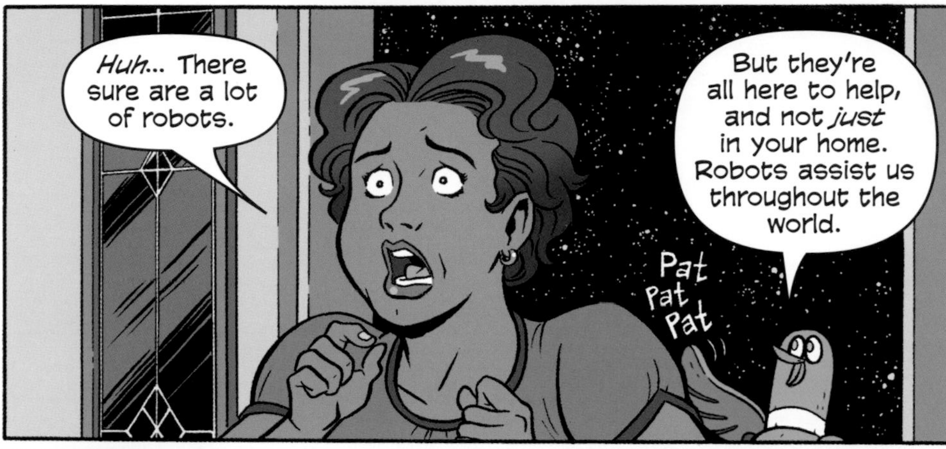
Huh... There sure are a lot of robots.
But they're all here to help, and not *just* in your home. Robots assist us throughout the world.
Pat Pat Pat

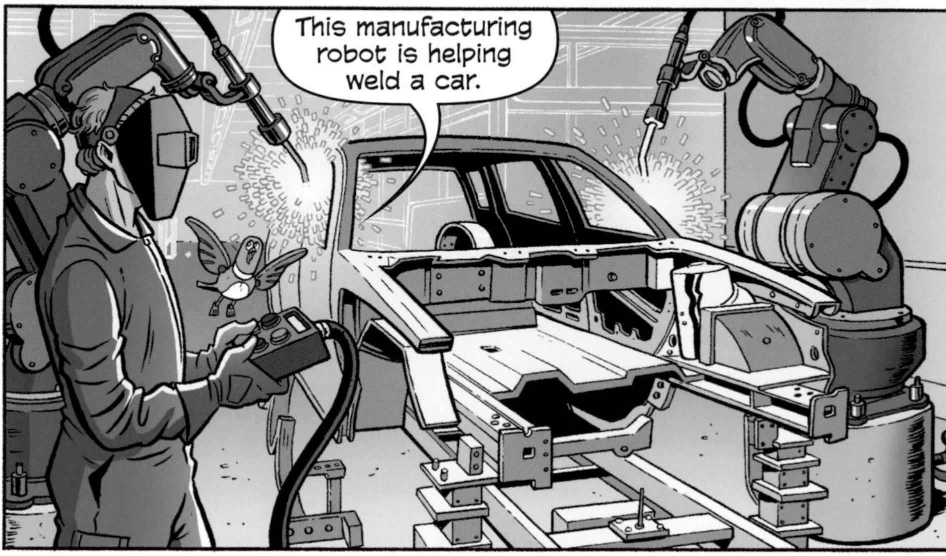
This manufacturing robot is helping weld a car.

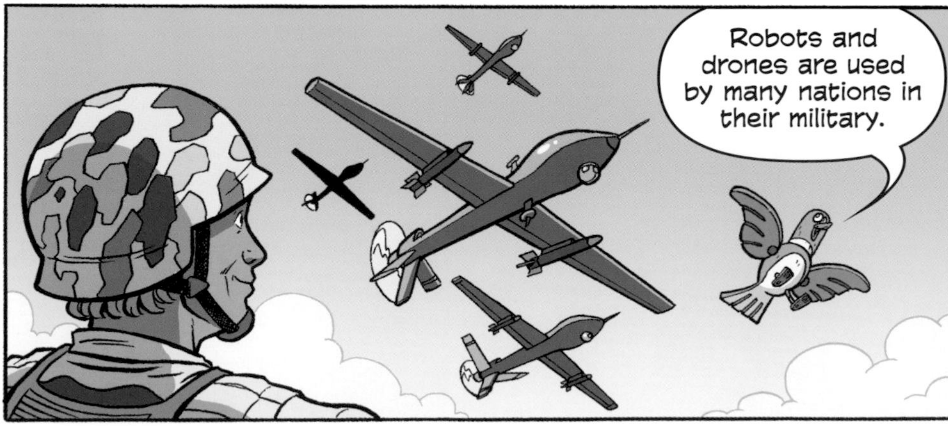
Robots and drones are used by many nations in their military.

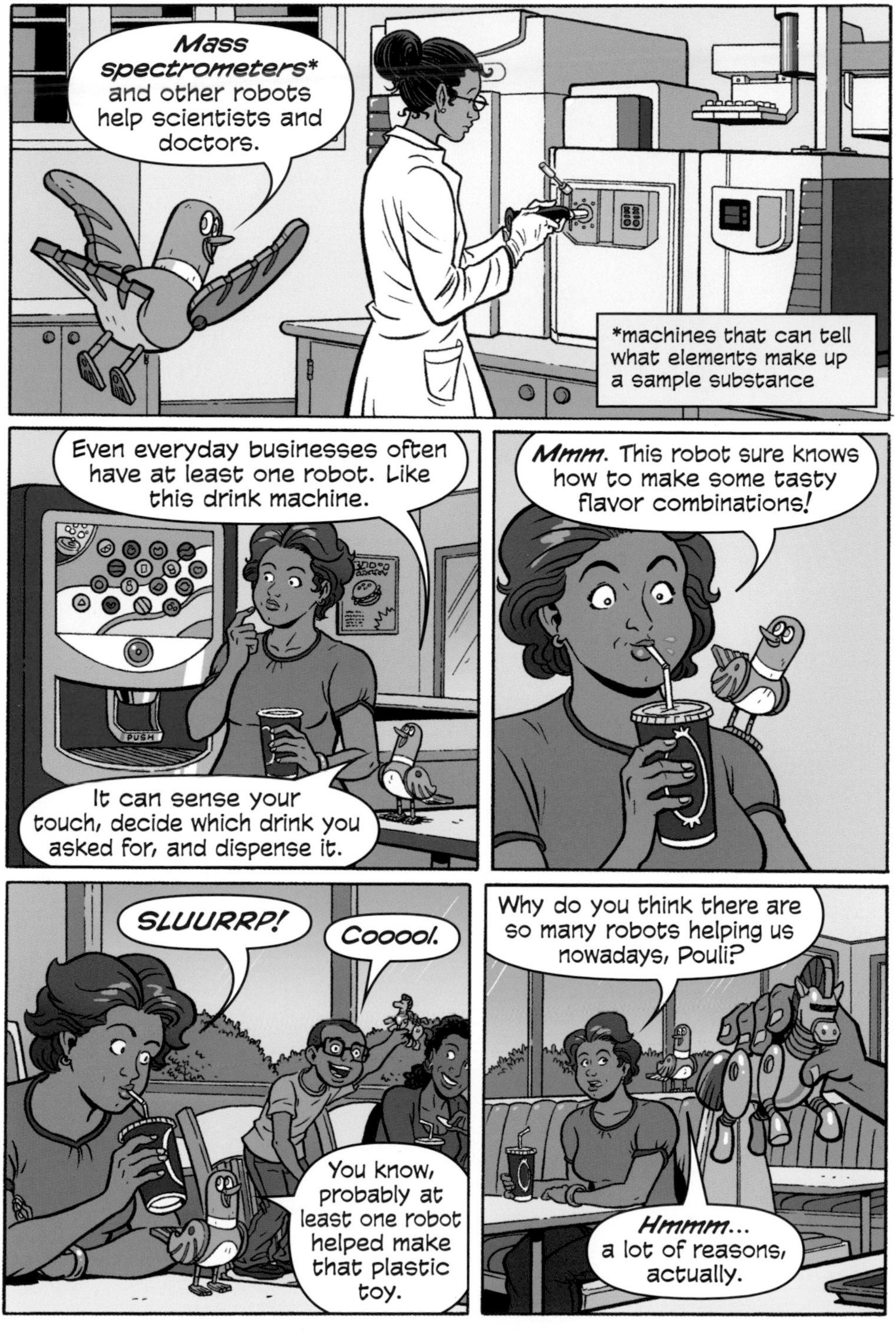

*Mass spectrometers** and other robots help scientists and doctors.
*machines that can tell what elements make up a sample substance
Even everyday businesses often have at least one robot. Like this drink machine.
PUSH
It can sense your touch, decide which drink you asked for, and dispense it.
Mmm. This robot sure knows how to make some tasty flavor combinations!
SLUURRP!
Cooool.
You know, probably at least one robot helped make that plastic toy.
Why do you think there are so many robots helping us nowadays, Pouli?
Hmmm... a lot of reasons, actually.

To understand why we use robots, you need to understand what robots are good at.

Let's imagine that we have a human worker and a robot worker making an engine.
TIM: Human worker
Tim
T1M: Robot worker
T1M
Part of building this engine involves attaching a nut to a bolt.
Tim and T1M can both attach a nut to a bolt.
T1M
4 hours later.
But T1m can do this all day for years without getting hurt or bored.
Human Tim, not so much.
T1M

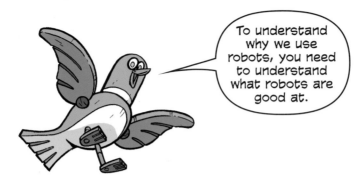

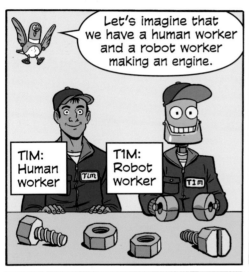

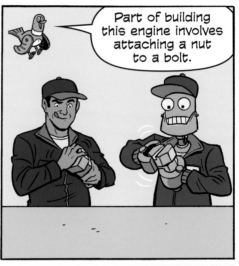

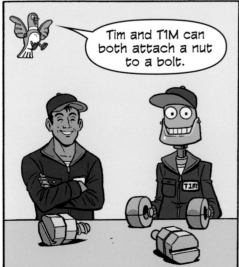

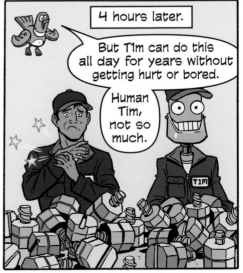

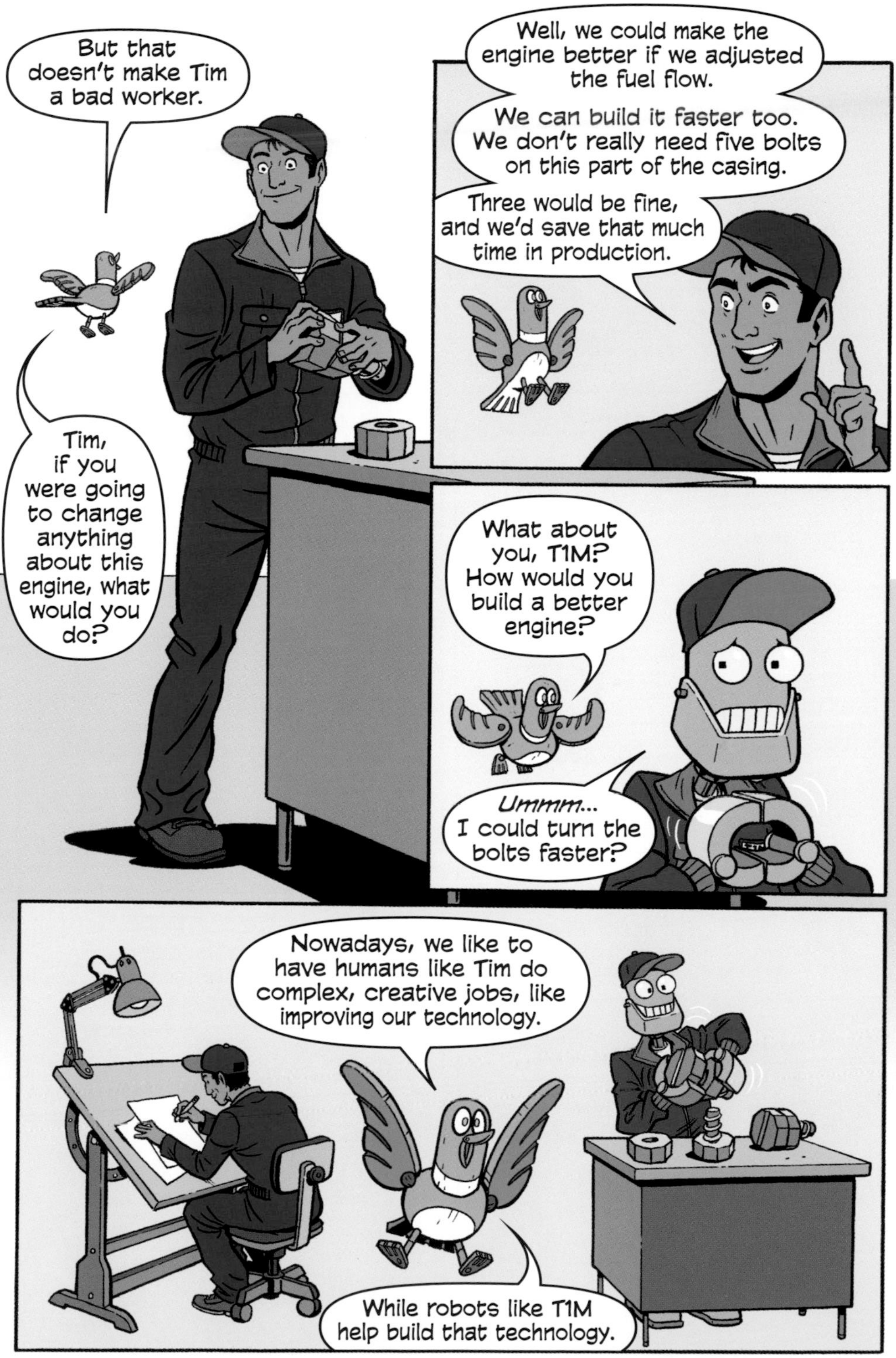

But that doesn't make Tim a bad worker.
Tim, if you were going to change anything about this engine, what would you do?
Well, we could make the engine better if we adjusted the fuel flow.
We can build it faster too. We don't really need five bolts on this part of the casing.
Three would be fine, and we'd save that much time in production.
What about you, T1M? How would you build a better engine?
Ummm... I could turn the bolts faster?
Nowadays, we like to have humans like Tim do complex, creative jobs, like improving our technology.
While robots like T1M help build that technology.

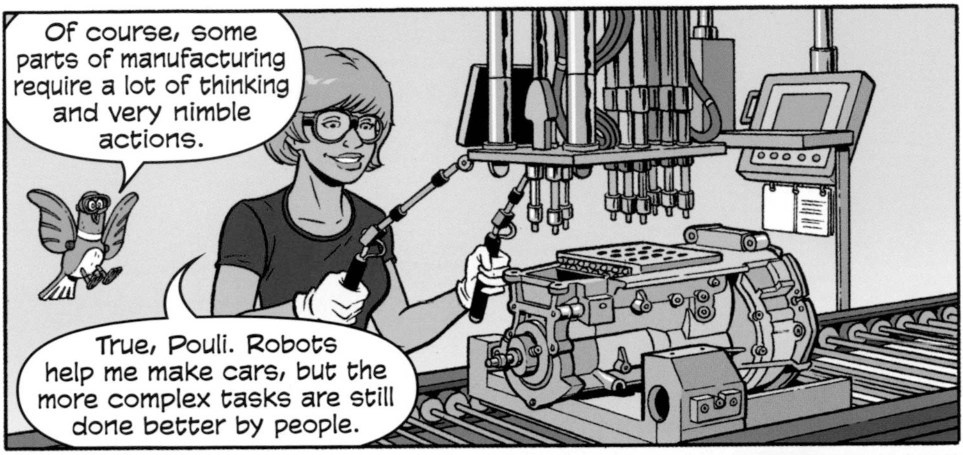
Of course, some parts of manufacturing require a lot of thinking and very nimble actions.
True, Pouli. Robots help me make cars, but the more complex tasks are still done better by people.

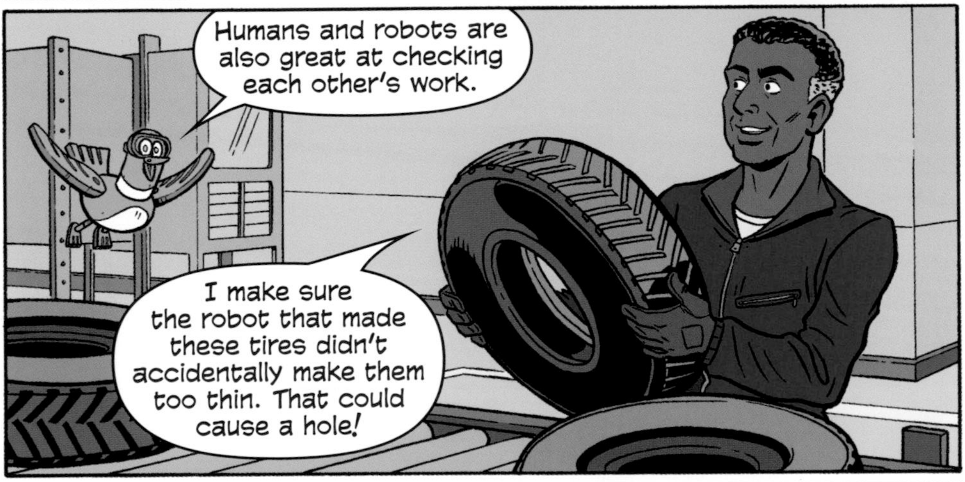
Humans and robots are also great at checking each other's work.
I make sure the robot that made these tires didn't accidentally make them too thin. That could cause a hole!

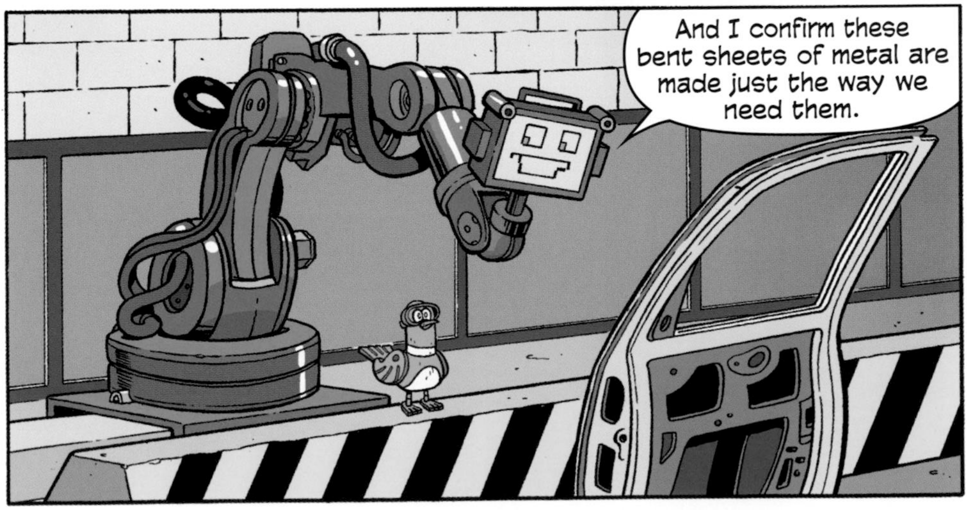
And I confirm these bent sheets of metal are made just the way we need them.

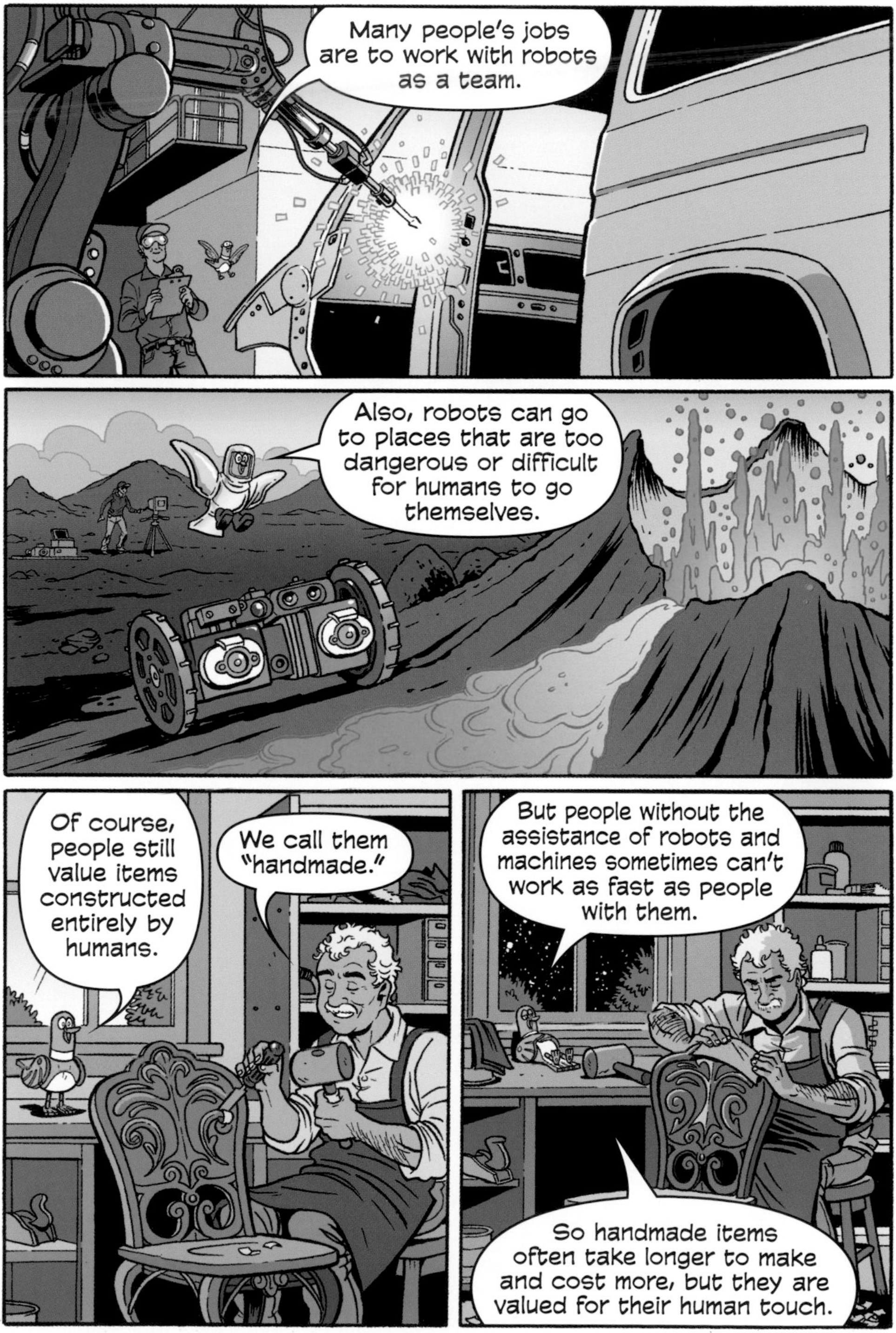
Many people's jobs are to work with robots as a team.
Also, robots can go to places that are too dangerous or difficult for humans to go themselves.
Of course, people still value items constructed entirely by humans.
We call them "handmade."
But people without the assistance of robots and machines sometimes can't work as fast as people with them.
So handmade items often take longer to make and cost more, but they are valued for their human touch.

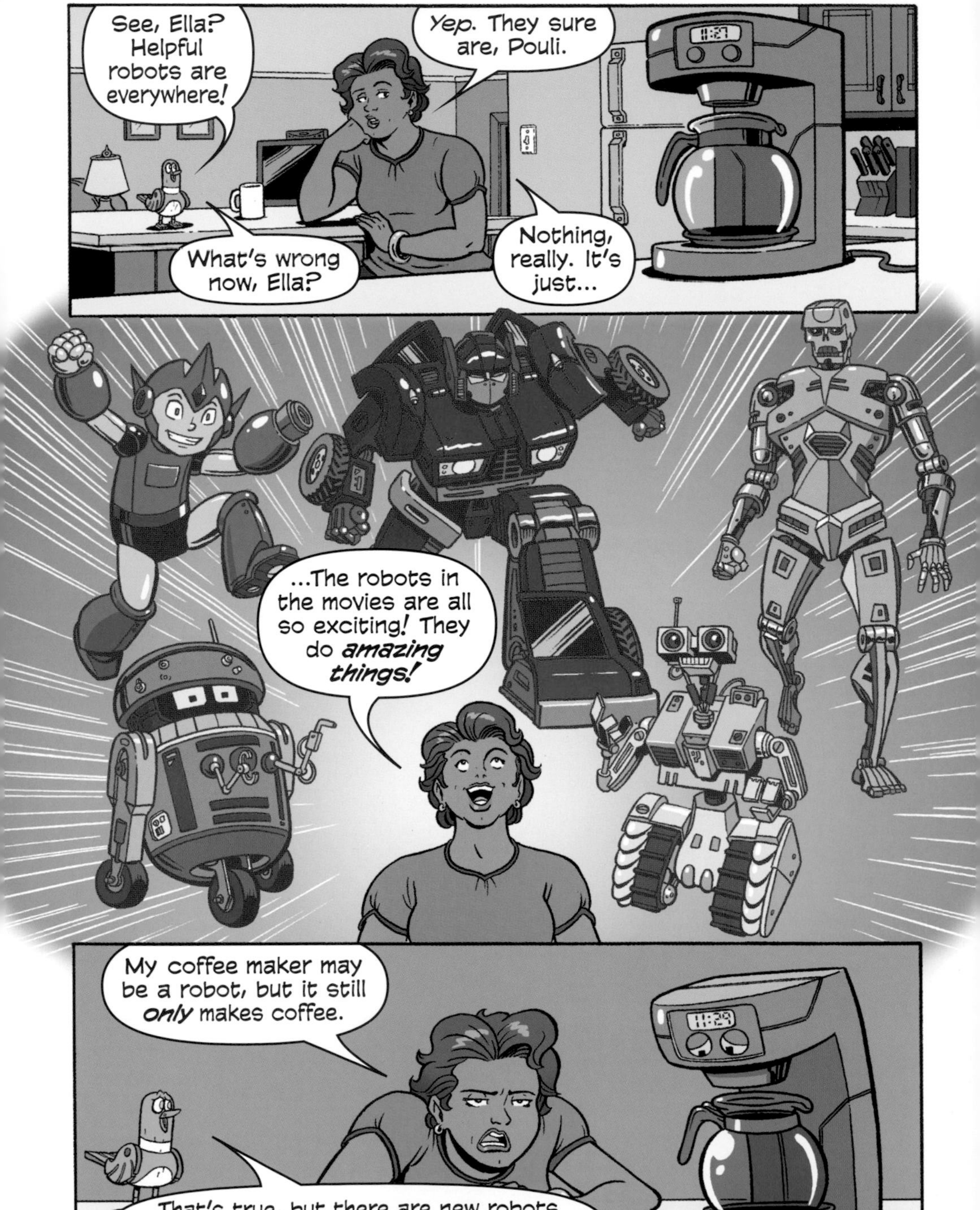

See, Ella? Helpful robots are everywhere!
Yep. They sure are, Pouli.
What's wrong now, Ella?
Nothing, really. It's just...
...The robots in the movies are all so exciting! They do amazing things!
My coffee maker may be a robot, but it still only makes coffee.
That's true, but there are new robots designed every day that are blazing trails and standing out from the crowd!

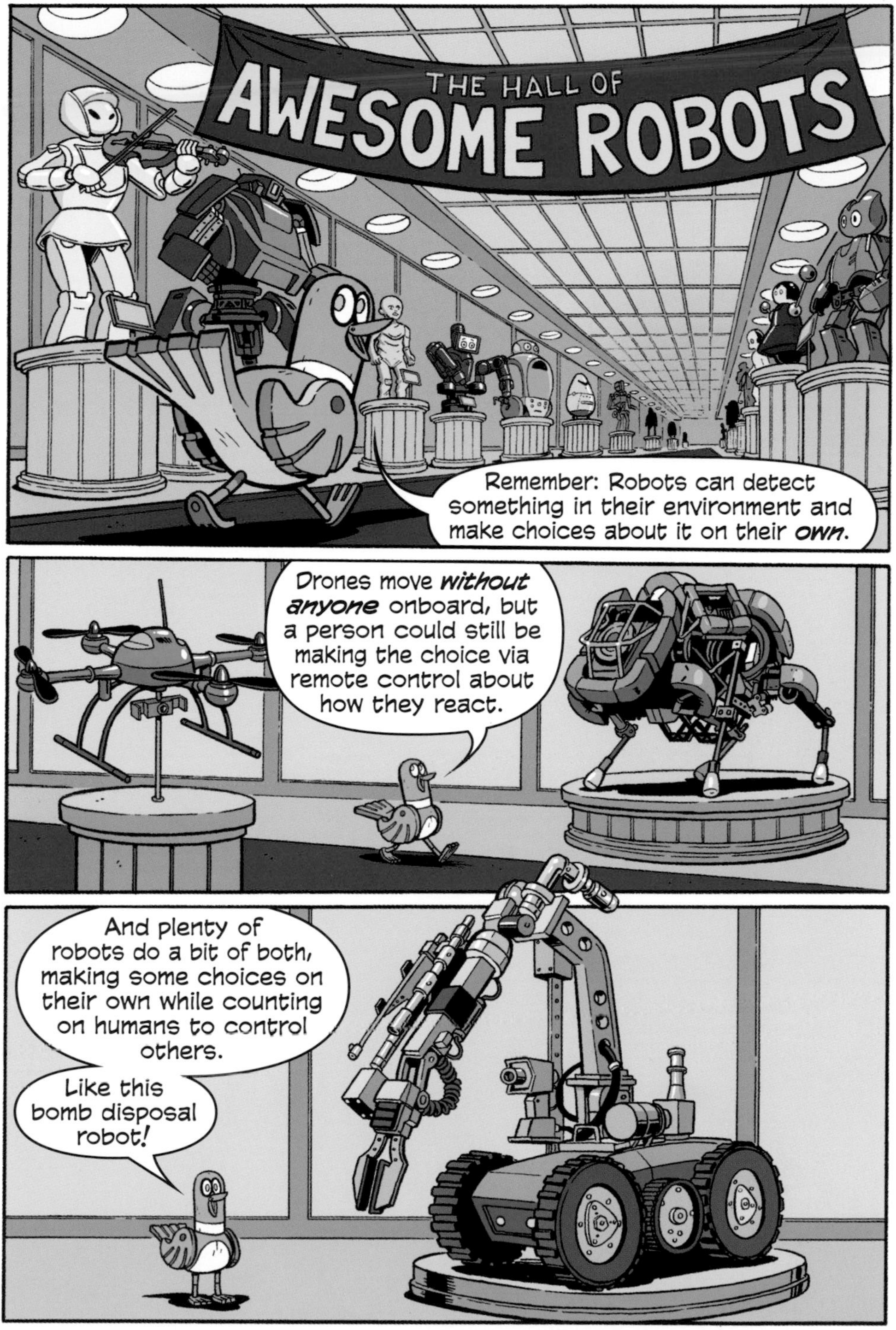
THE HALL OF
AWESOME ROBOTS
Remember: Robots can detect something in their environment and make choices about it on their *own*.
Drones move ***without anyone*** onboard, but a person could still be making the choice via remote control about how they react.
And plenty of robots do a bit of both, making some choices on their own while counting on humans to control others.
Like this bomb disposal robot!

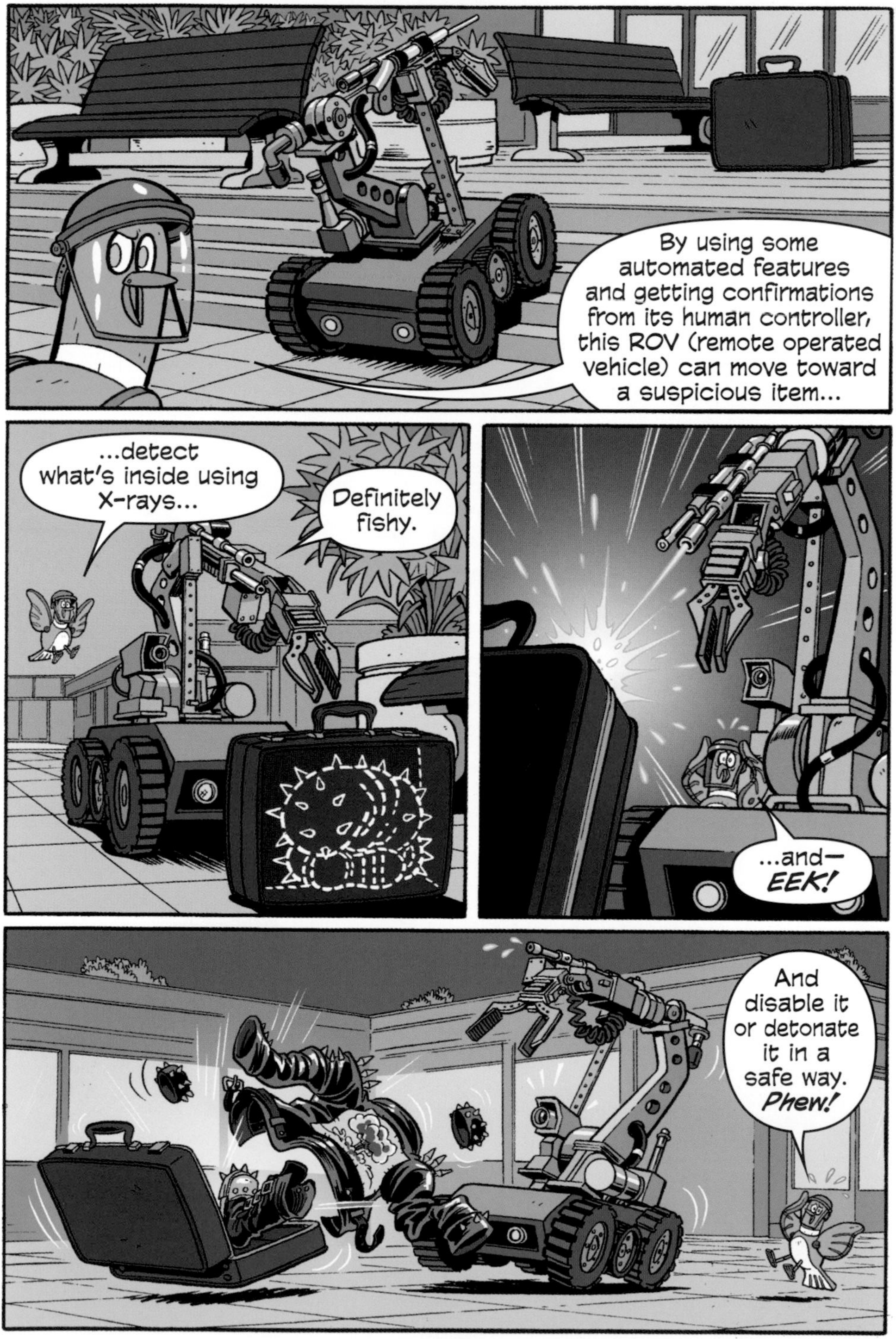
By using some automated features and getting confirmations from its human controller, this ROV (remote operated vehicle) can move toward a suspicious item...
...detect what's inside using X-rays...
Definitely fishy.
...and—
EEK!
And disable it or detonate it in a safe way.
Phew!

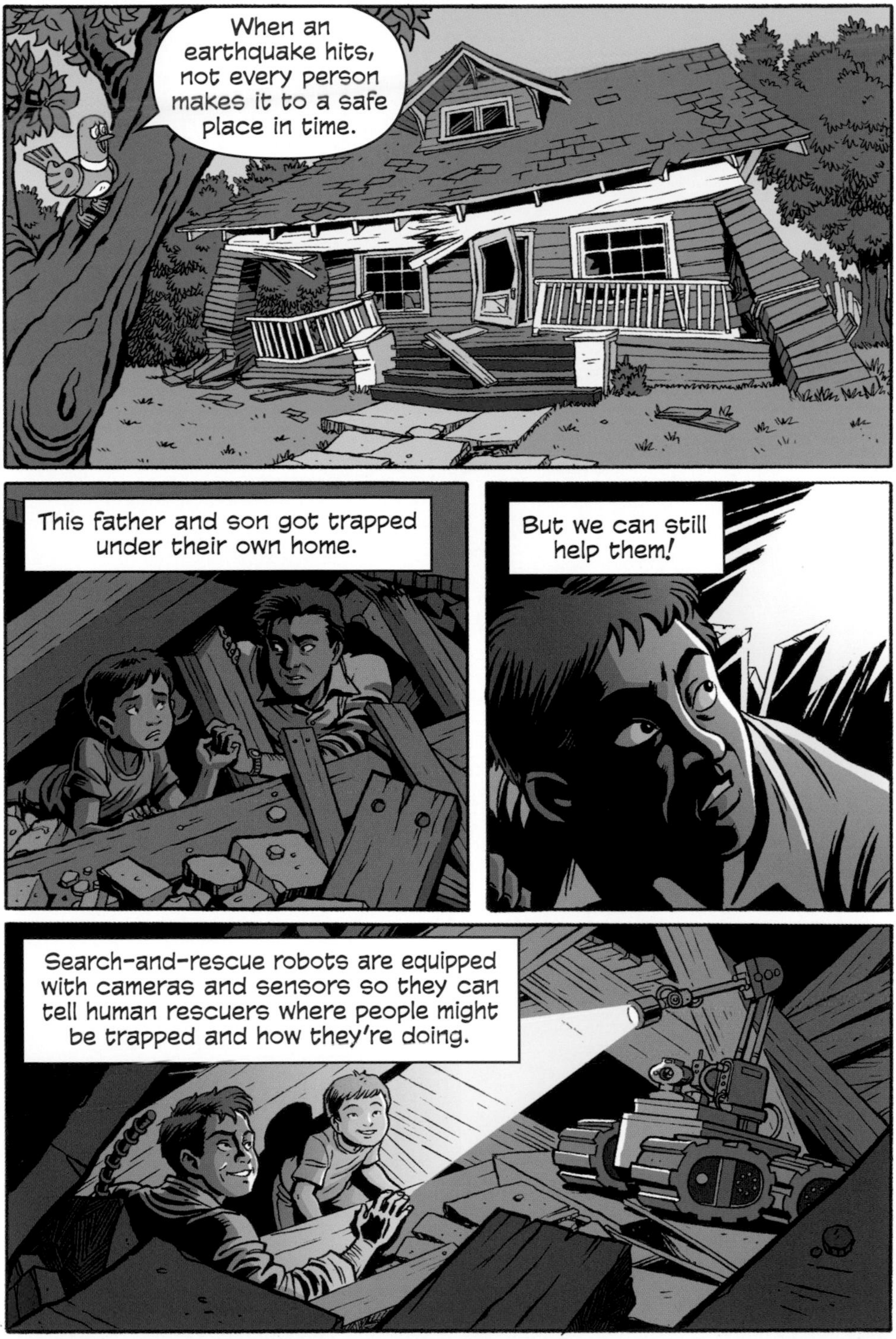
When an earthquake hits, not every person makes it to a safe place in time.
This father and son got trapped under their own home.
But we can still help them!
Search-and-rescue robots are equipped with cameras and sensors so they can tell human rescuers where people might be trapped and how they're doing.

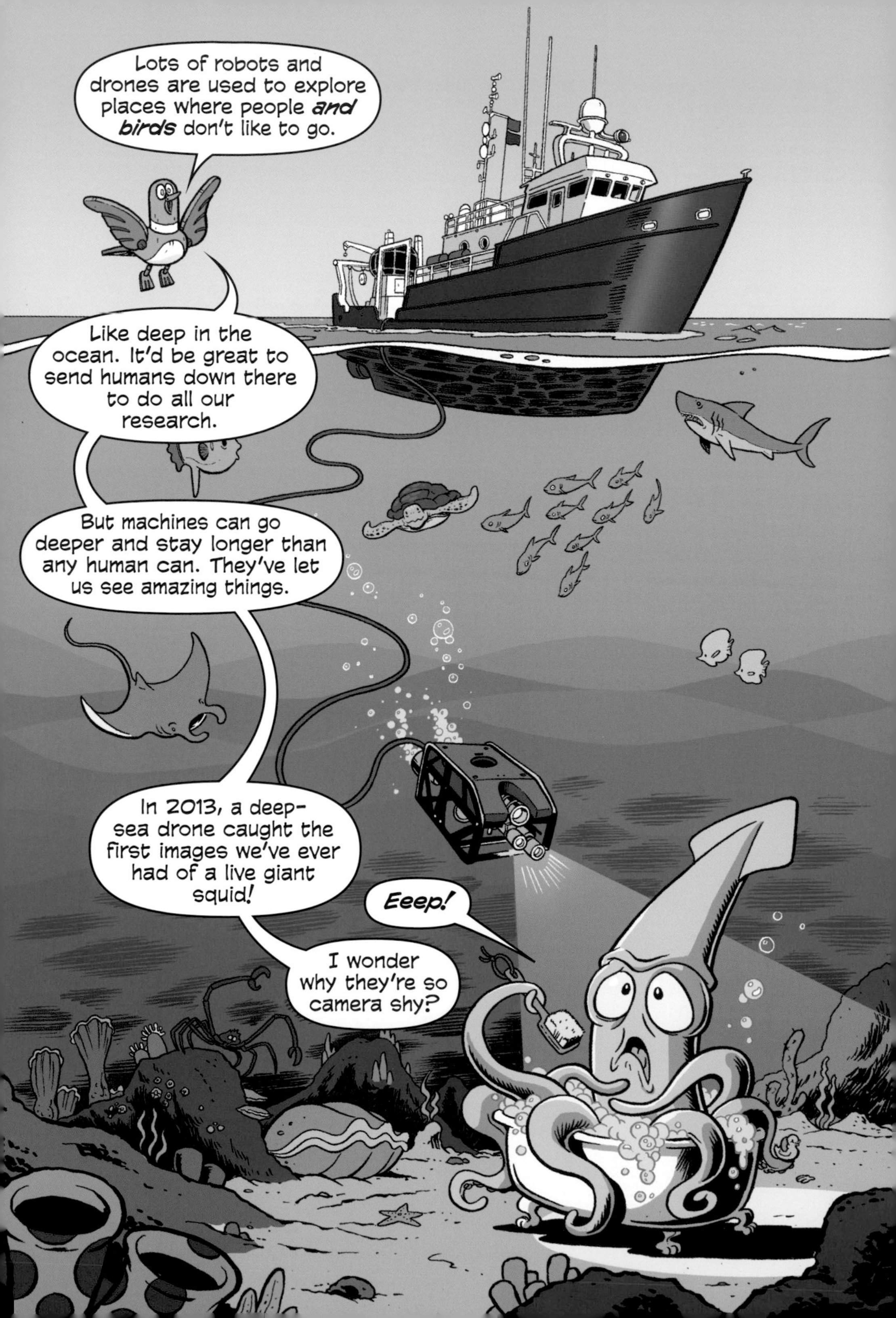
Lots of robots and drones are used to explore places where people ***and birds*** don't like to go.
Like deep in the ocean. It'd be great to send humans down there to do all our research.
But machines can go deeper and stay longer than any human can. They've let us see amazing things.
In 2013, a deep-sea drone caught the first images we've ever had of a live giant squid!
Eeep!
I wonder why they're so camera shy?

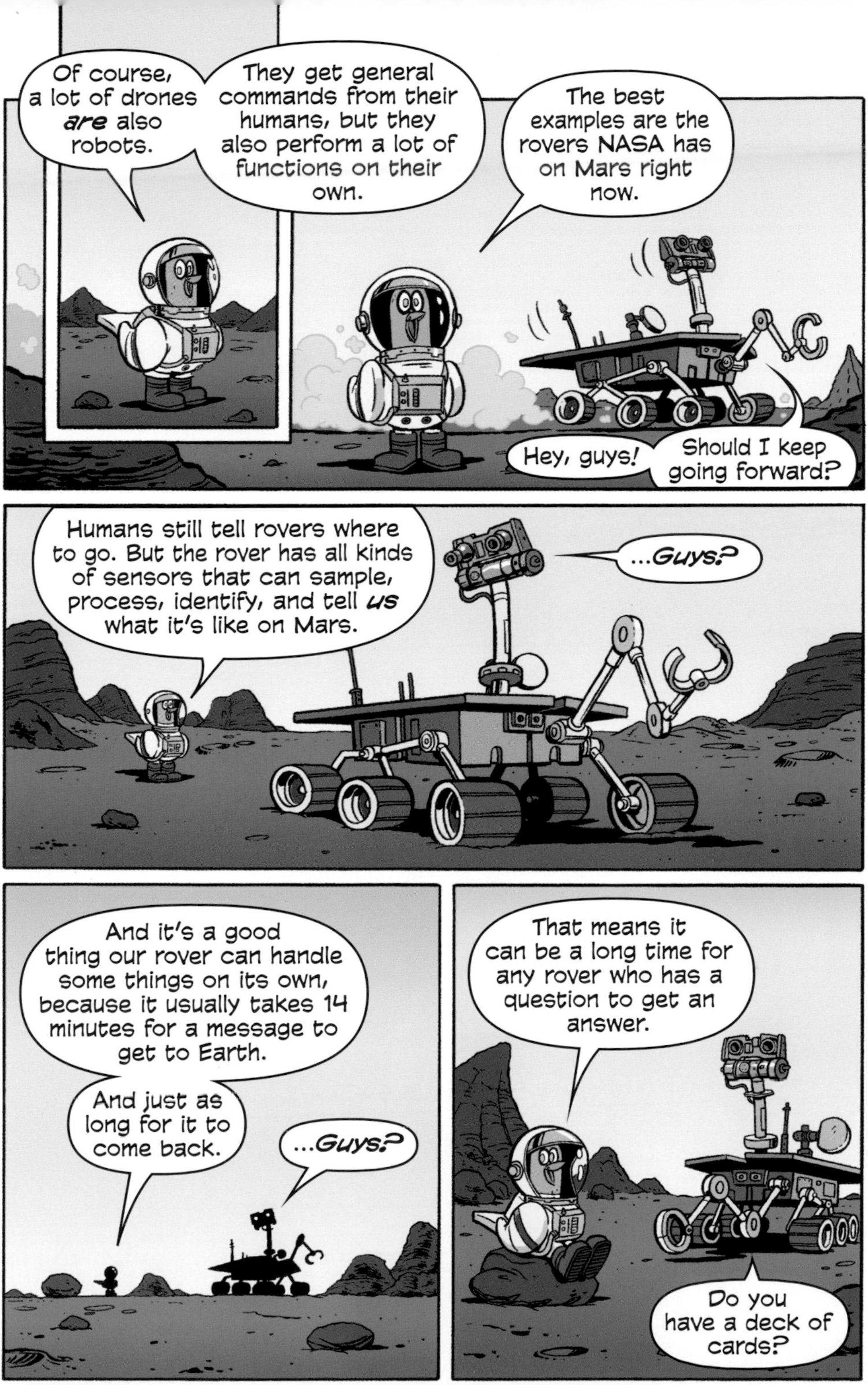
Of course, a lot of drones *are* also robots.
They get general commands from their humans, but they also perform a lot of functions on their own.
The best examples are the rovers NASA has on Mars right now.
Hey, guys!
Should I keep going forward?
Humans still tell rovers where to go. But the rover has all kinds of sensors that can sample, process, identify, and tell *us* what it's like on Mars.
...*Guys?*
And it's a good thing our rover can handle some things on its own, because it usually takes 14 minutes for a message to get to Earth.
And just as long for it to come back.
...*Guys?*
That means it can be a long time for any rover who has a question to get an answer.
Do you have a deck of cards?

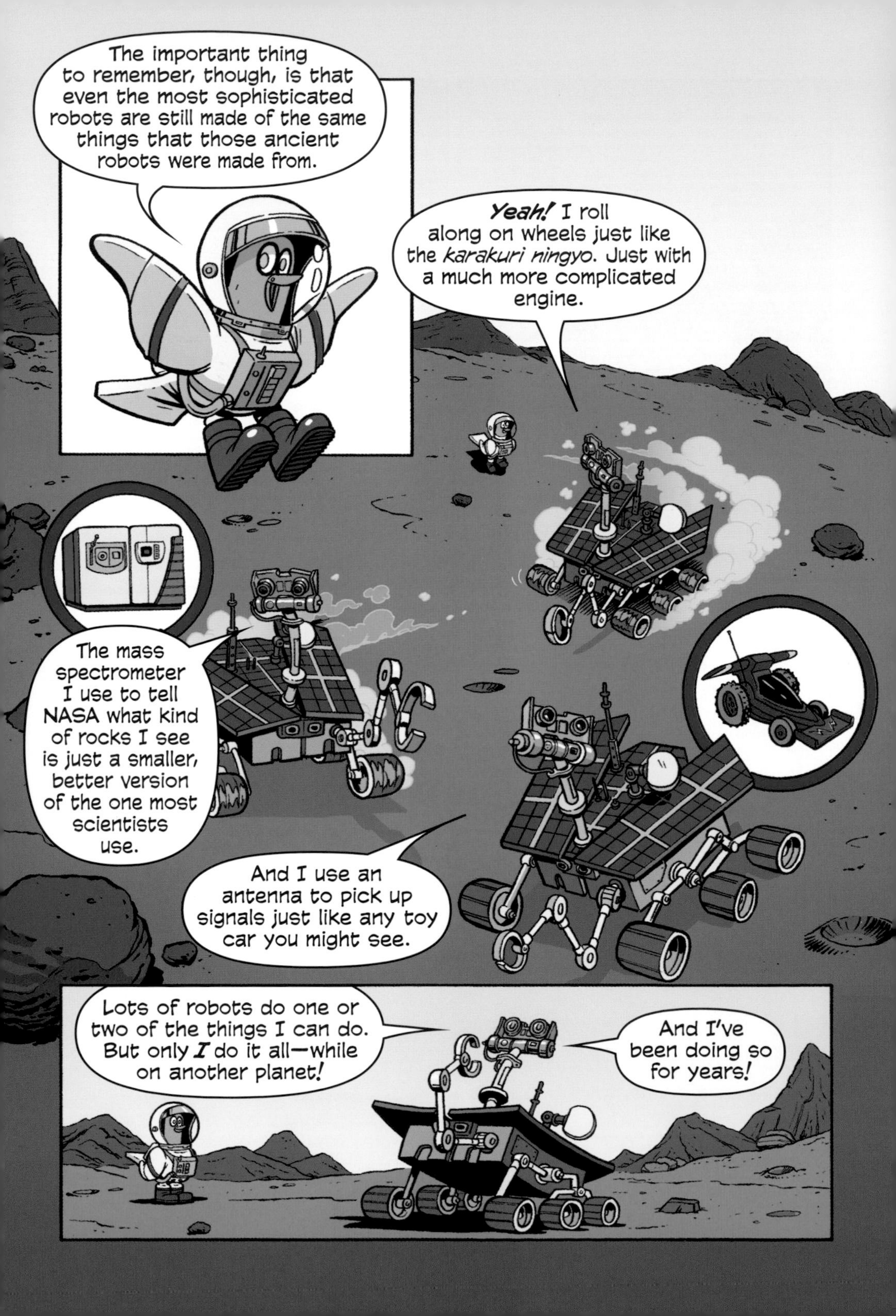
The important thing to remember, though, is that even the most sophisticated robots are still made of the same things that those ancient robots were made from.
Yeah! I roll along on wheels just like the karakuri ningyo. Just with a much more complicated engine.
The mass spectrometer I use to tell NASA what kind of rocks I see is just a smaller, better version of the one most scientists use.
And I use an antenna to pick up signals just like any toy car you might see.
Lots of robots do one or two of the things I can do. But only I do it all—while on another planet!
And I've been doing so for years!

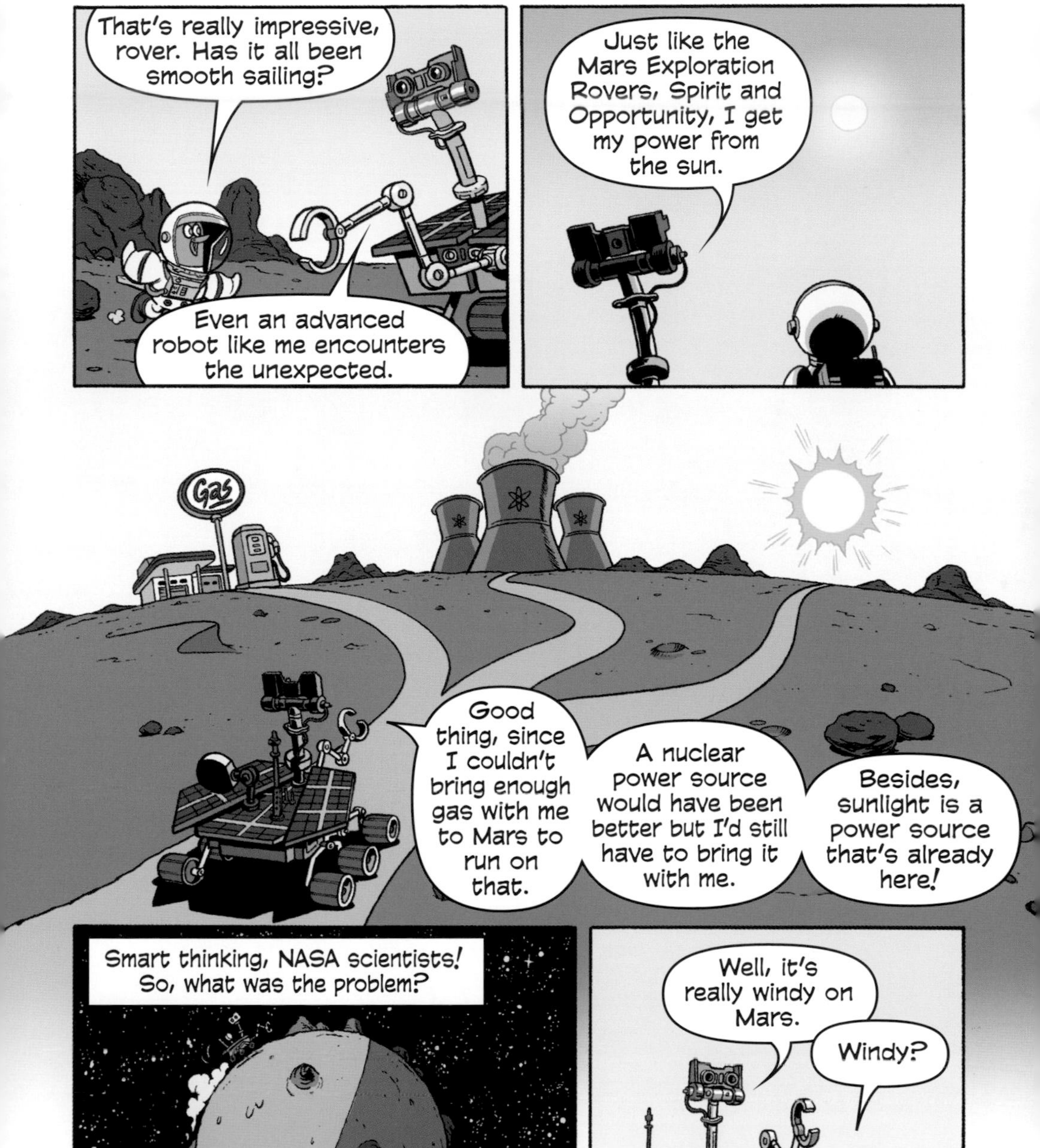
That's really impressive, rover. Has it all been smooth sailing?
Even an advanced robot like me encounters the unexpected.
Just like the Mars Exploration Rovers, Spirit and Opportunity, I get my power from the sun.
Gas
Good thing, since I couldn't bring enough gas with me to Mars to run on that.
A nuclear power source would have been better but I'd still have to bring it with me.
Besides, sunlight is a power source that's already here!
Smart thinking, NASA scientists! So, what was the problem?
Z.
Well, it's really windy on Mars.
Windy?

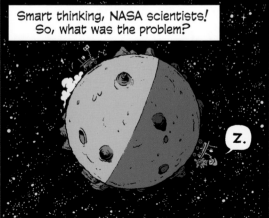

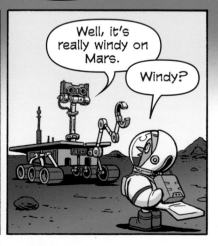

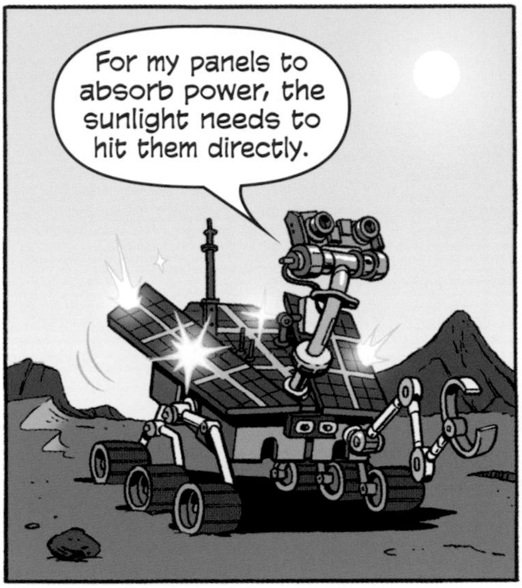
For my panels to absorb power, the sunlight needs to hit them directly.

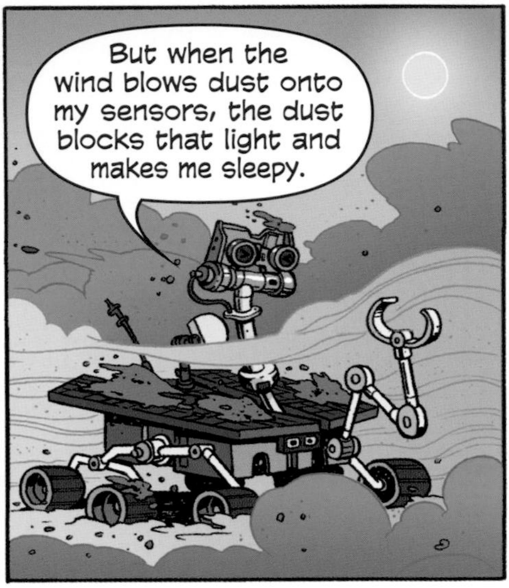
But when the wind blows dust onto my sensors, the dust blocks that light and makes me sleepy.

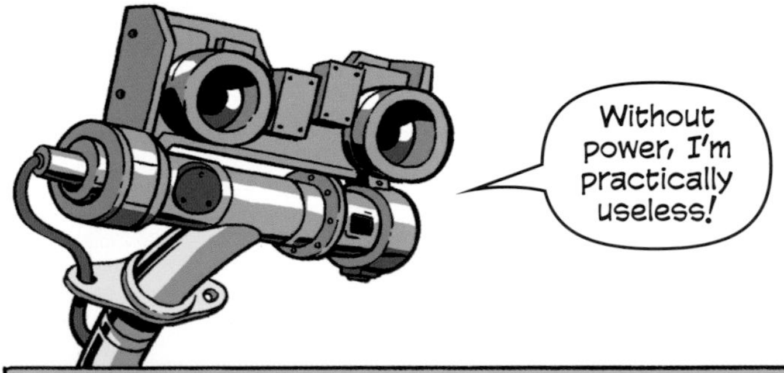
Without power, I'm practically useless!

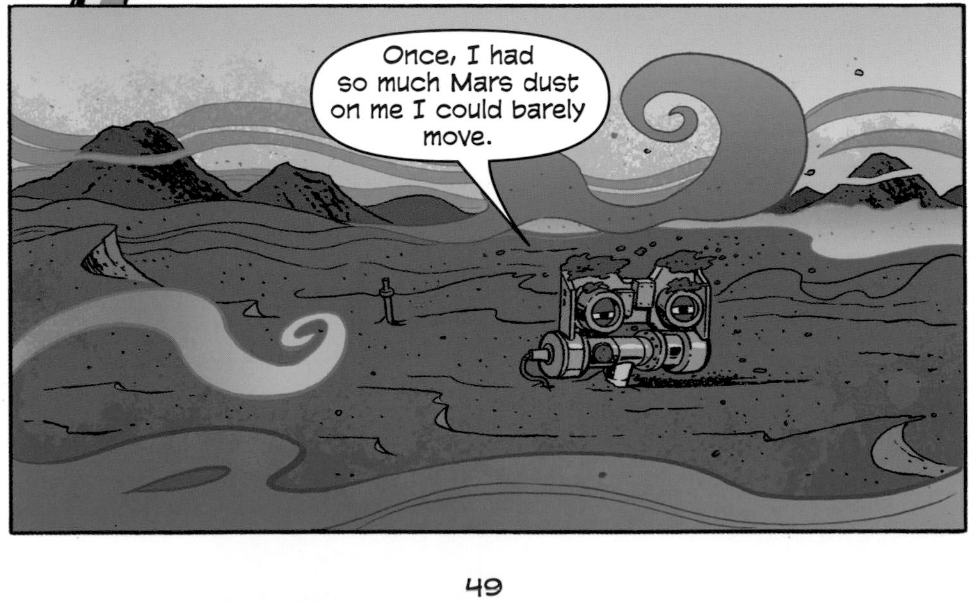
Once, I had so much Mars dust on me I could barely move.

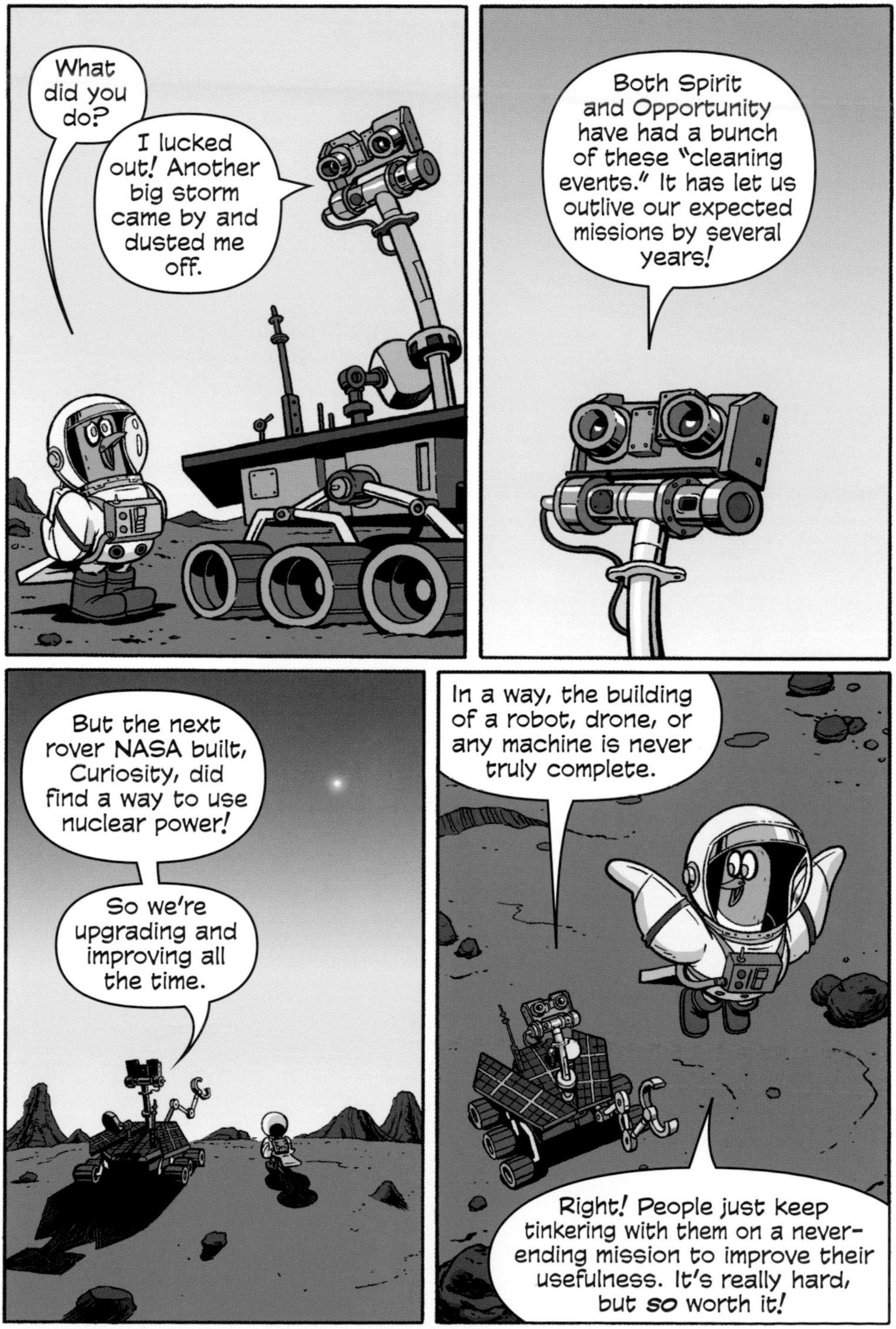
What did you do?
I lucked out! Another big storm came by and dusted me off.
Both Spirit and Opportunity have had a bunch of these "cleaning events." It has let us outlive our expected missions by several years!
But the next rover NASA built, Curiosity, did find a way to use nuclear power!
So we're upgrading and improving all the time.
In a way, the building of a robot, drone, or any machine is never truly complete.
Right! People just keep tinkering with them on a never-ending mission to improve their usefulness. It's really hard, but *so* worth it!

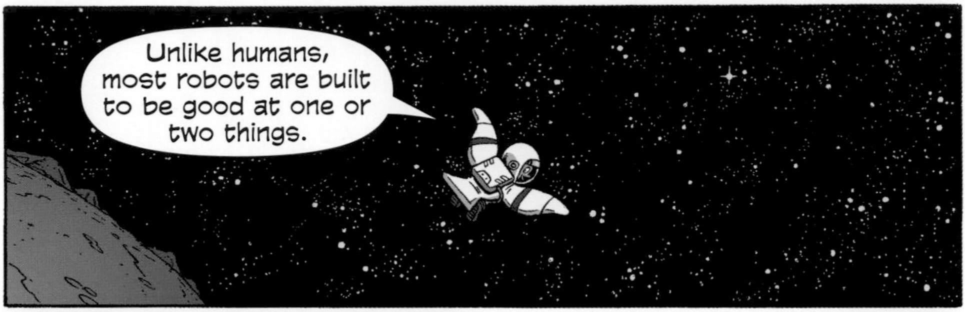
Unlike humans, most robots are built to be good at one or two things.

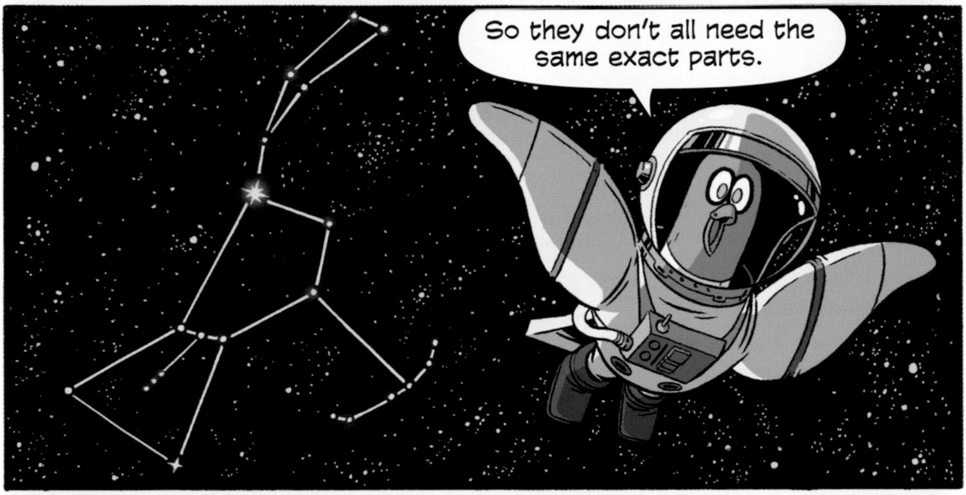
So they don't all need the same exact parts.

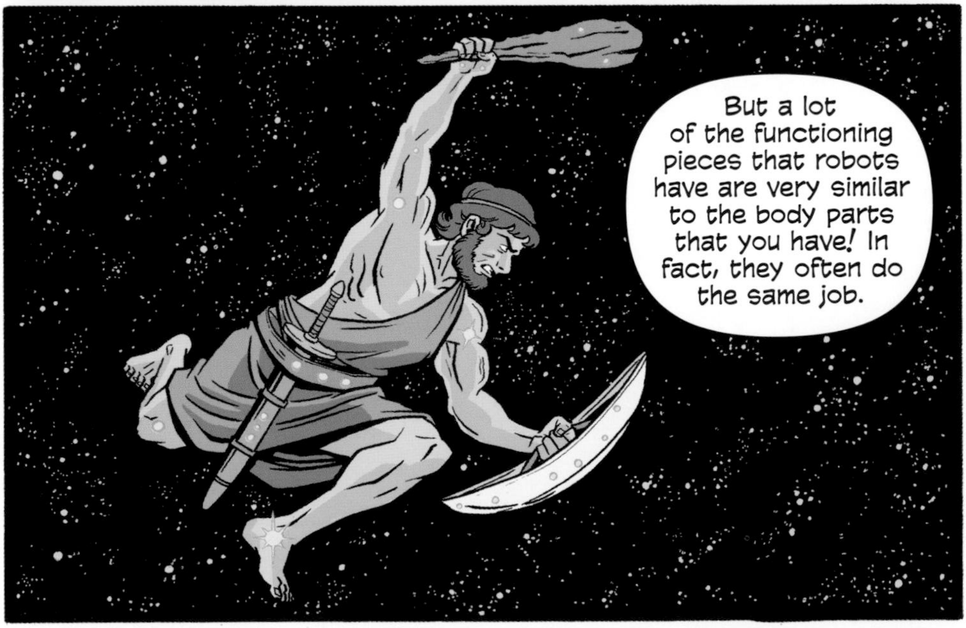
But a lot of the functioning pieces that robots have are very similar to the body parts that you have! In fact, they often do the same job.

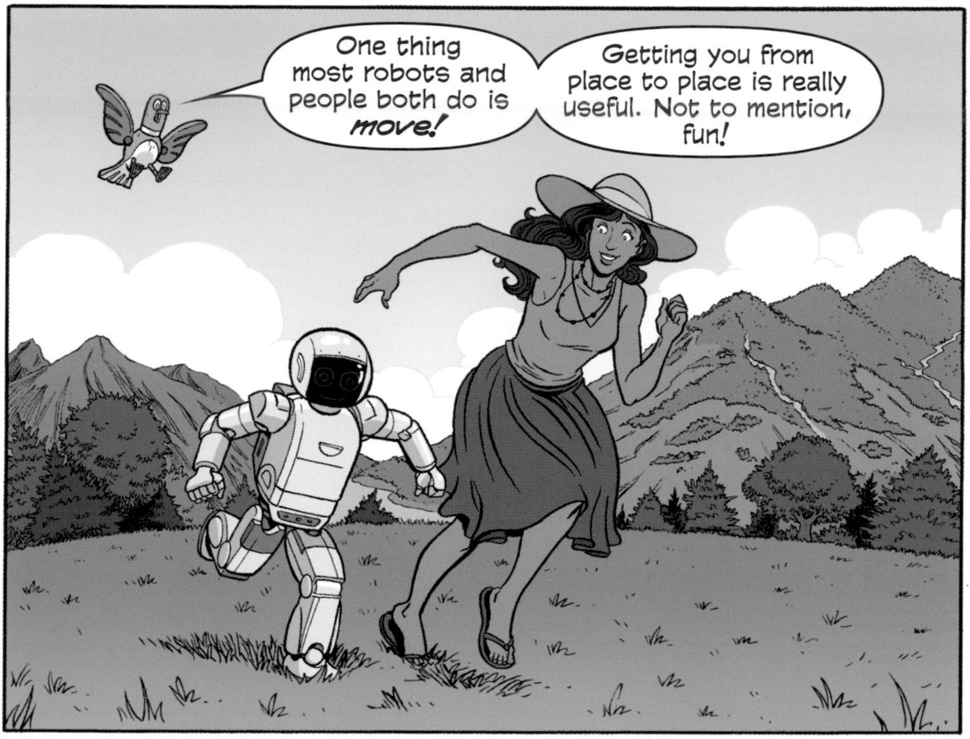
One thing most robots and people both do is *move!*
Getting you from place to place is really useful. Not to mention, fun!

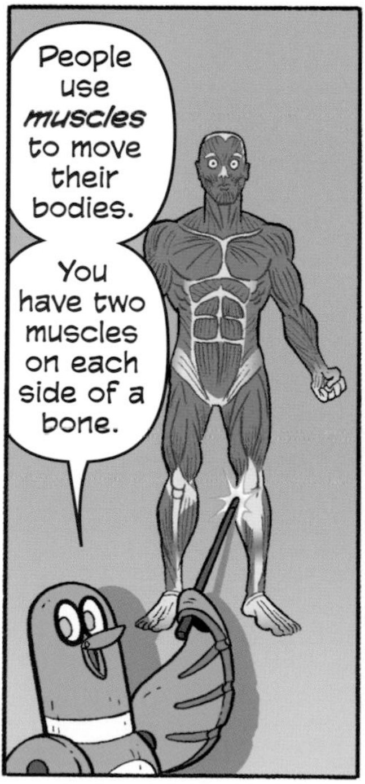
People use *muscles* to move their bodies.
You have two muscles on each side of a bone.

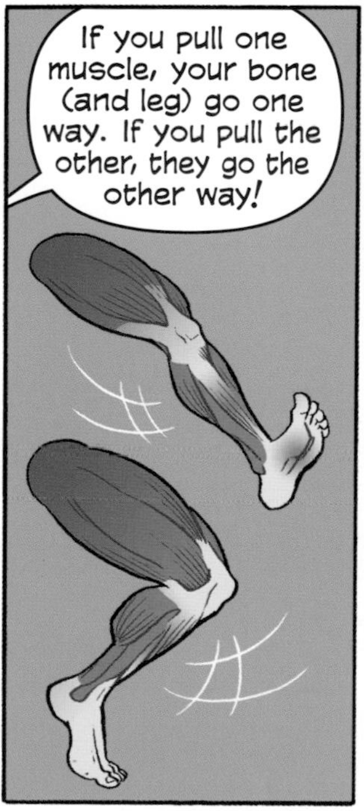
If you pull one muscle, your bone (and leg) go one way. If you pull the other, they go the other way!

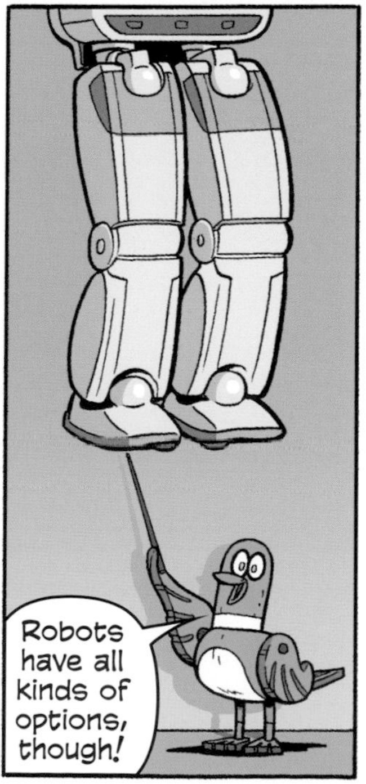
Robots have all kinds of options, though!

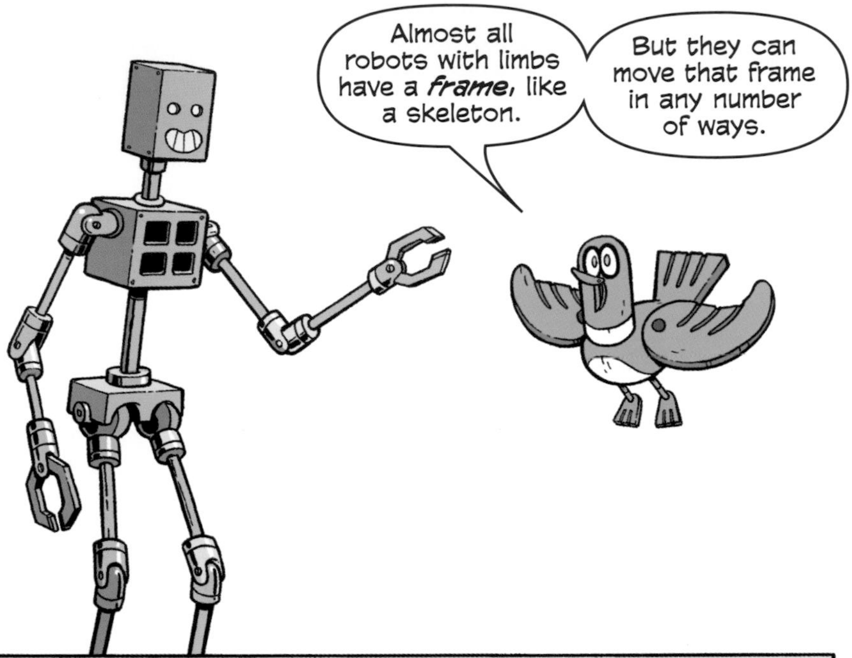
Almost all robots with limbs have a *frame*, like a skeleton.
But they can move that frame in any number of ways.

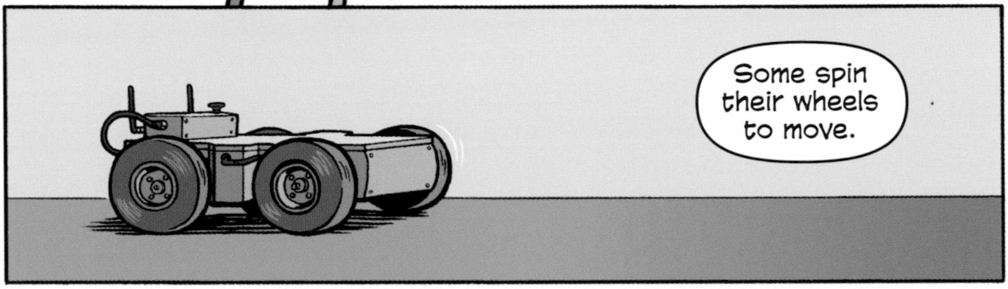
Some spin their wheels to move.

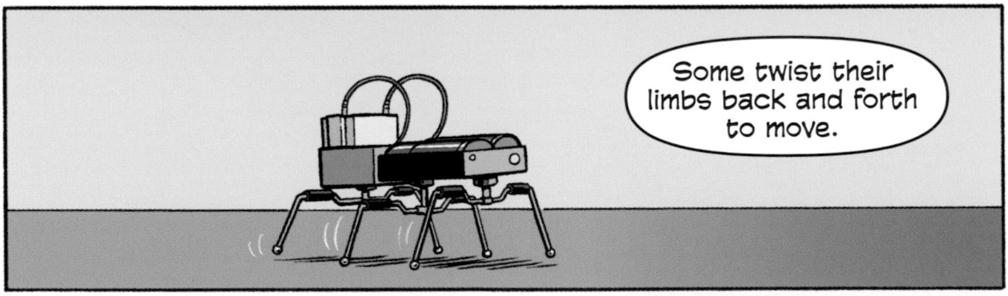
Some twist their limbs back and forth to move.

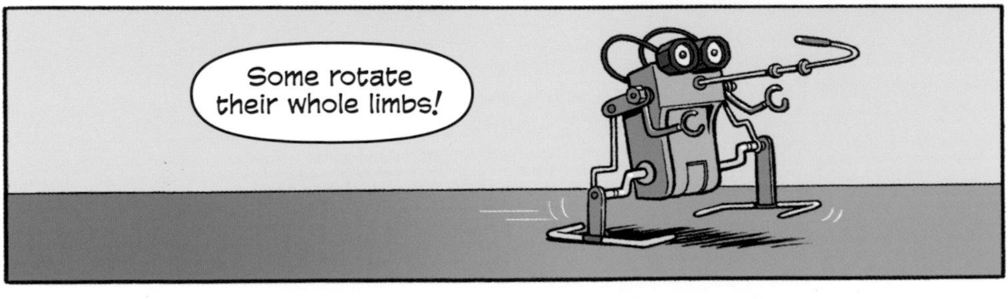
Some rotate their whole limbs!

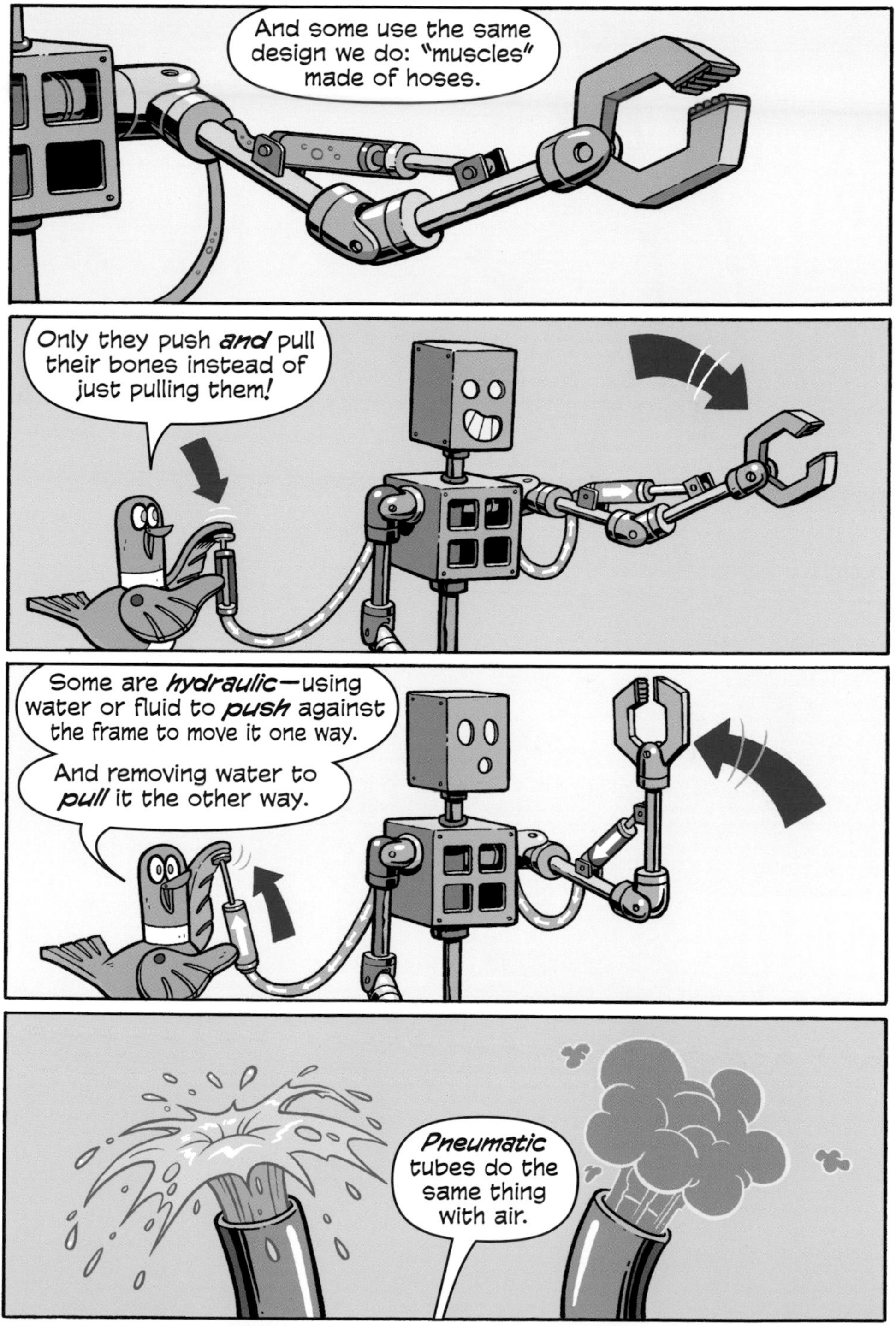
And some use the same design we do: "muscles" made of hoses.
Only they push *and* pull their bones instead of just pulling them!
Some are *hydraulic*—using water or fluid to *push* against the frame to move it one way.
And removing water to *pull* it the other way.
Pneumatic tubes do the same thing with air.

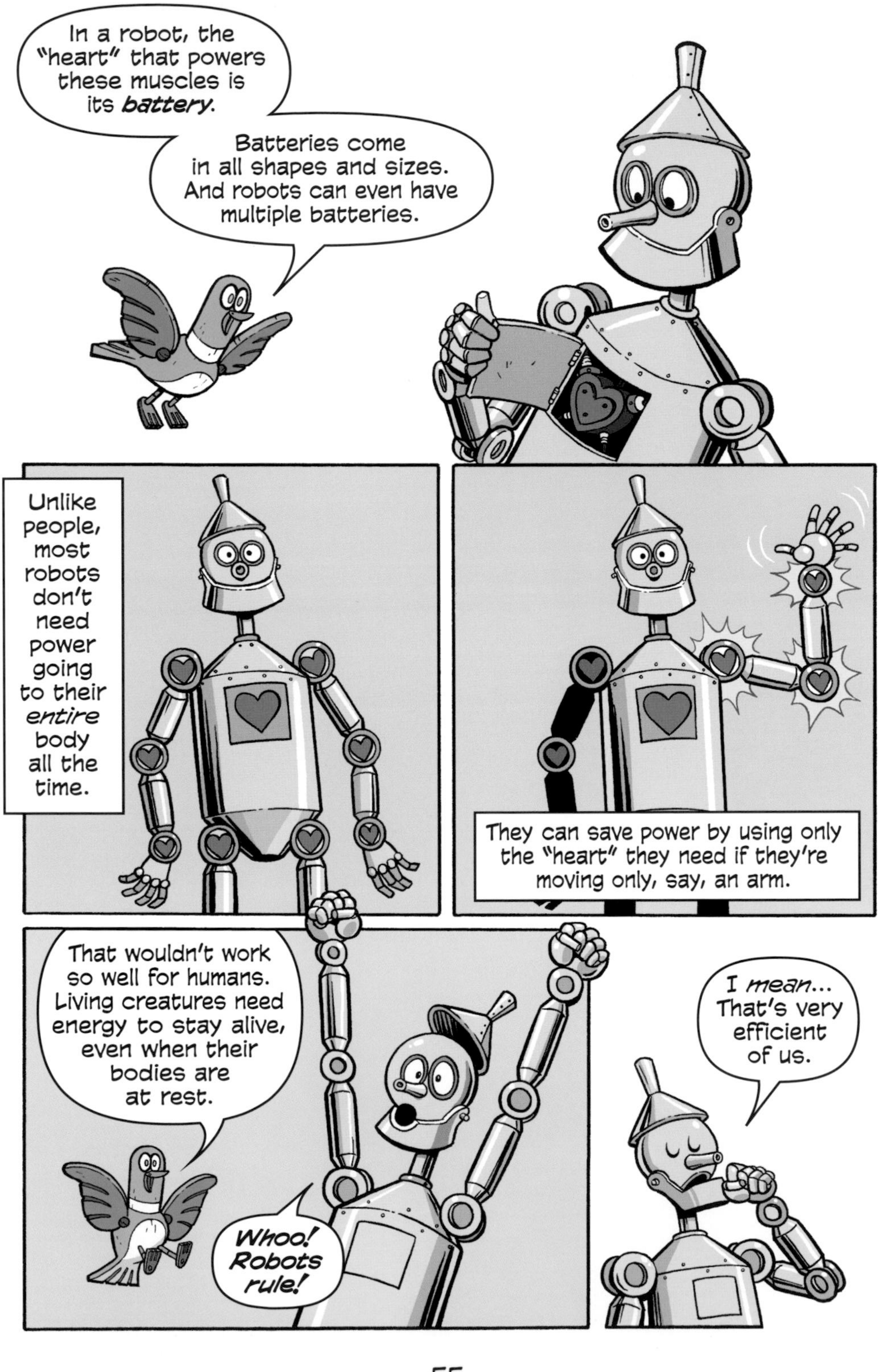
In a robot, the "heart" that powers these muscles is its ***battery***.
Batteries come in all shapes and sizes. And robots can even have multiple batteries.
Unlike people, most robots don't need power going to their *entire* body all the time.
They can save power by using only the "heart" they need if they're moving only, say, an arm.
That wouldn't work so well for humans. Living creatures need energy to stay alive, even when their bodies are at rest.
Whoo! Robots rule!
I *mean*... That's very efficient of us.

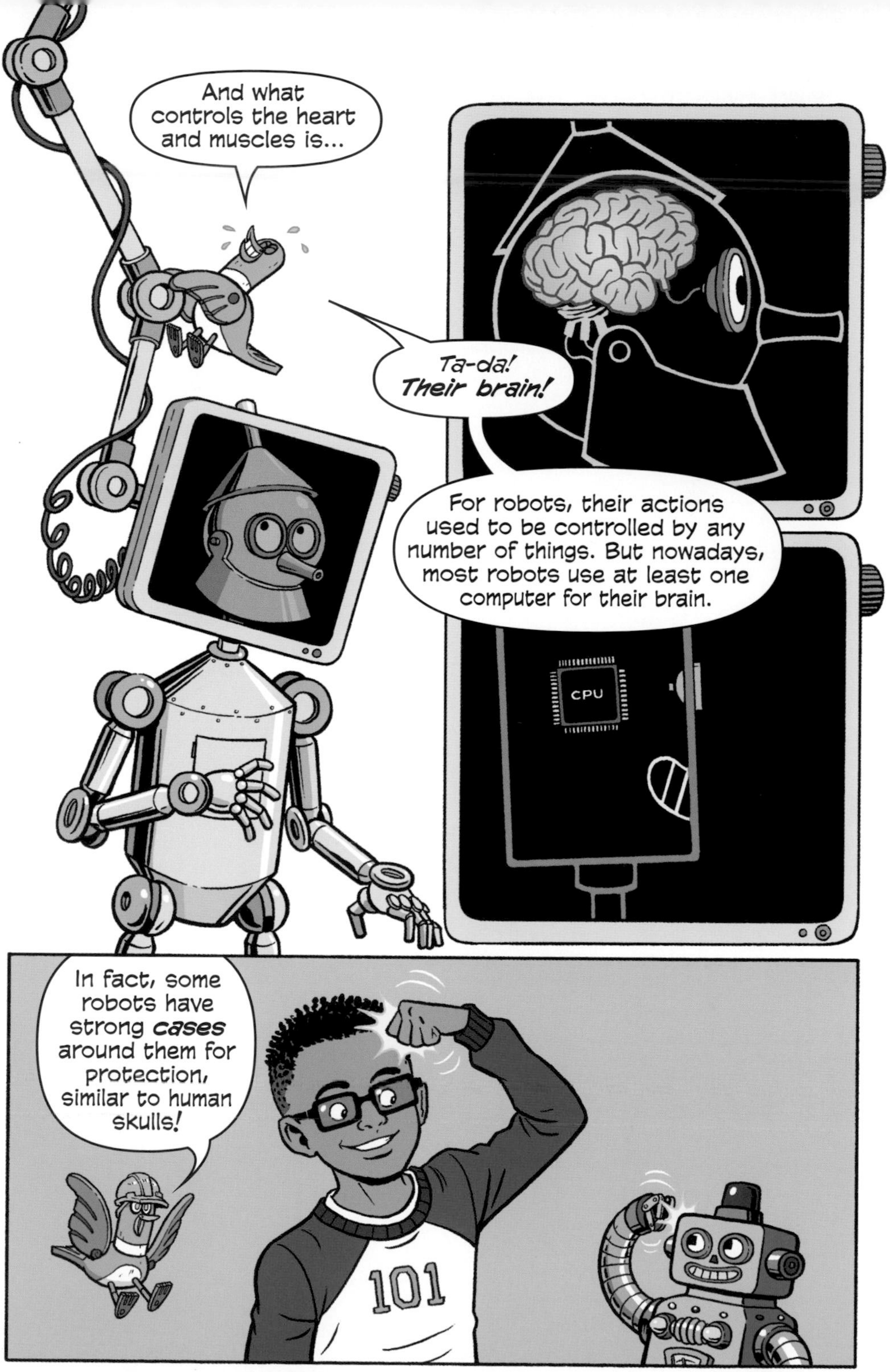
And what controls the heart and muscles is...
Ta-da! *Their brain!*
For robots, their actions used to be controlled by any number of things. But nowadays, most robots use at least one computer for their brain.
CPU
In fact, some robots have strong ***cases*** around them for protection, similar to human skulls!
101

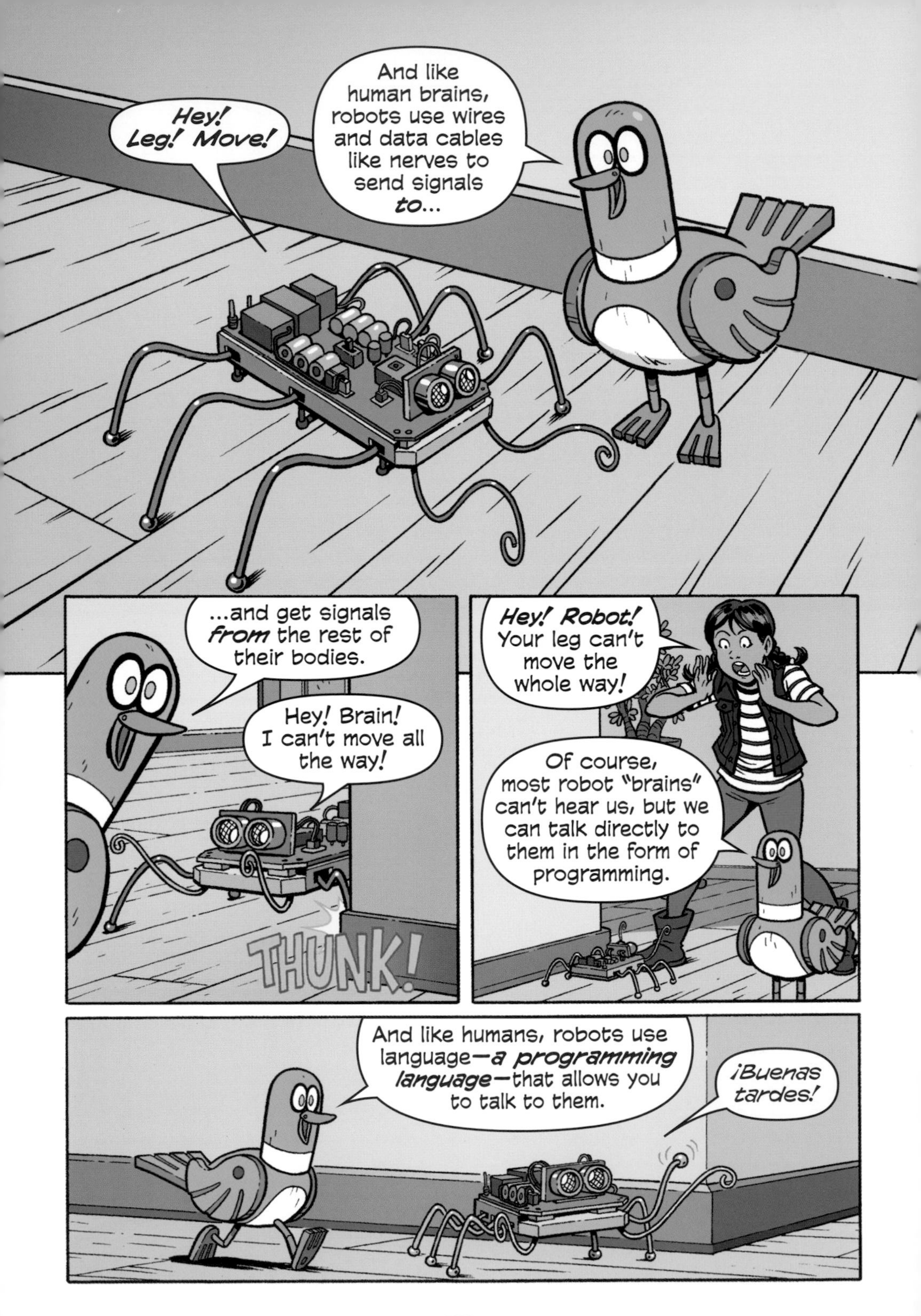
Hey! Leg! Move!
And like human brains, robots use wires and data cables like nerves to send signals *to*...
...and get signals *from* the rest of their bodies.
Hey! Brain! I can't move all the way!
THUNK!
Hey! Robot! Your leg can't move the whole way!
Of course, most robot "brains" can't hear us, but we can talk directly to them in the form of programming.
And like humans, robots use language—*a programming language*—that allows you to talk to them.
¡Buenas tardes!

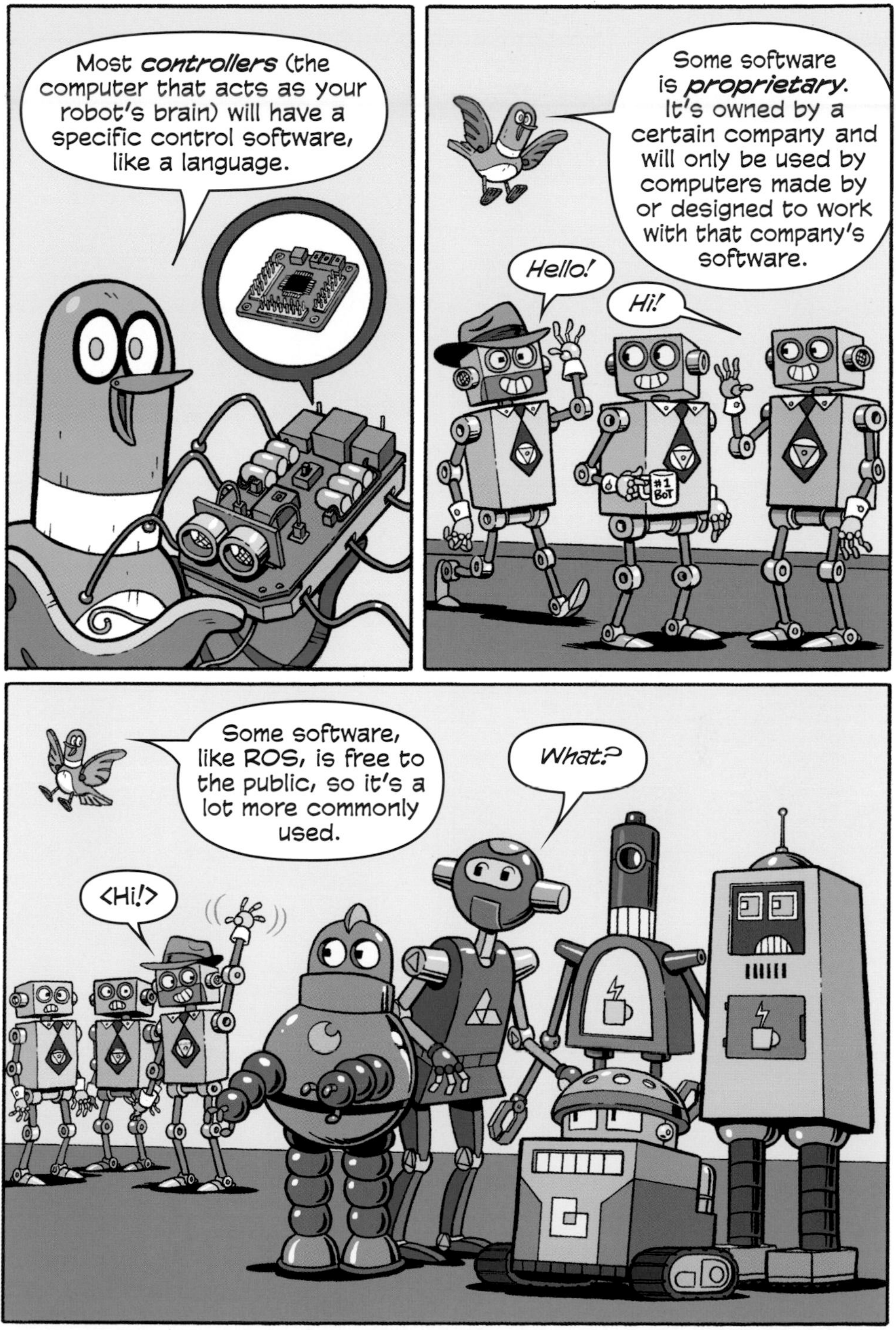
Most controllers (the computer that acts as your robot's brain) will have a specific control software, like a language.
Some software is proprietary. It's owned by a certain company and will only be used by computers made by or designed to work with that company's software.
Hello!
Hi!
#1 BoT
Some software, like ROS, is free to the public, so it's a lot more commonly used.
What?
<Hi!>

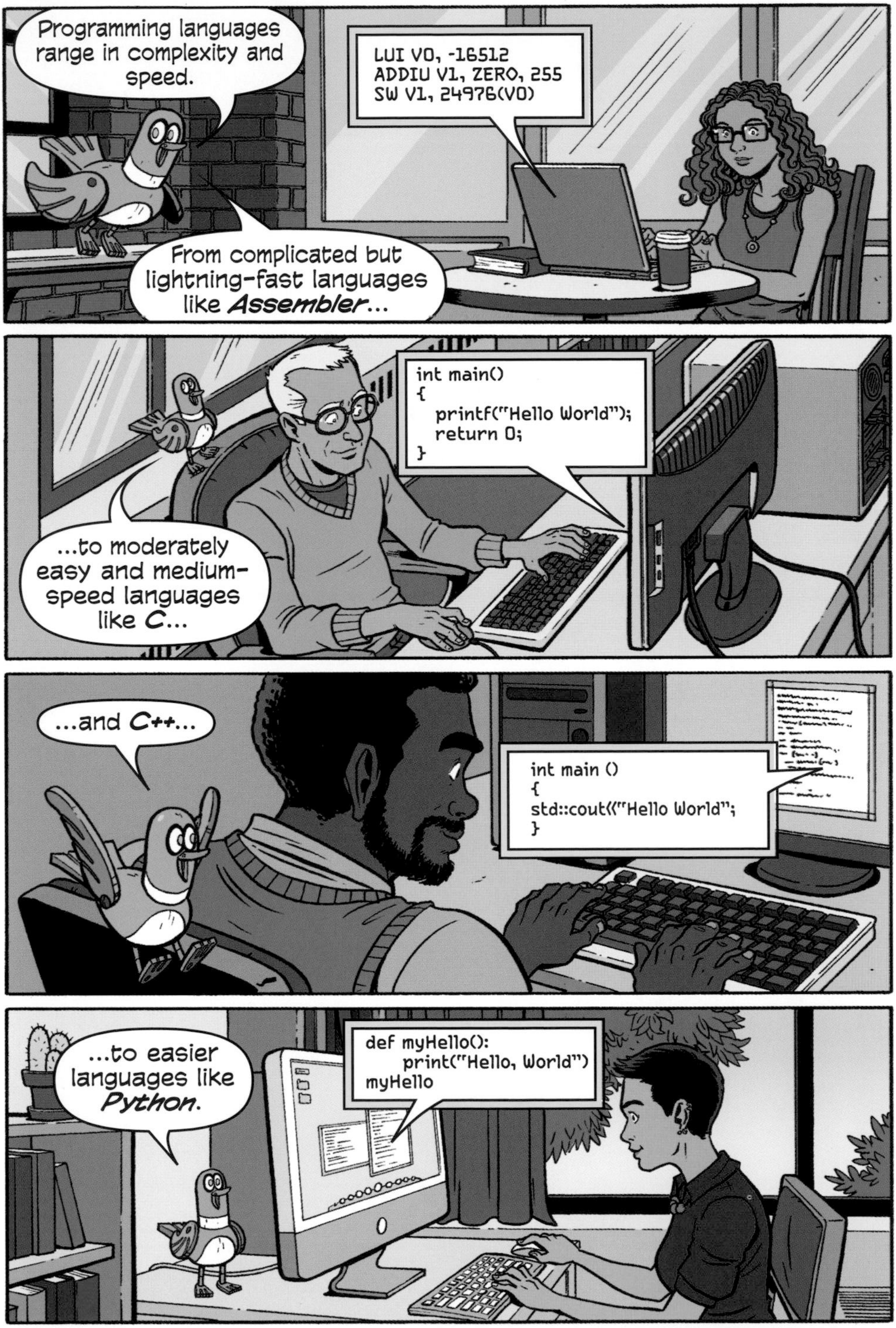
Programming languages range in complexity and speed.
LUI V0, -16512
ADDIU V1, ZERO, 255
SW V1, 24976(V0)
From complicated but lightning-fast languages like *Assembler*...
...to moderately easy and medium-speed languages like *C*...
int main()
{
printf("Hello World");
return 0;
}
...and *C++*...
int main ()
{
std::cout<<"Hello World";
}
...to easier languages like *Python*.
def myHello():
print("Hello, World")
myHello

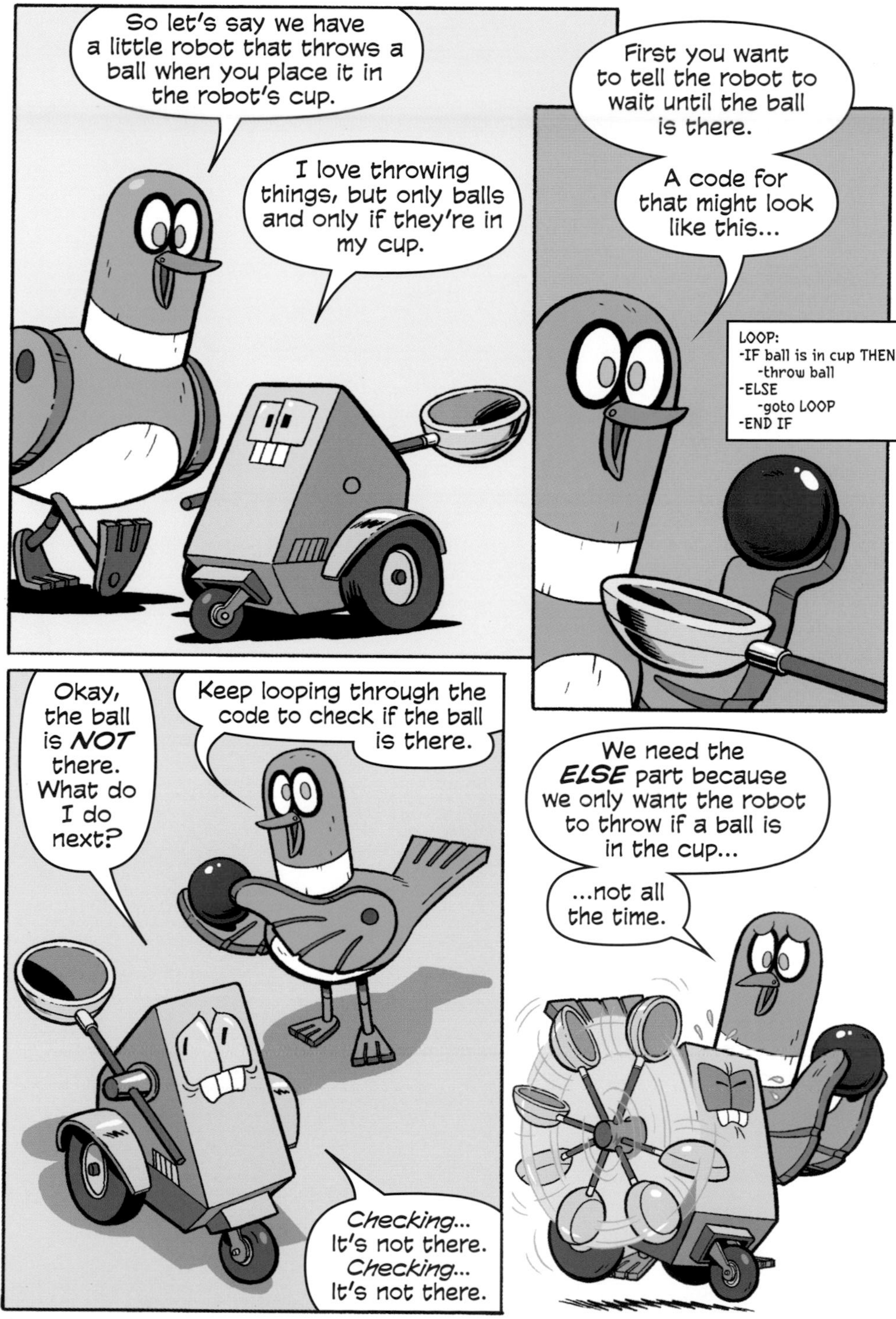
So let's say we have a little robot that throws a ball when you place it in the robot's cup.
I love throwing things, but only balls and only if they're in my cup.
First you want to tell the robot to wait until the ball is there.
A code for that might look like this...
LOOP:
-IF ball is in cup THEN
-throw ball
-ELSE
-goto LOOP
-END IF
Okay, the ball is *NOT* there. What do I do next?
Keep looping through the code to check if the ball is there.
Checking... It's not there. *Checking*... It's not there.
We need the *ELSE* part because we only want the robot to throw if a ball is in the cup...
...not all the time.

So we ask the robot to keep checking for the ball. But once it senses the ball...
Hey! There IS a ball in my cup.
Okay, I'm supposed to... um..."IF ball is in cup THEN..."
THROW THE BALL!
YES! Throw the ball!

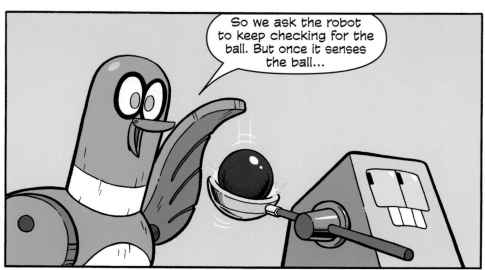

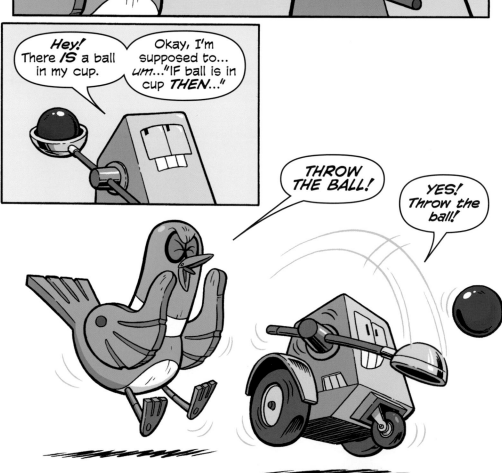

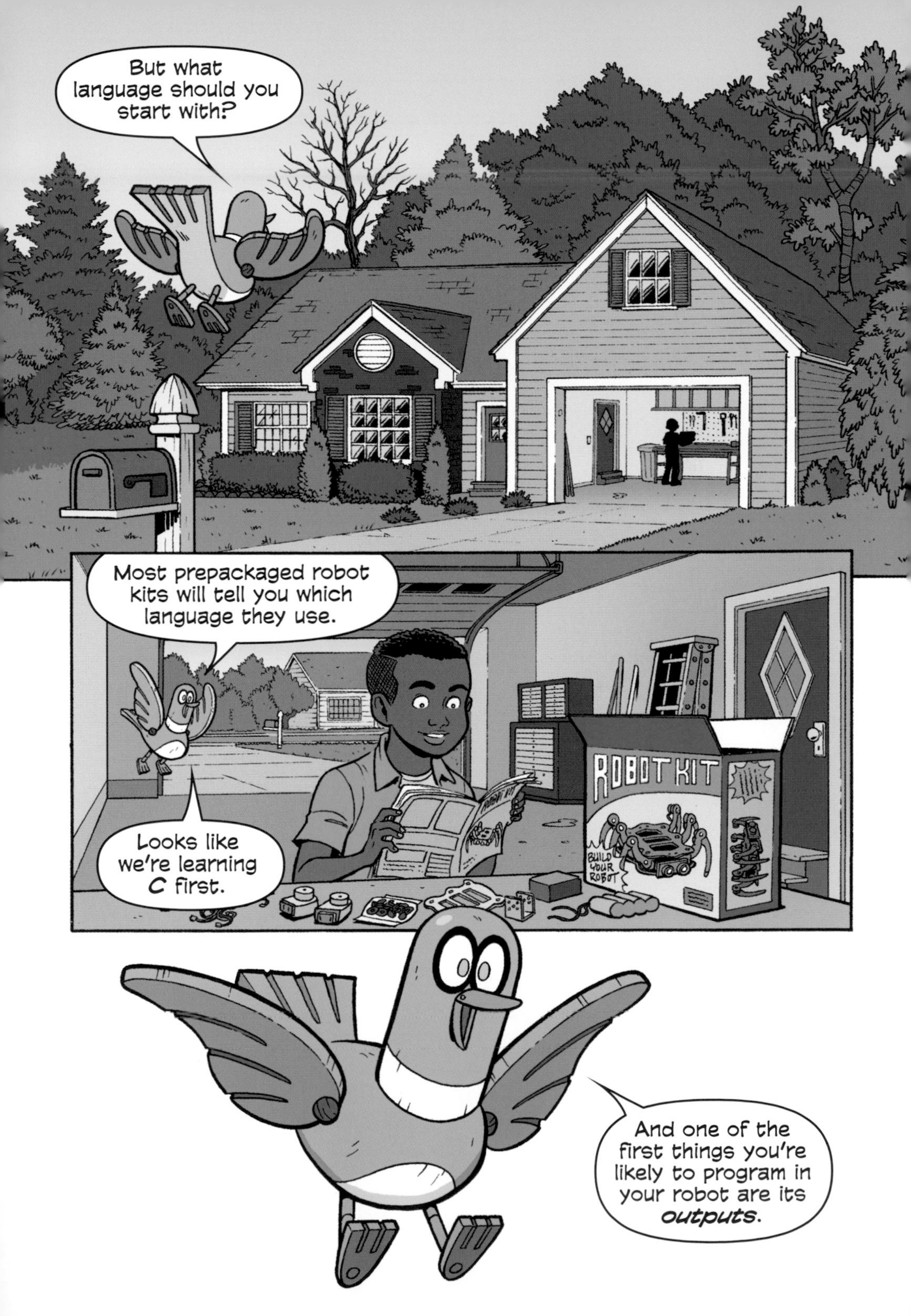
But what language should you start with?
Most prepackaged robot kits will tell you which language they use.
Looks like we're learning *C* first.
ROBOT KIT
BUILD YOUR ROBOT
And one of the first things you're likely to program in your robot are its ***outputs***.

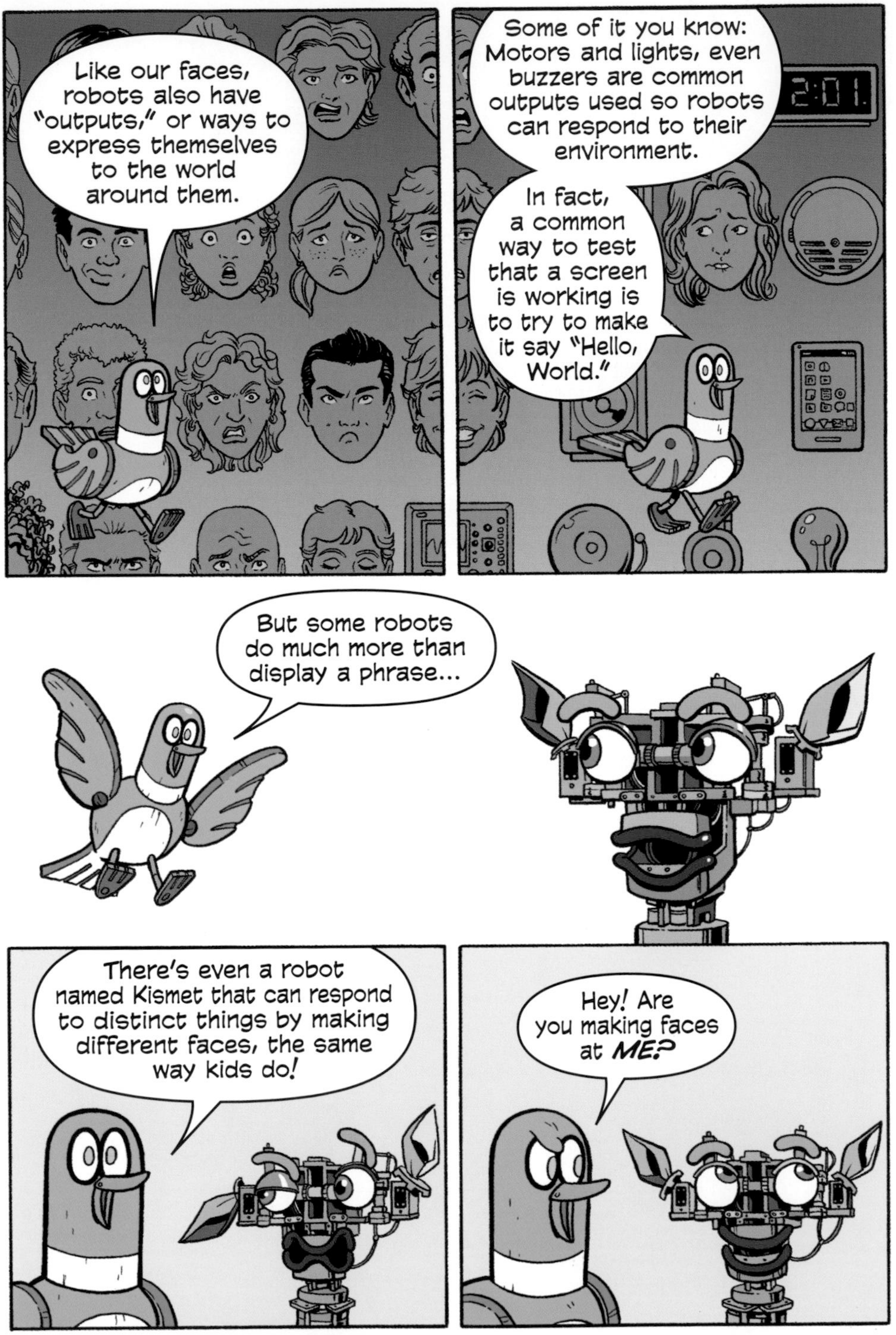
Like our faces, robots also have "outputs," or ways to express themselves to the world around them.
Some of it you know: Motors and lights, even buzzers are common outputs used so robots can respond to their environment.
2:01
In fact, a common way to test that a screen is working is to try to make it say "Hello, World."
But some robots do much more than display a phrase...
There's even a robot named Kismet that can respond to distinct things by making different faces, the same way kids do!
Hey! Are you making faces at ***ME?***

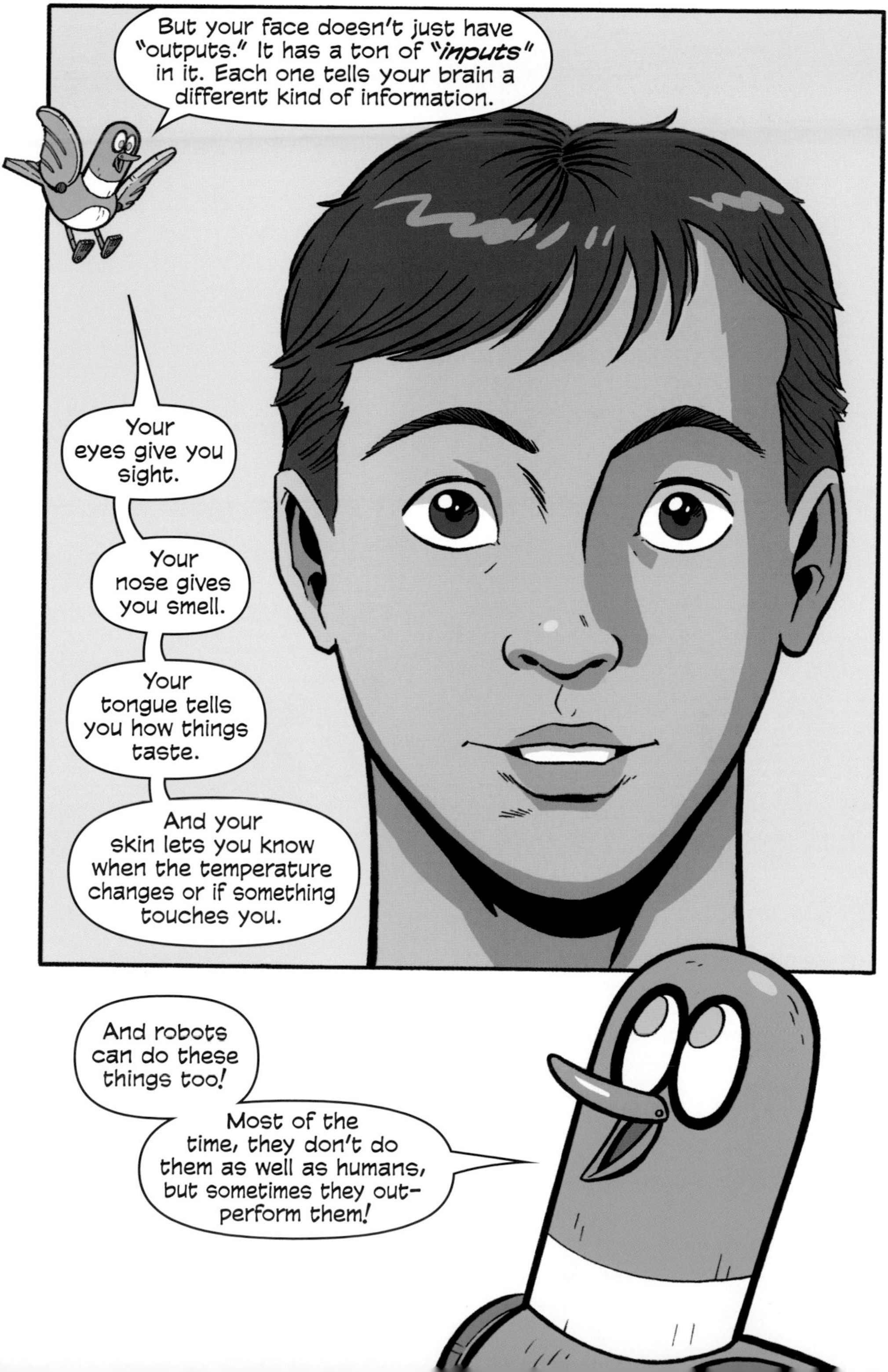
But your face doesn't just have "outputs." It has a ton of "*inputs*" in it. Each one tells your brain a different kind of information.
Your eyes give you sight.
Your nose gives you smell.
Your tongue tells you how things taste.
And your skin lets you know when the temperature changes or if something touches you.
And robots can do these things too!
Most of the time, they don't do them as well as humans, but sometimes they out-perform them!

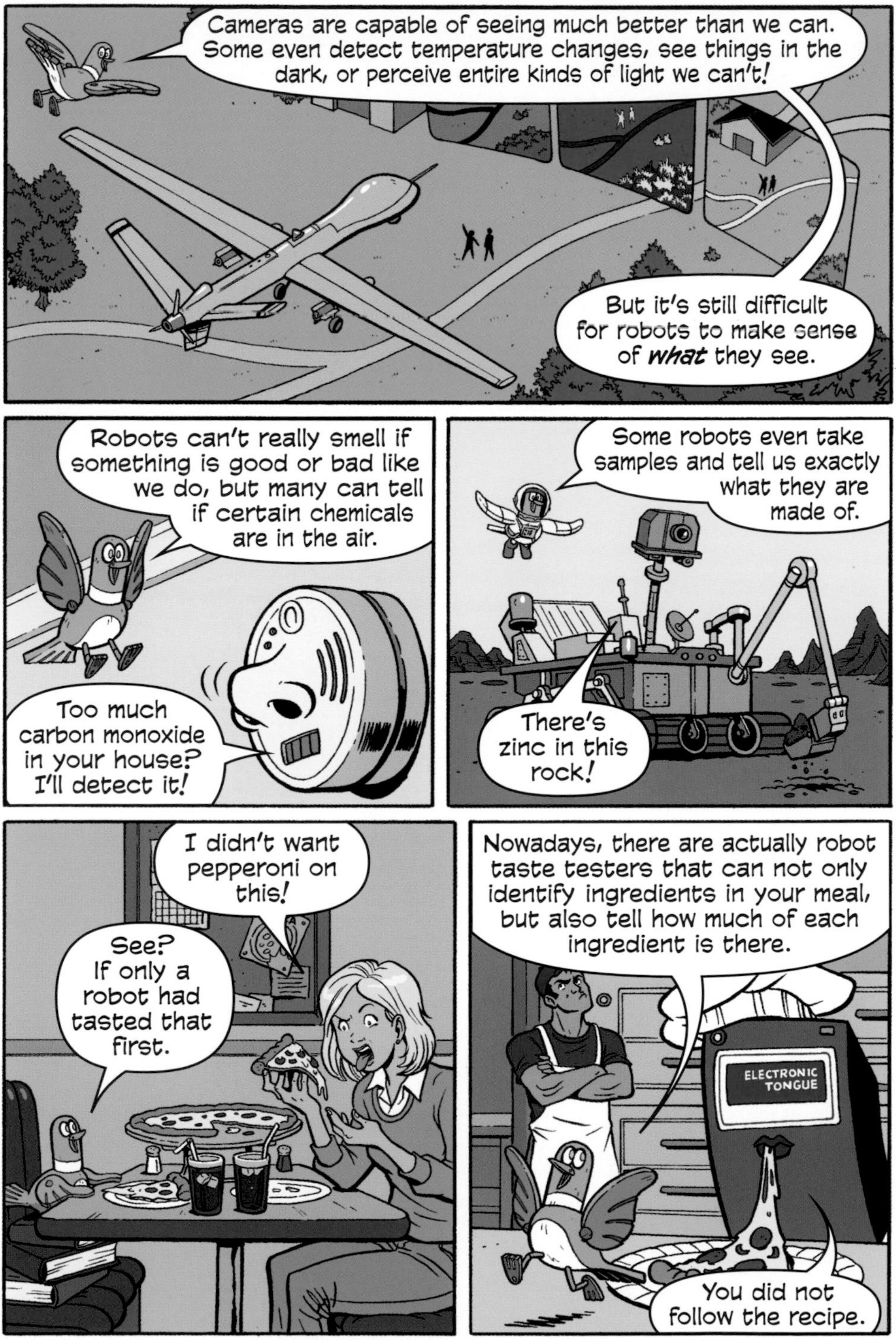
Cameras are capable of seeing much better than we can. Some even detect temperature changes, see things in the dark, or perceive entire kinds of light we can't!
But it's still difficult for robots to make sense of ***what*** they see.
Robots can't really smell if something is good or bad like we do, but many can tell if certain chemicals are in the air.
Too much carbon monoxide in your house? I'll detect it!
Some robots even take samples and tell us exactly what they are made of.
There's zinc in this rock!
I didn't want pepperoni on this!
See? If only a robot had tasted that first.
Nowadays, there are actually robot taste testers that can not only identify ingredients in your meal, but also tell how much of each ingredient is there.
ELECTRONIC TONGUE
You did not follow the recipe.

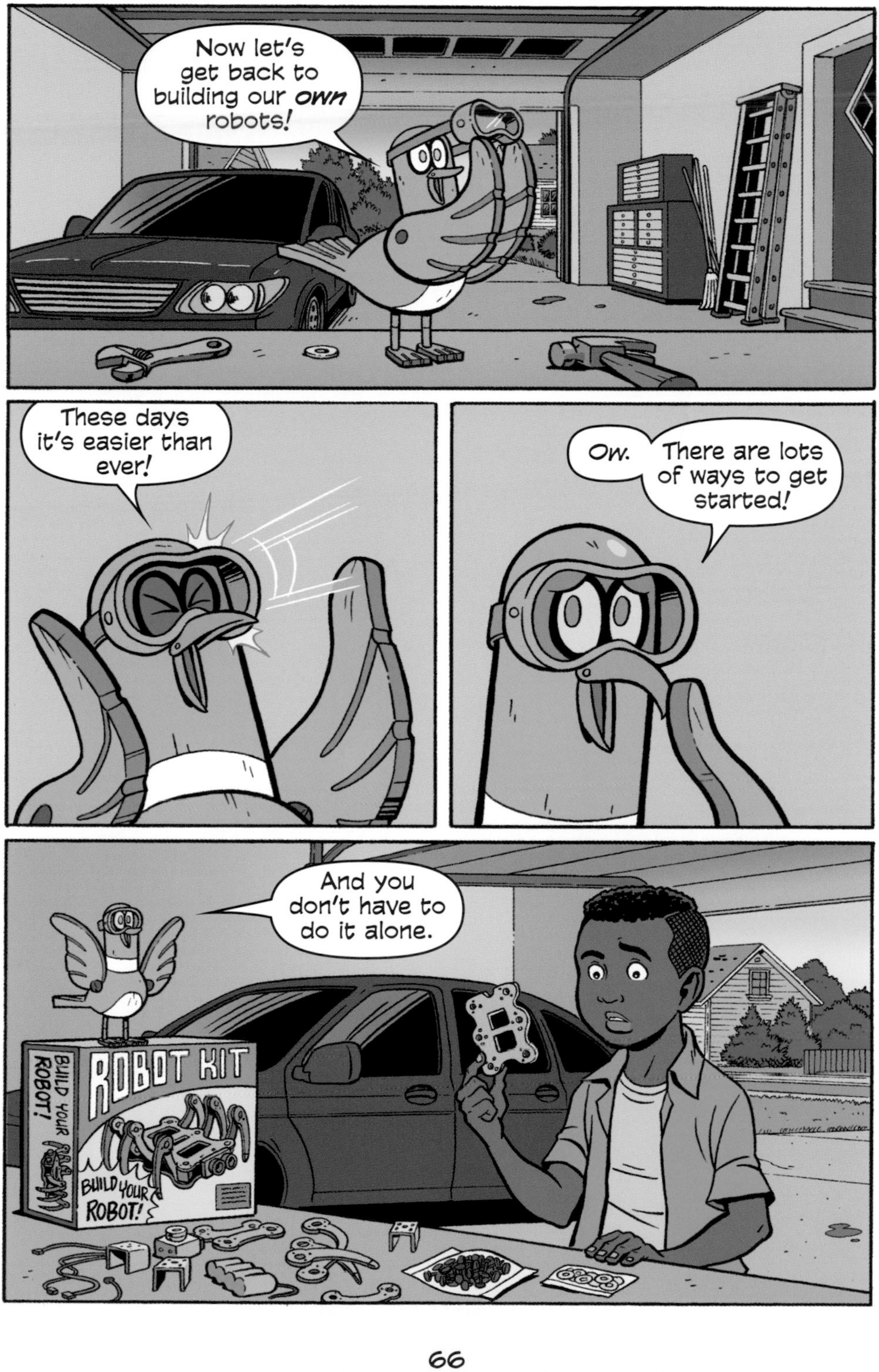
Now let's get back to building our *own* robots!
These days it's easier than ever!
Ow.
There are lots of ways to get started!
And you don't have to do it alone.
ROBOT KIT
BUILD YOUR ROBOT!
BUILD YOUR ROBOT!

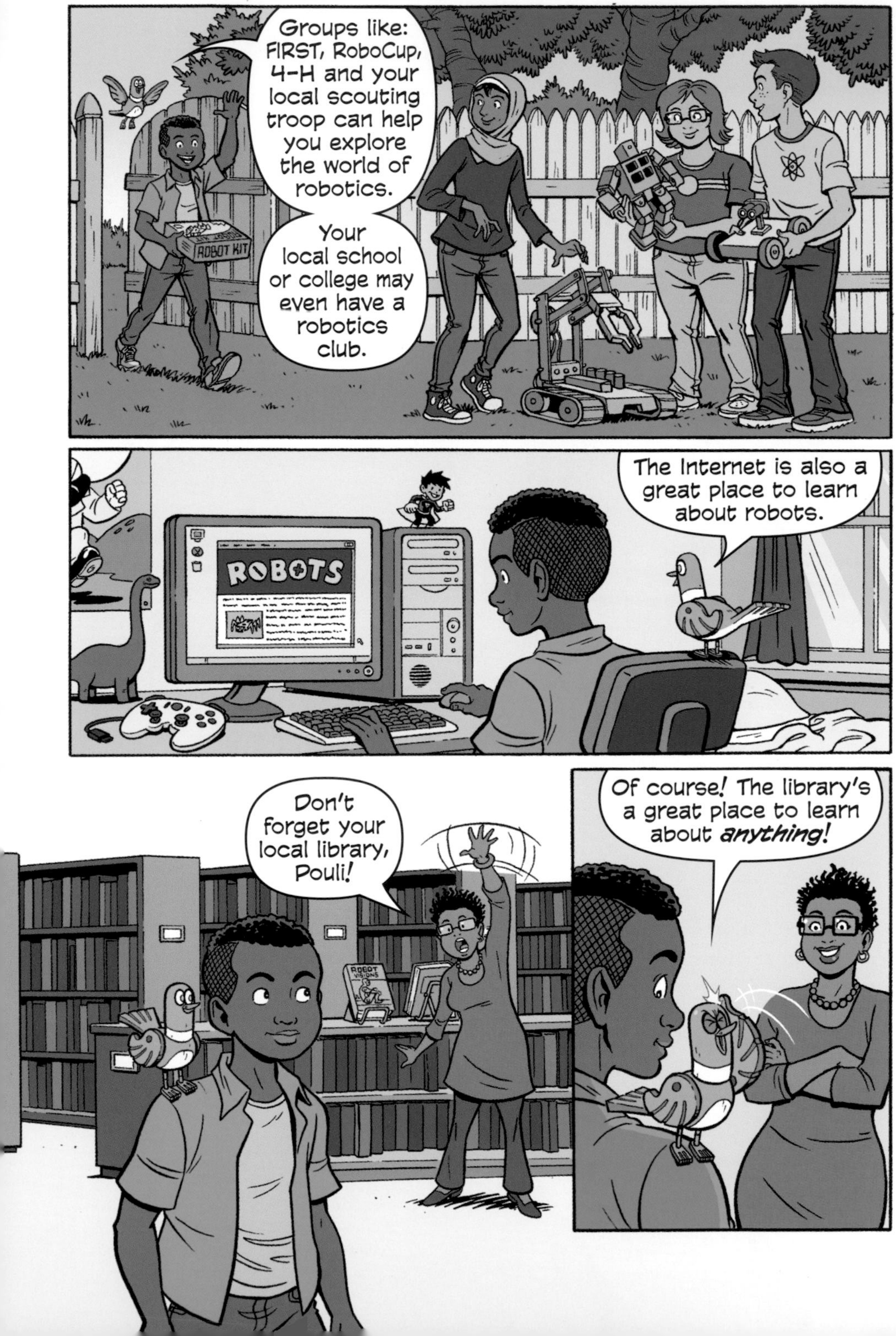
Groups like: FIRST, RoboCup, 4-H and your local scouting troop can help you explore the world of robotics.
Your local school or college may even have a robotics club.
ROBOT KIT
ROBOTS
The Internet is also a great place to learn about robots.
ROBOT VISIONS
Don't forget your local library, Pouli!
Of course! The library's a great place to learn about *anything*!

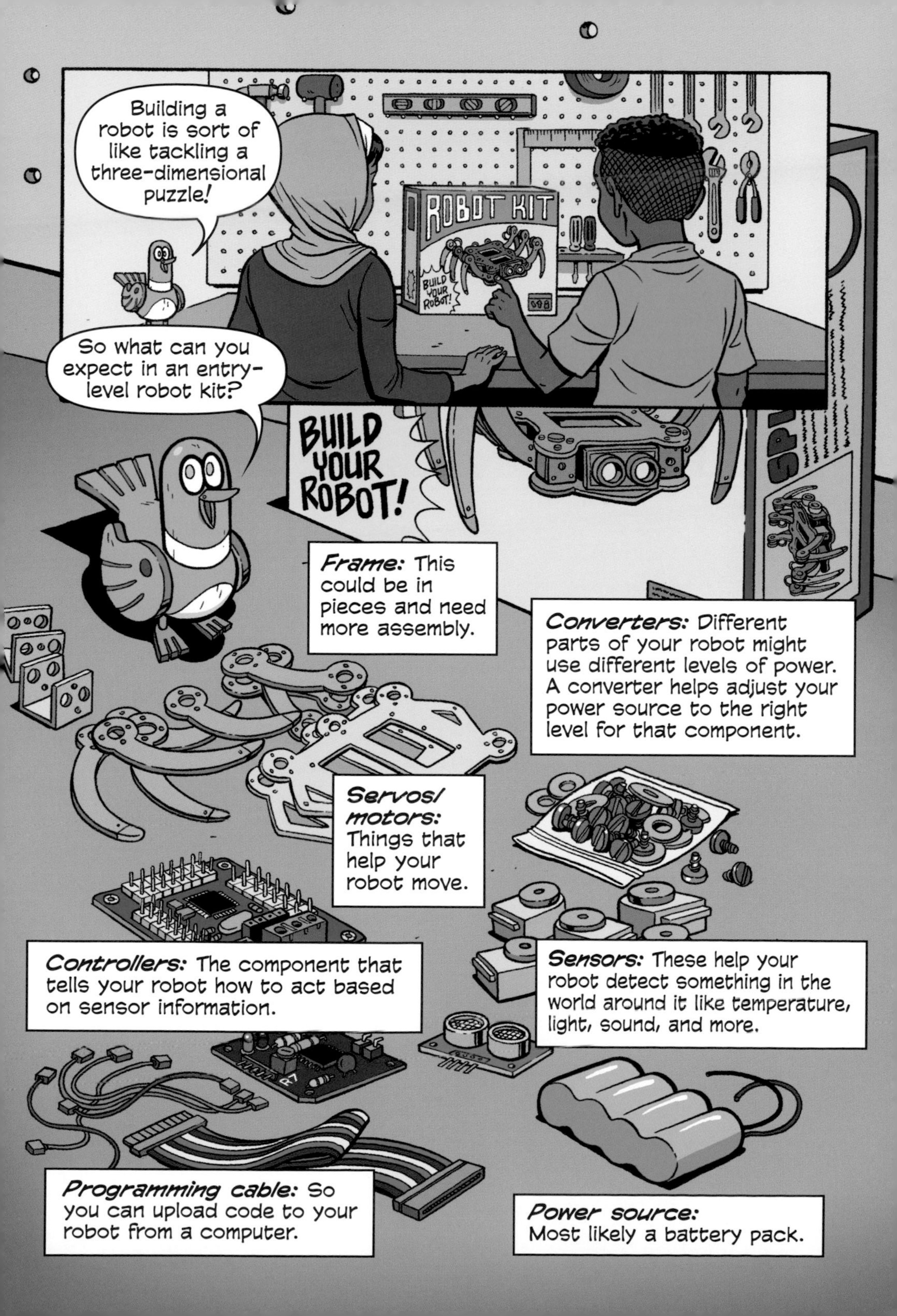

Building a robot is sort of like tackling a three-dimensional puzzle!
ROBOT KIT
BUILD YOUR ROBOT!
So what can you expect in an entry-level robot kit?
BUILD YOUR ROBOT!
Frame: This could be in pieces and need more assembly.
Converters: Different parts of your robot might use different levels of power. A converter helps adjust your power source to the right level for that component.
Servos/motors: Things that help your robot move.
Controllers: The component that tells your robot how to act based on sensor information.
Sensors: These help your robot detect something in the world around it like temperature, light, sound, and more.
Programming cable: So you can upload code to your robot from a computer.
Power source: Most likely a battery pack.

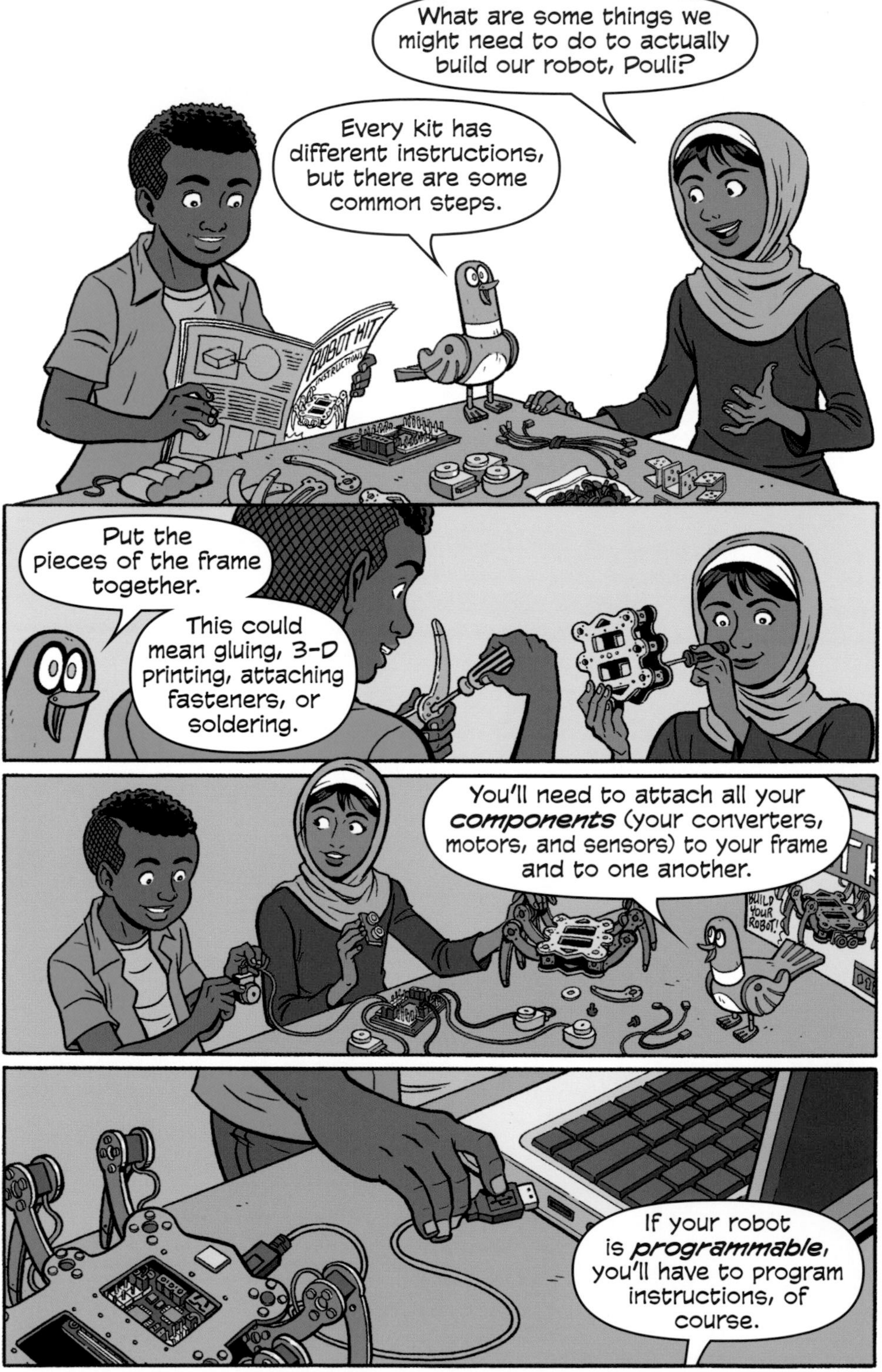
What are some things we might need to do to actually build our robot, Pouli?
Every kit has different instructions, but there are some common steps.
ROBOT KIT INSTRUCTIONS
Put the pieces of the frame together.
This could mean gluing, 3-D printing, attaching fasteners, or soldering.
You'll need to attach all your ***components*** (your converters, motors, and sensors) to your frame and to one another.
BUILD YOUR ROBOT!
If your robot is ***programmable***, you'll have to program instructions, of course.

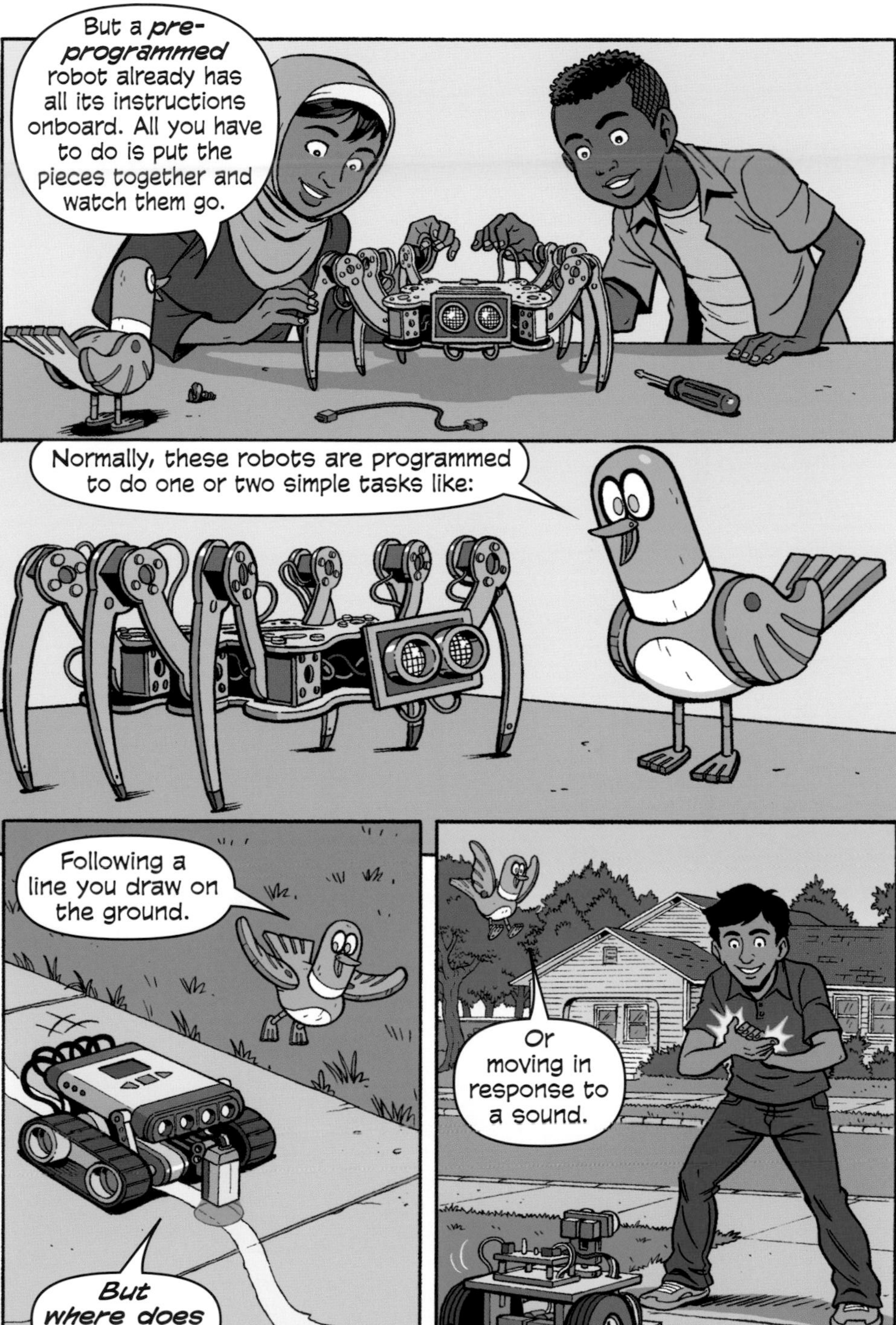
But a *pre-programmed* robot already has all its instructions onboard. All you have to do is put the pieces together and watch them go.
Normally, these robots are programmed to do one or two simple tasks like:
Following a line you draw on the ground.
But where does it go?!
Or moving in response to a sound.

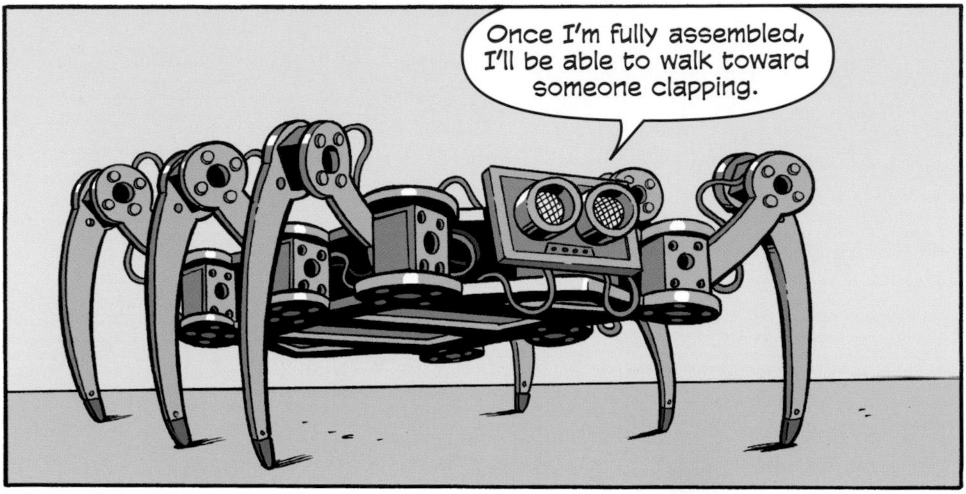
Once I'm fully assembled, I'll be able to walk toward someone clapping.

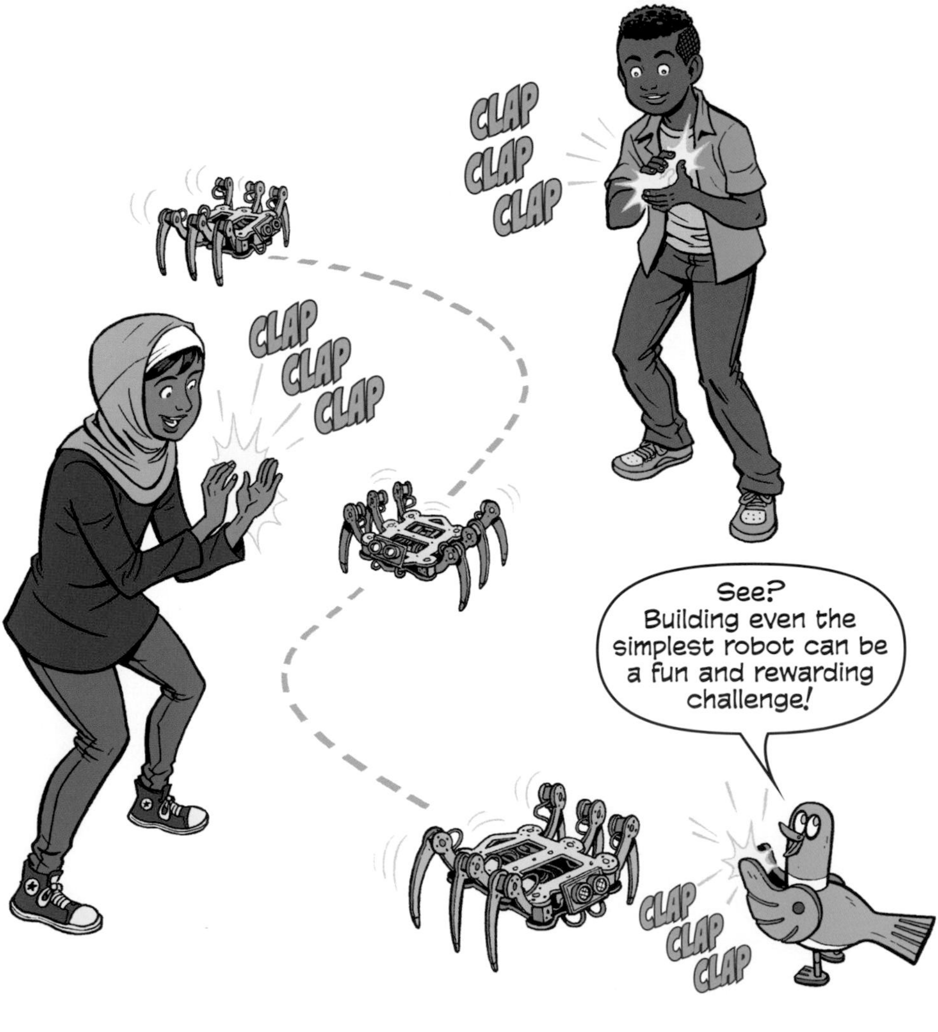
CLAP CLAP CLAP
CLAP CLAP CLAP
See? Building even the simplest robot can be a fun and rewarding challenge!
CLAP CLAP CLAP

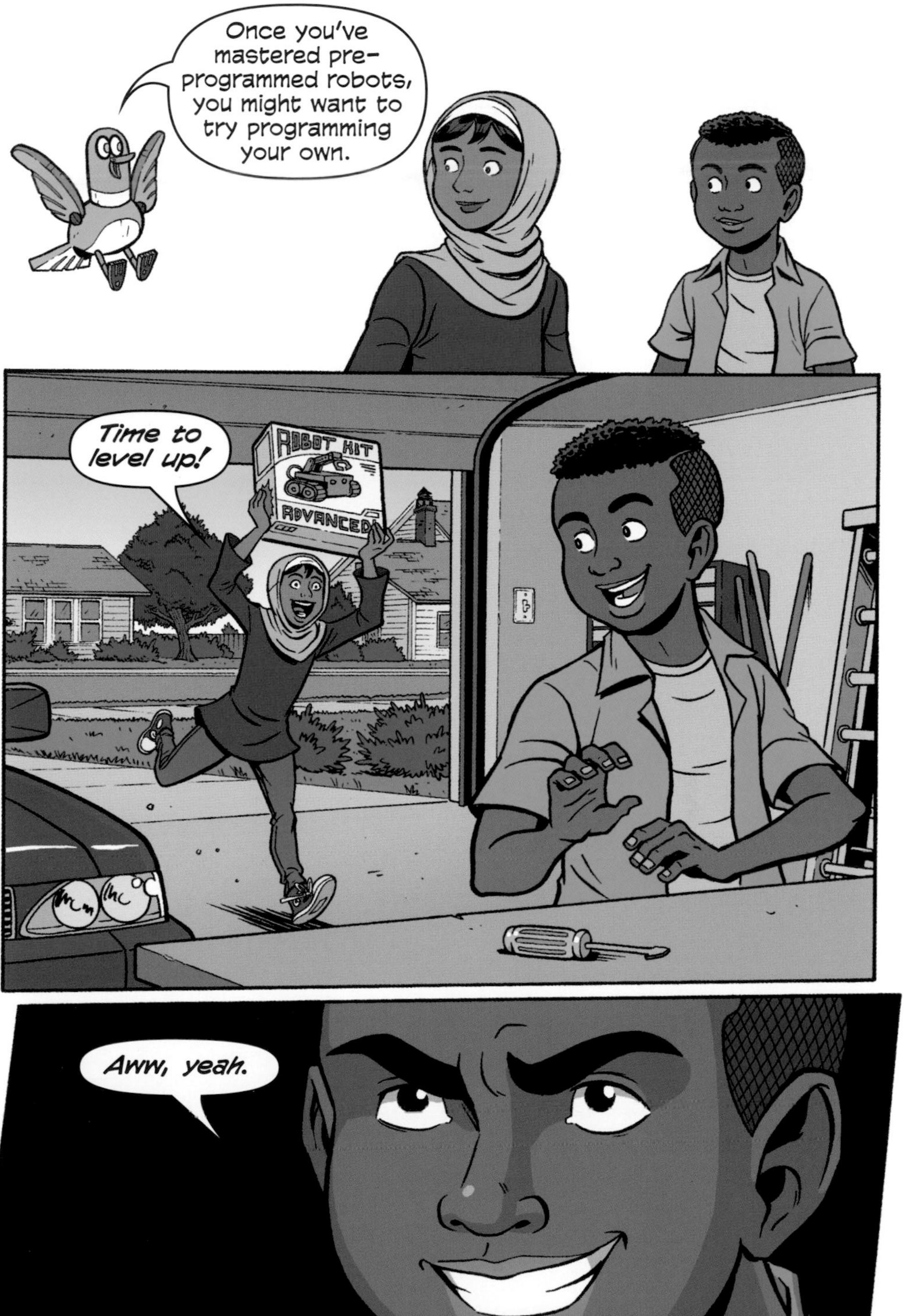
Once you've mastered pre-programmed robots, you might want to try programming your own.
Time to level up!
ROBOT KIT
ADVANCED
Aww, yeah.

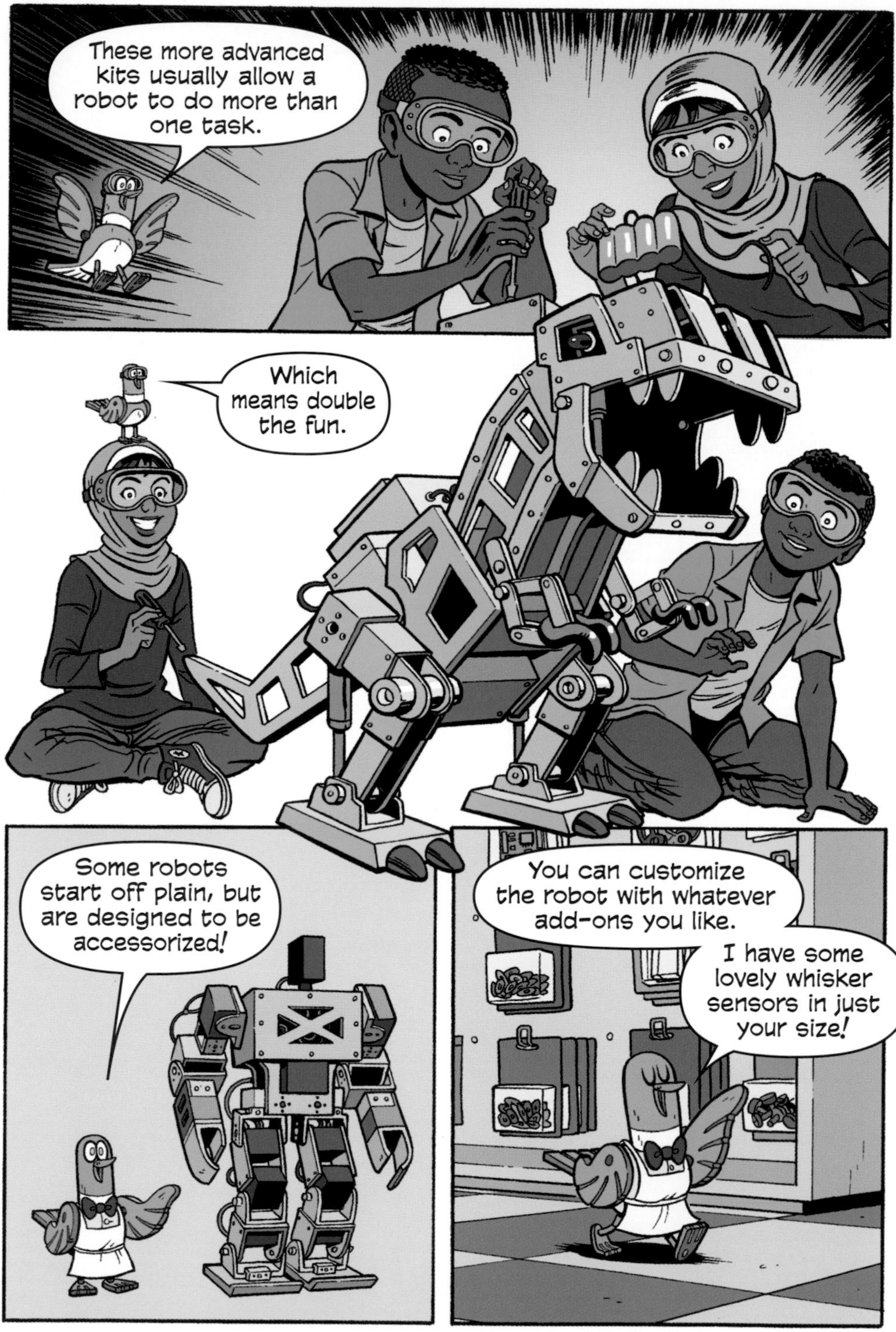
These more advanced kits usually allow a robot to do more than one task.
Which means double the fun.
Some robots start off plain, but are designed to be accessorized!
You can customize the robot with whatever add-ons you like.
I have some lovely whisker sensors in just your size!

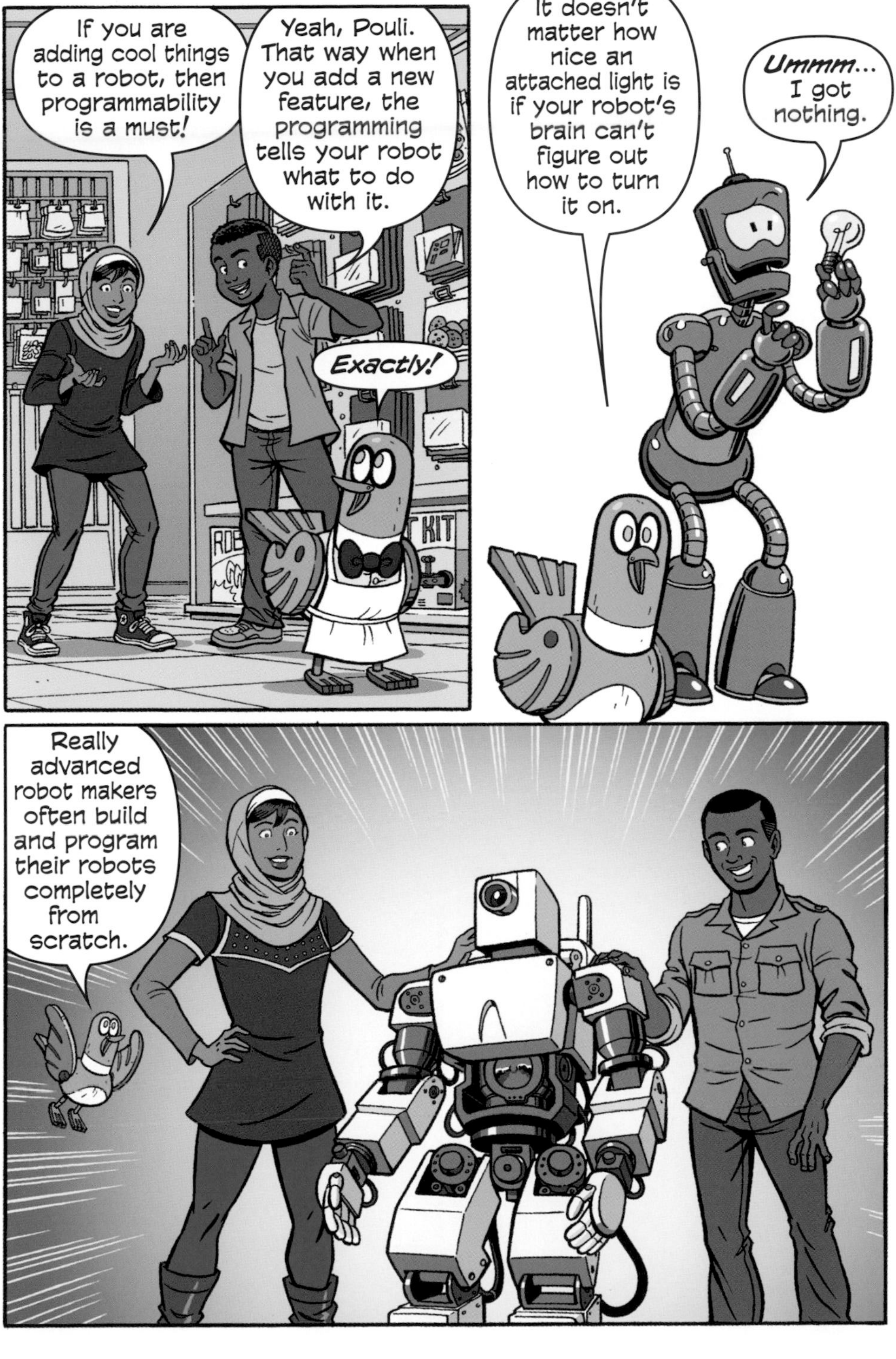
If you are adding cool things to a robot, then programmability is a must!
Yeah, Pouli. That way when you add a new feature, the programming tells your robot what to do with it.
Exactly!
It doesn't matter how nice an attached light is if your robot's brain can't figure out how to turn it on.
Ummm... I got nothing.
Really advanced robot makers often build and program their robots completely from scratch.

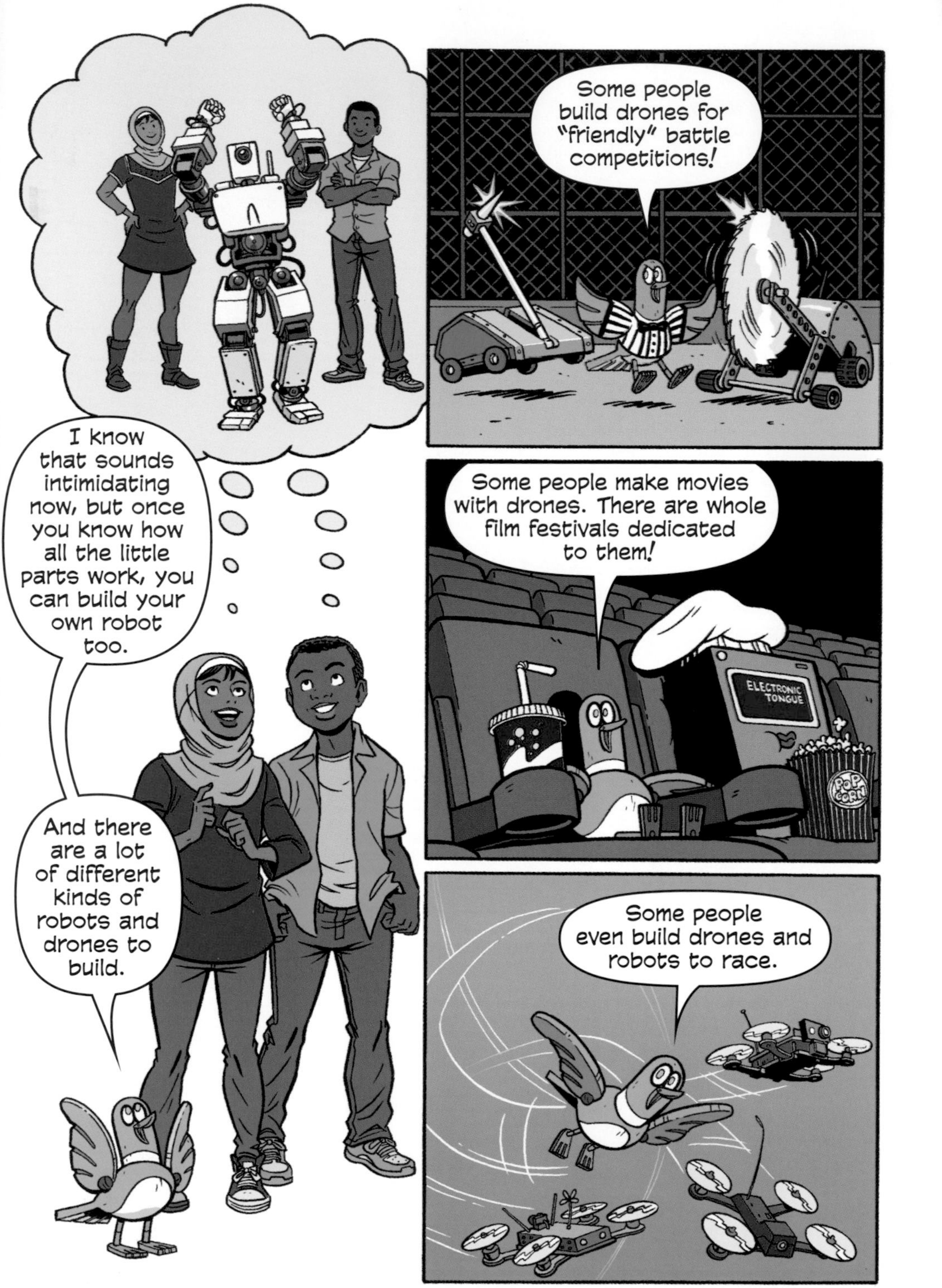
I know that sounds intimidating now, but once you know how all the little parts work, you can build your own robot too.
And there are a lot of different kinds of robots and drones to build.
Some people build drones for "friendly" battle competitions!
Some people make movies with drones. There are whole film festivals dedicated to them!
ELECTRONIC TONGUE
POP CORN
Some people even build drones and robots to race.

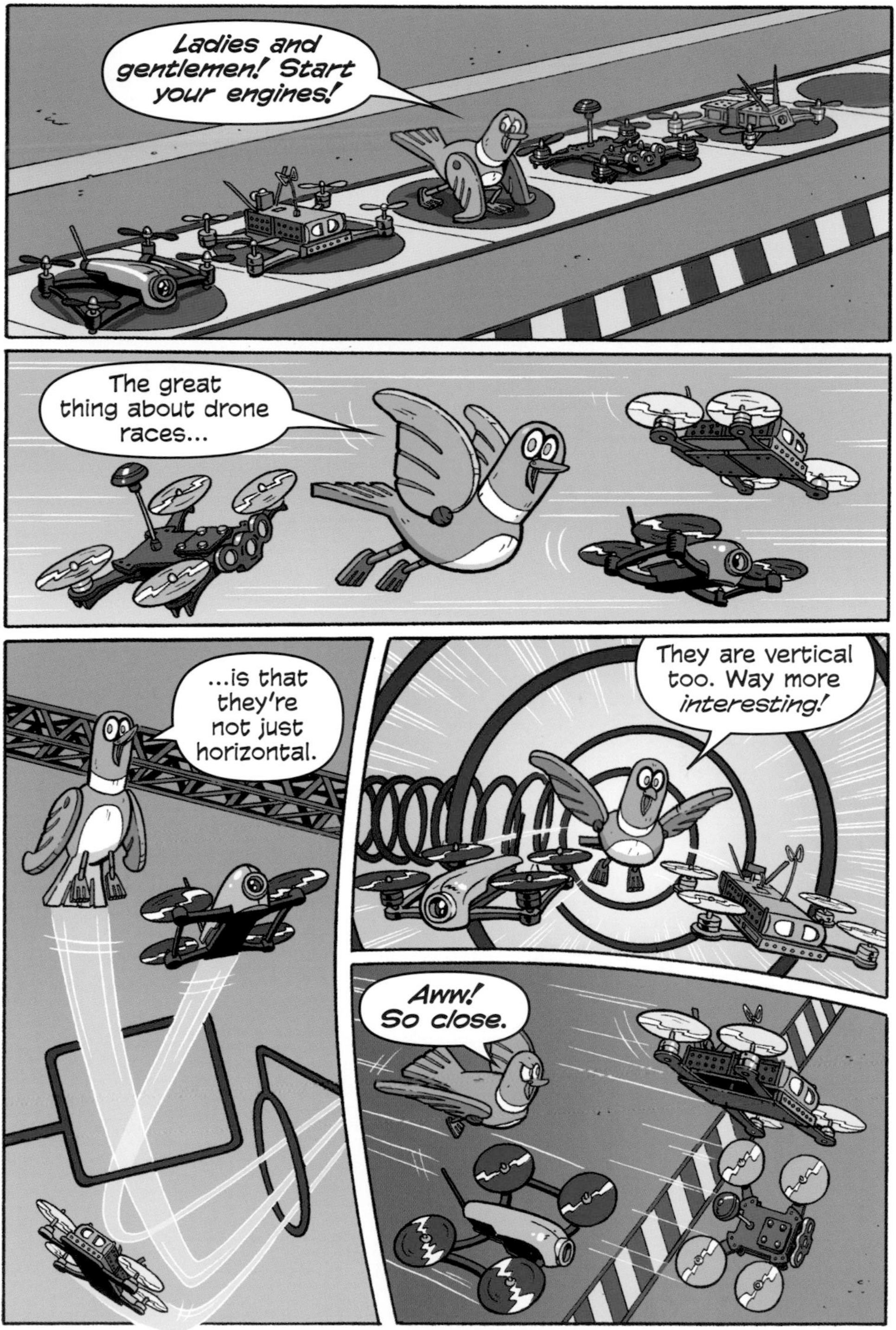

Ladies and gentlemen! Start your engines!
The great thing about drone races...
...is that they're not just horizontal.
They are vertical too. Way more *interesting!*
Aww! So close.

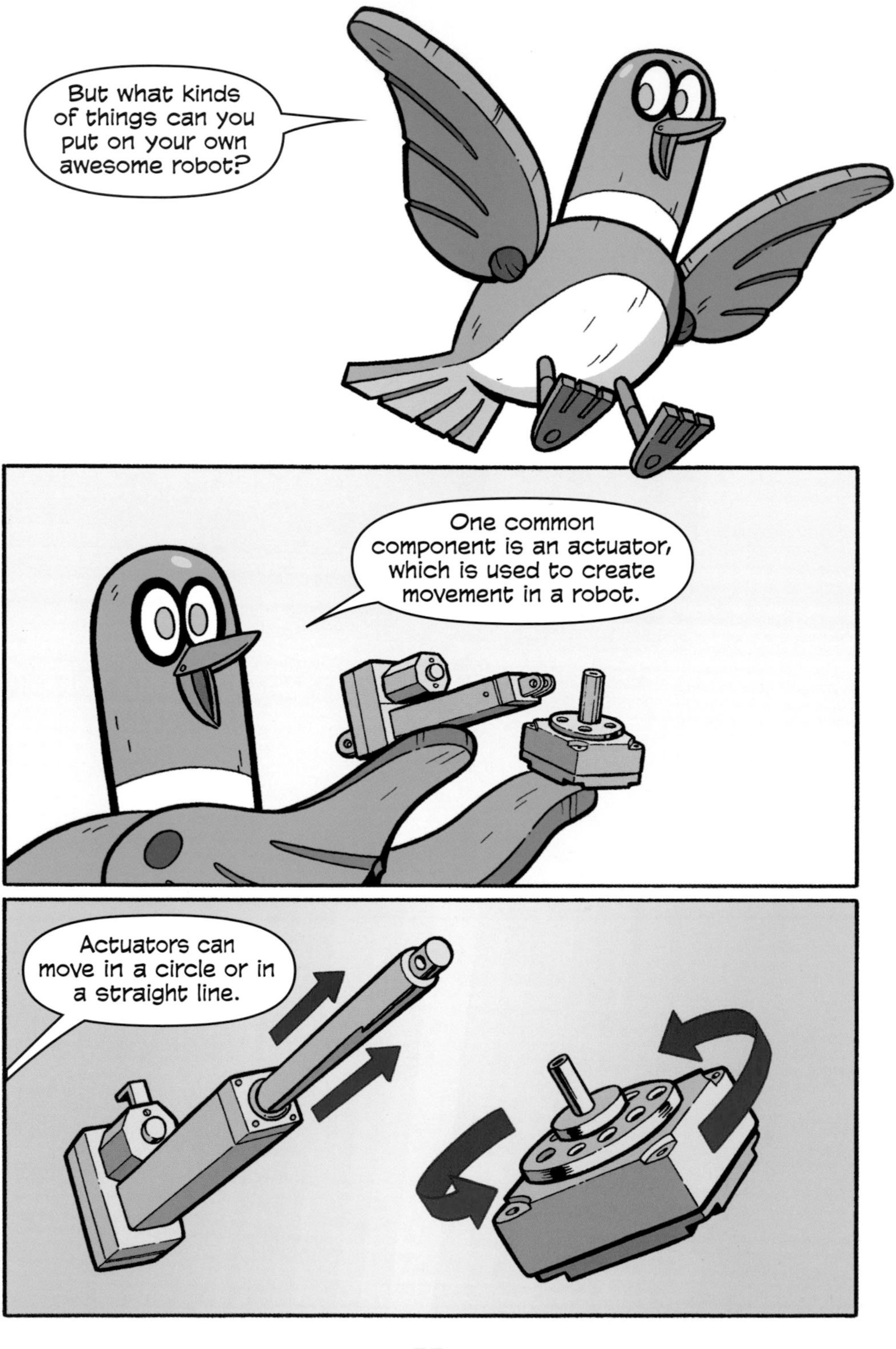
But what kinds of things can you put on your own awesome robot?
One common component is an actuator, which is used to create movement in a robot.
Actuators can move in a circle or in a straight line.

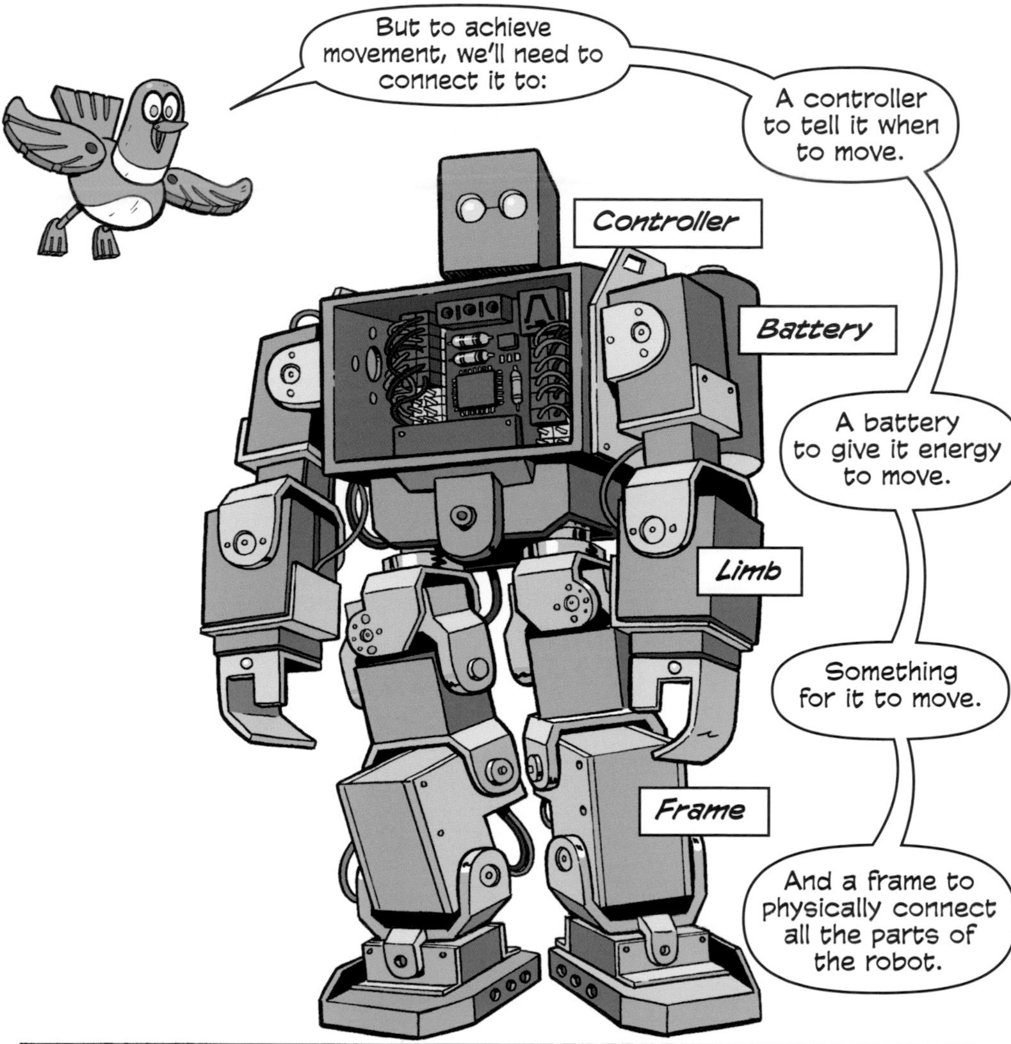

But to achieve movement, we'll need to connect it to:
A controller to tell it when to move.
Controller
Battery
A battery to give it energy to move.
Limb
Something for it to move.
Frame
And a frame to physically connect all the parts of the robot.

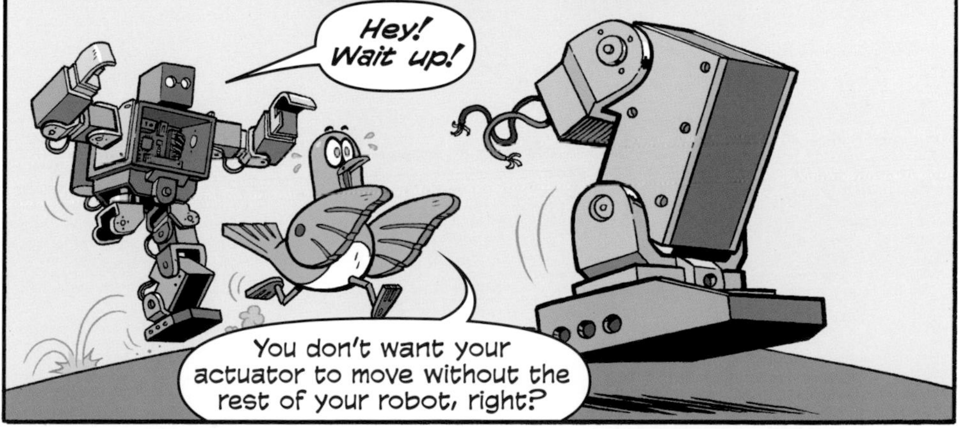

Hey! Wait up!
You don't want your actuator to move without the rest of your robot, right?

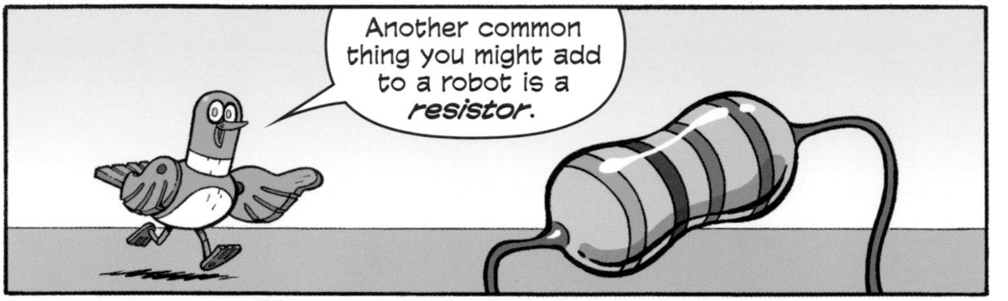
Another common thing you might add to a robot is a *resistor*.

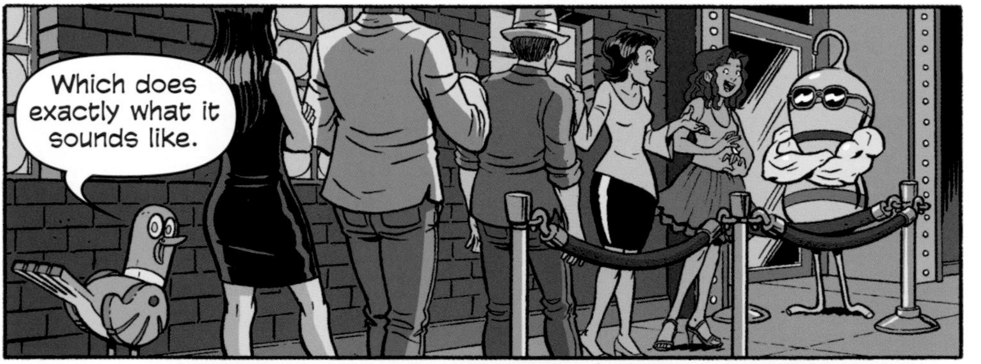
Which does exactly what it sounds like.

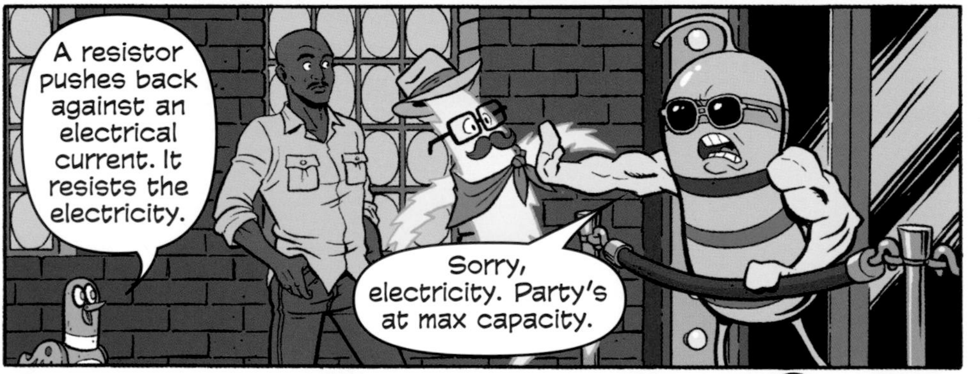
A resistor pushes back against an electrical current. It resists the electricity.
Sorry, electricity. Party's at max capacity.

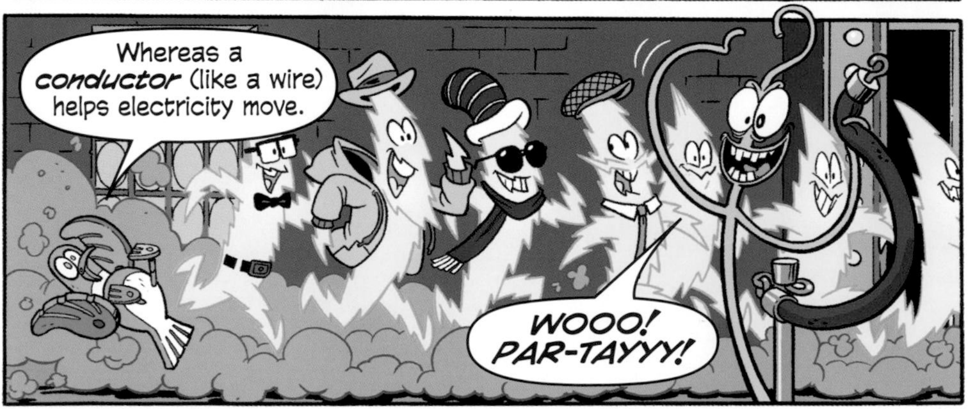
Whereas a *conductor* (like a wire) helps electricity move.
WOOO! PAR-TAYYY!

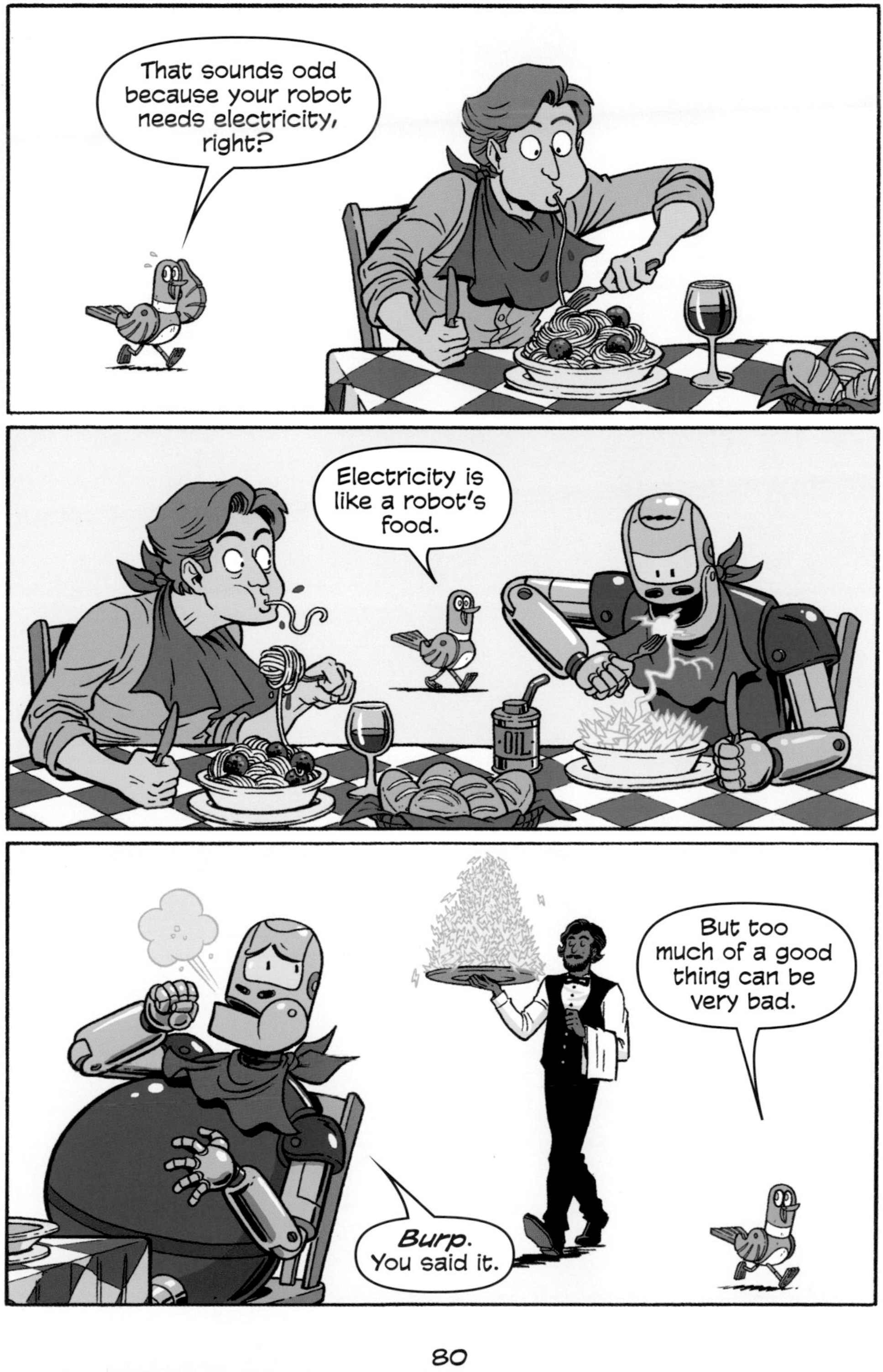
That sounds odd because your robot needs electricity, right?
Electricity is like a robot's food.
OIL
But too much of a good thing can be very bad.
Burp. You said it.

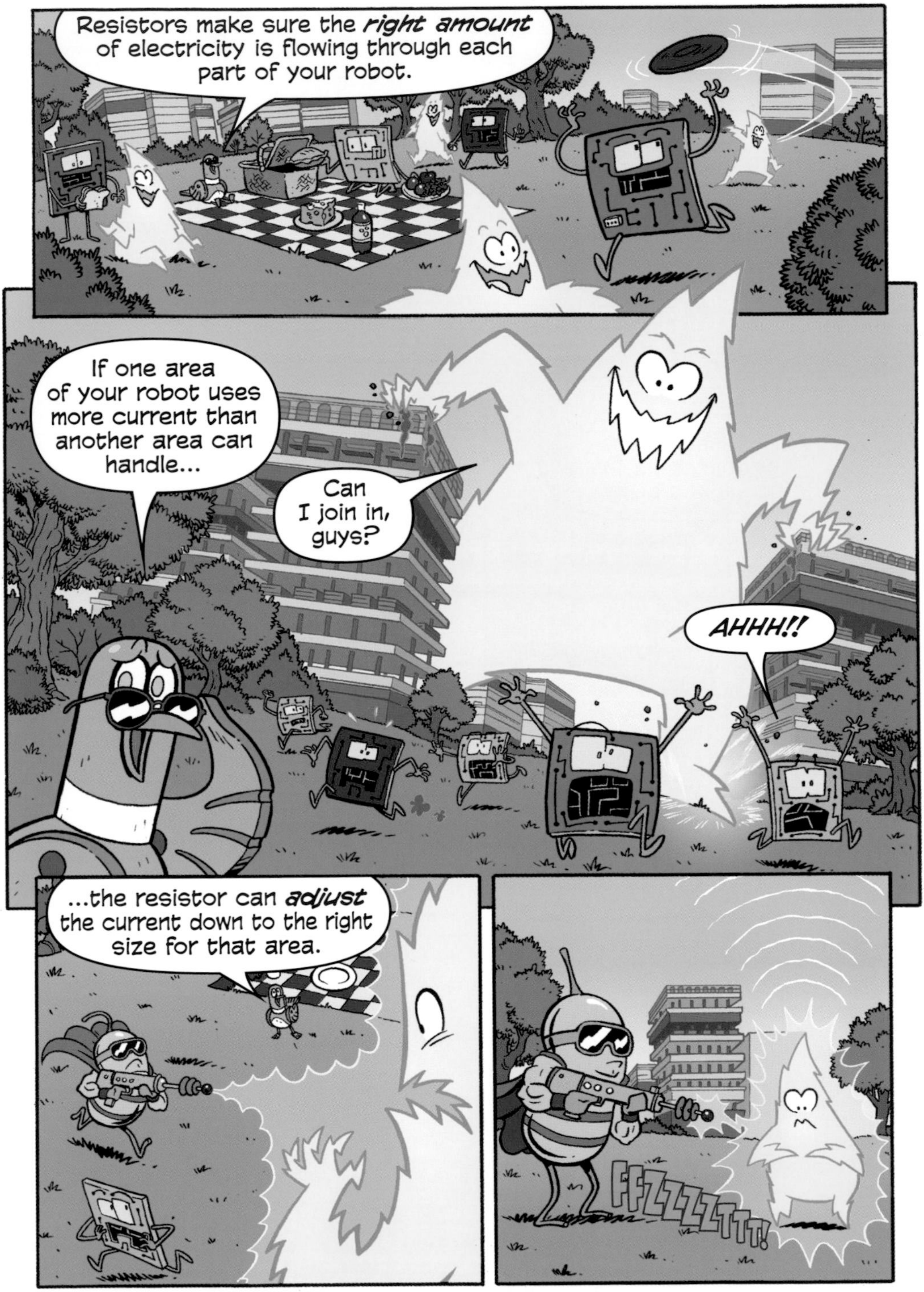
Resistors make sure the *right amount* of electricity is flowing through each part of your robot.
If one area of your robot uses more current than another area can handle...
Can I join in, guys?
AHHH!!
...the resistor can *adjust* the current down to the right size for that area.
FFZZZZZTTTT!

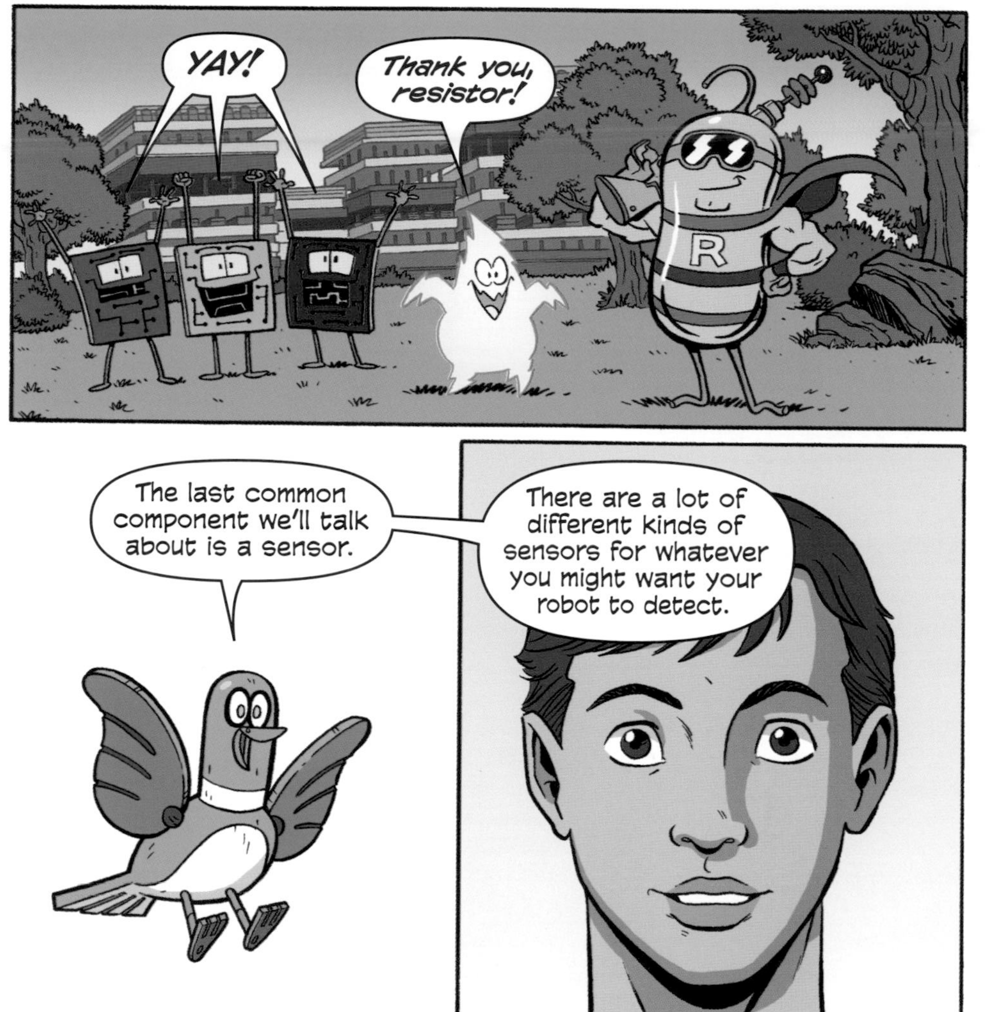
YAY!
Thank you, resistor!
The last common component we'll talk about is a sensor.
There are a lot of different kinds of sensors for whatever you might want your robot to detect.
You could install a temperature sensor that can tell a display how hot it is.
You could even build a robot that points to, or moves toward, the hottest thing in the room.
Give me your heat!

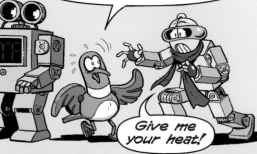

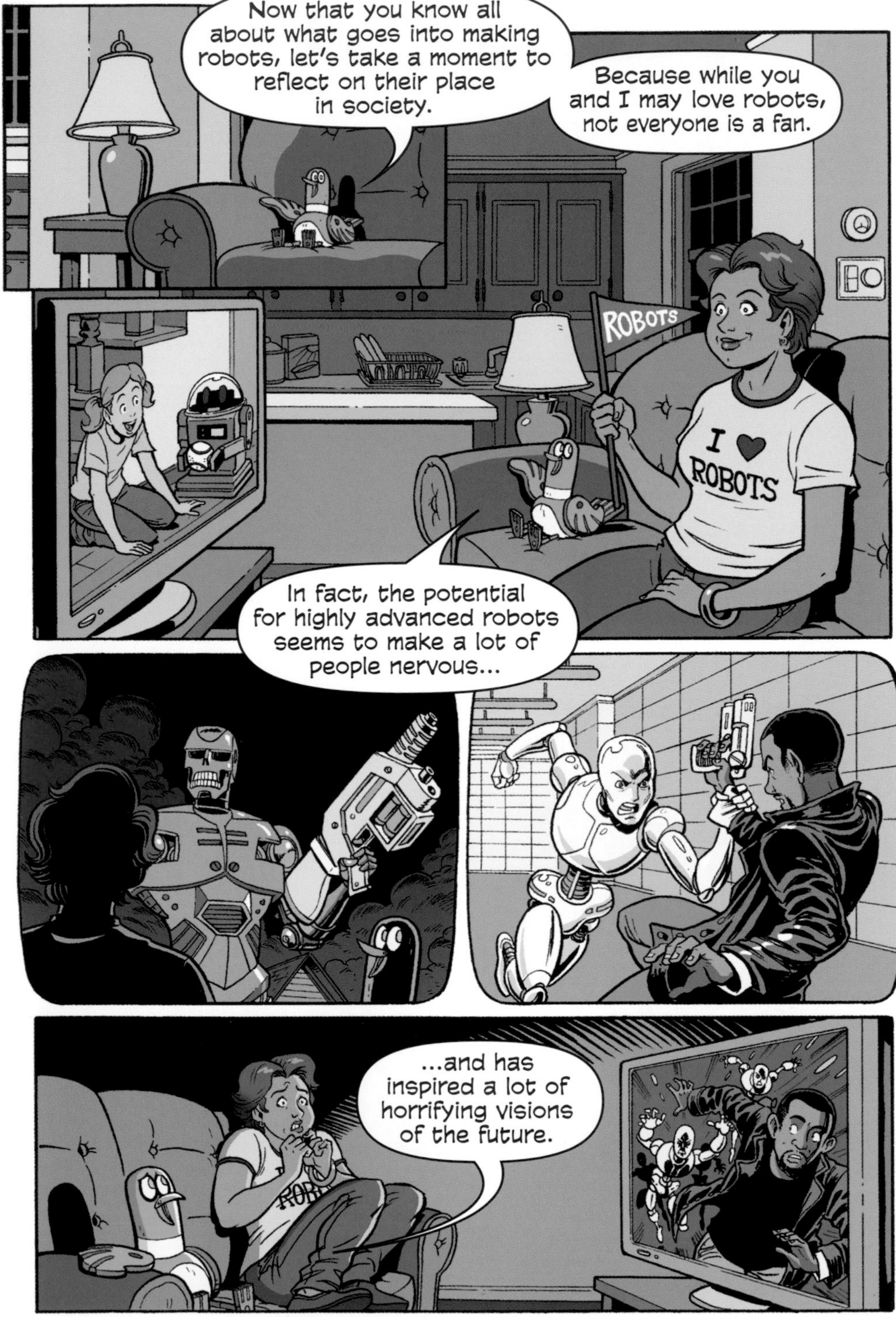

Now that you know all about what goes into making robots, let's take a moment to reflect on their place in society.
Because while you and I may love robots, not everyone is a fan.
ROBOTS
I ♥ ROBOTS
In fact, the potential for highly advanced robots seems to make a lot of people nervous...
...and has inspired a lot of horrifying visions of the future.

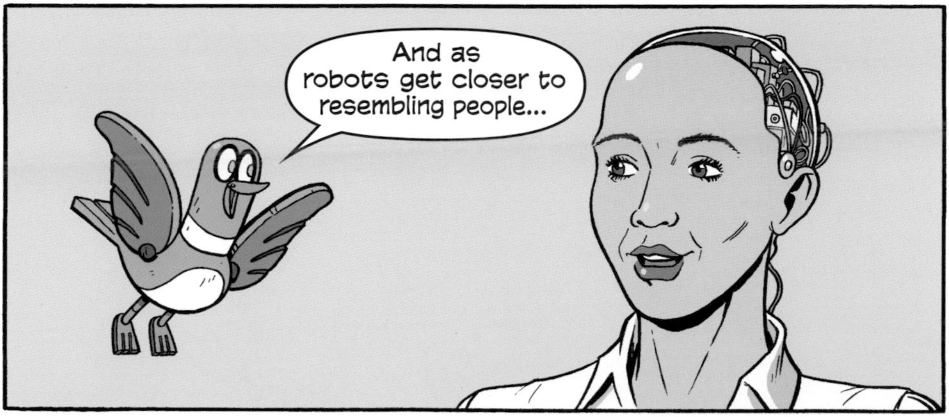
And as robots get closer to resembling people...

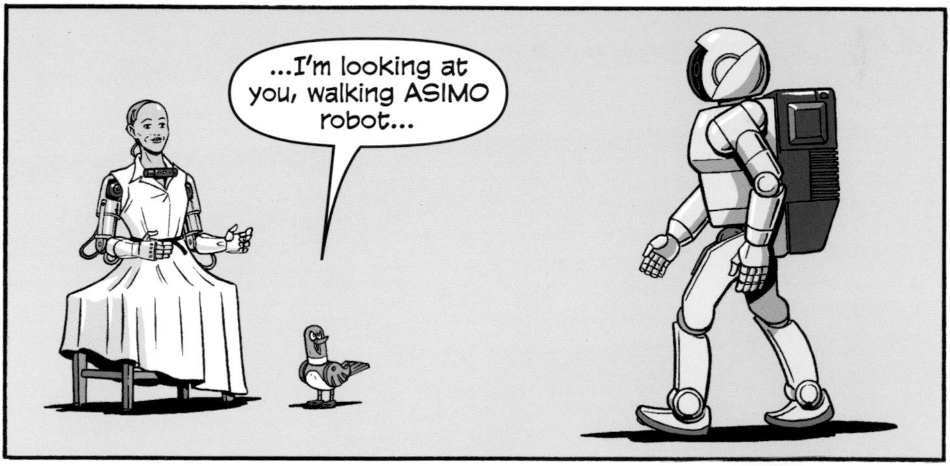
...I'm looking at you, walking ASIMO robot...

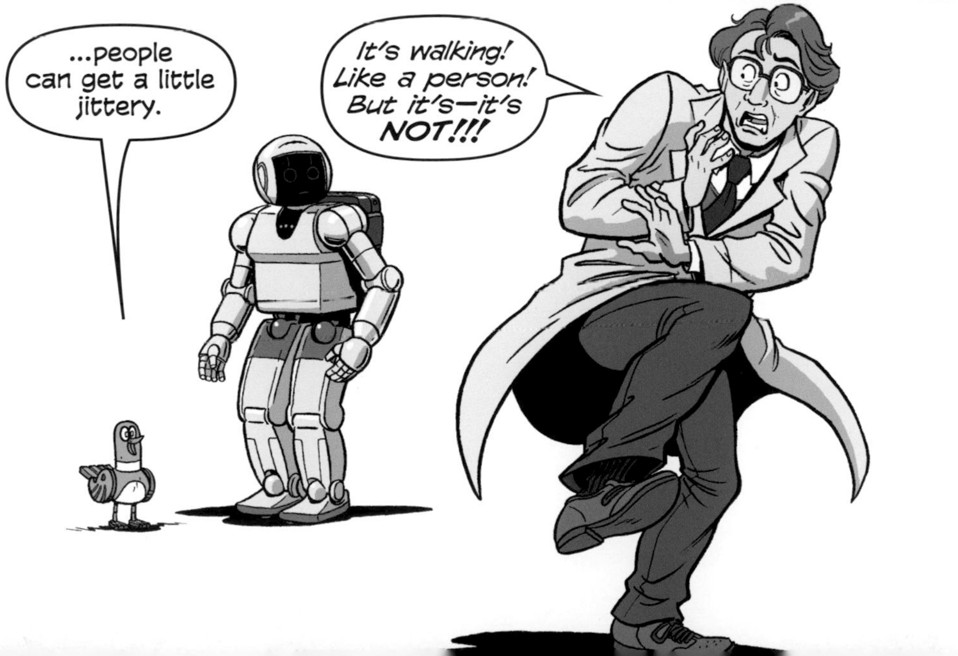
...people can get a little jittery.
It's walking! Like a person! But it's—it's ***NOT!!!***

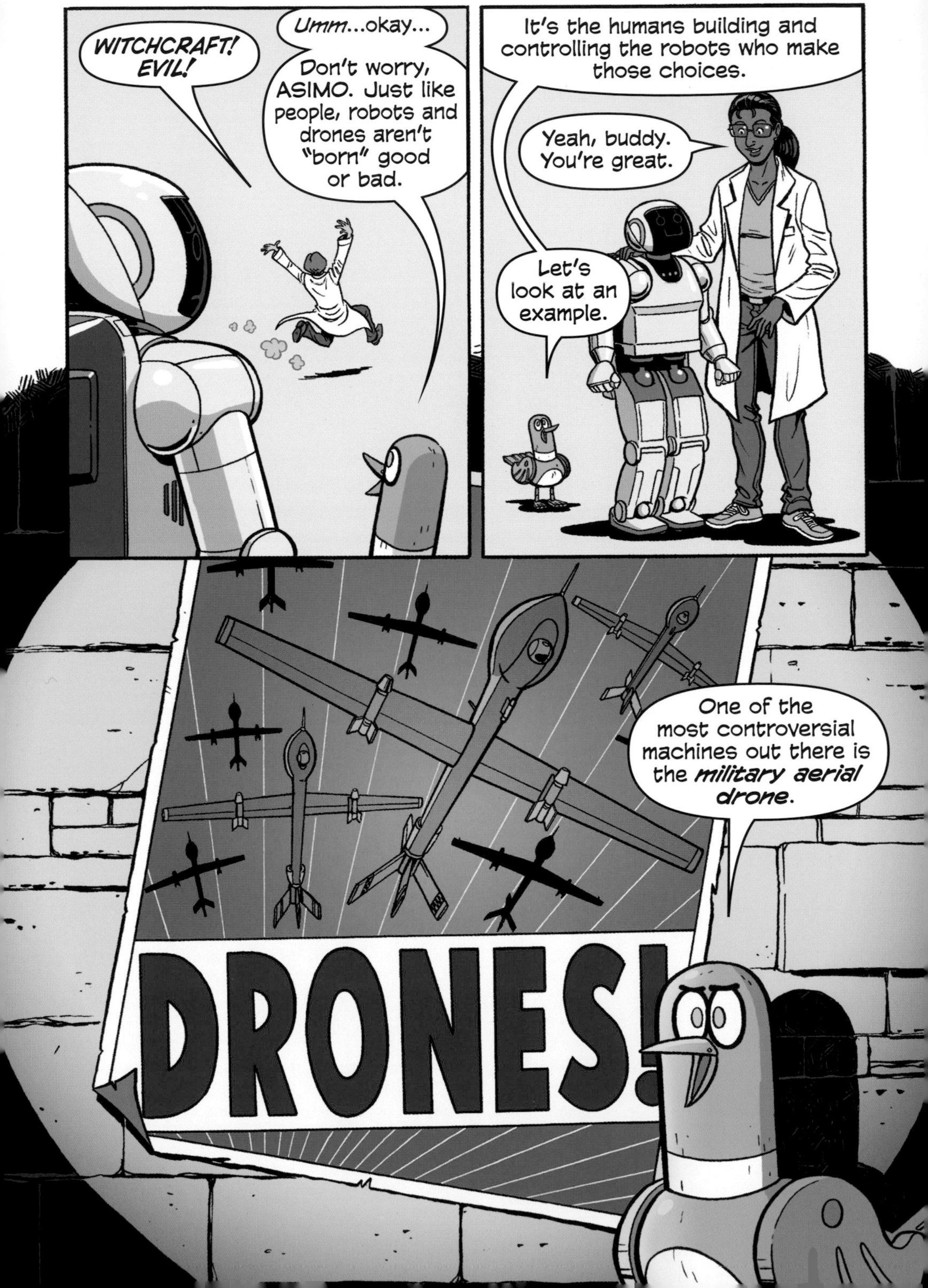
WITCHCRAFT! EVIL!
Umm...okay...
Don't worry, ASIMO. Just like people, robots and drones aren't "born" good or bad.
It's the humans building and controlling the robots who make those choices.
Yeah, buddy. You're great.
Let's look at an example.
One of the most controversial machines out there is the *military aerial drone*.
DRONES!

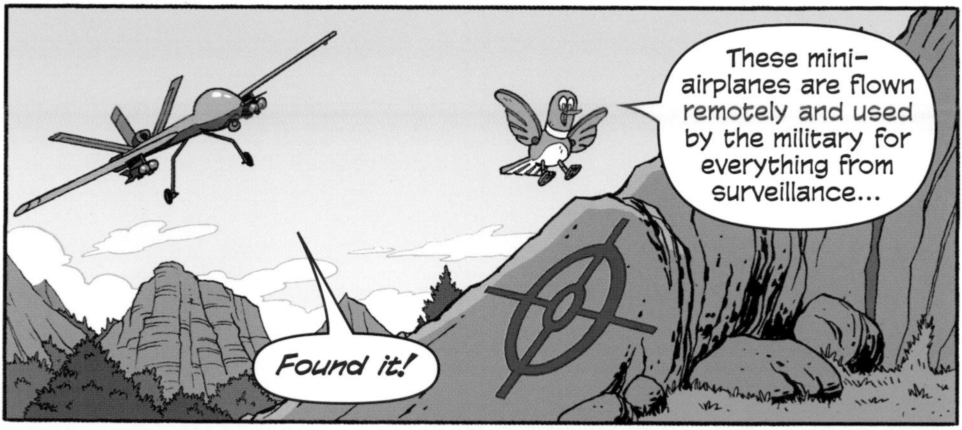
These mini-airplanes are flown remotely and used by the military for everything from surveillance...
Found it!

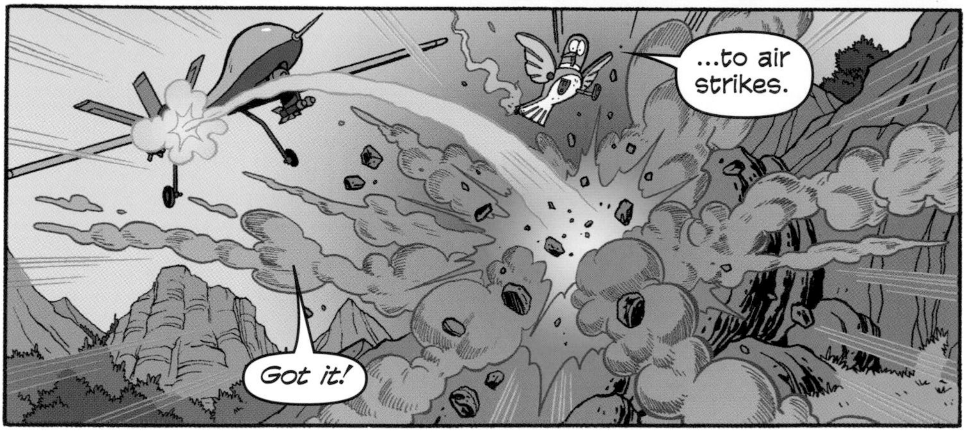
...to air strikes.
Got it!

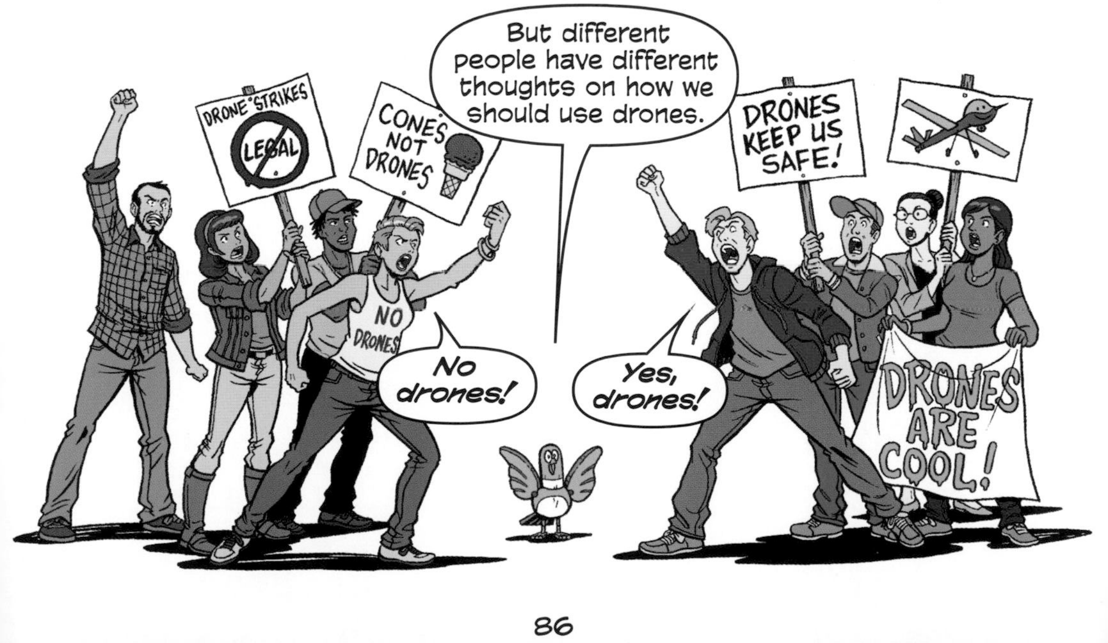
DRONE STRIKES LEGAL
CONES NOT DRONES
But different people have different thoughts on how we should use drones.
DRONES KEEP US SAFE!
NO DRONES
No drones!
Yes, drones!
DRONES ARE COOL!

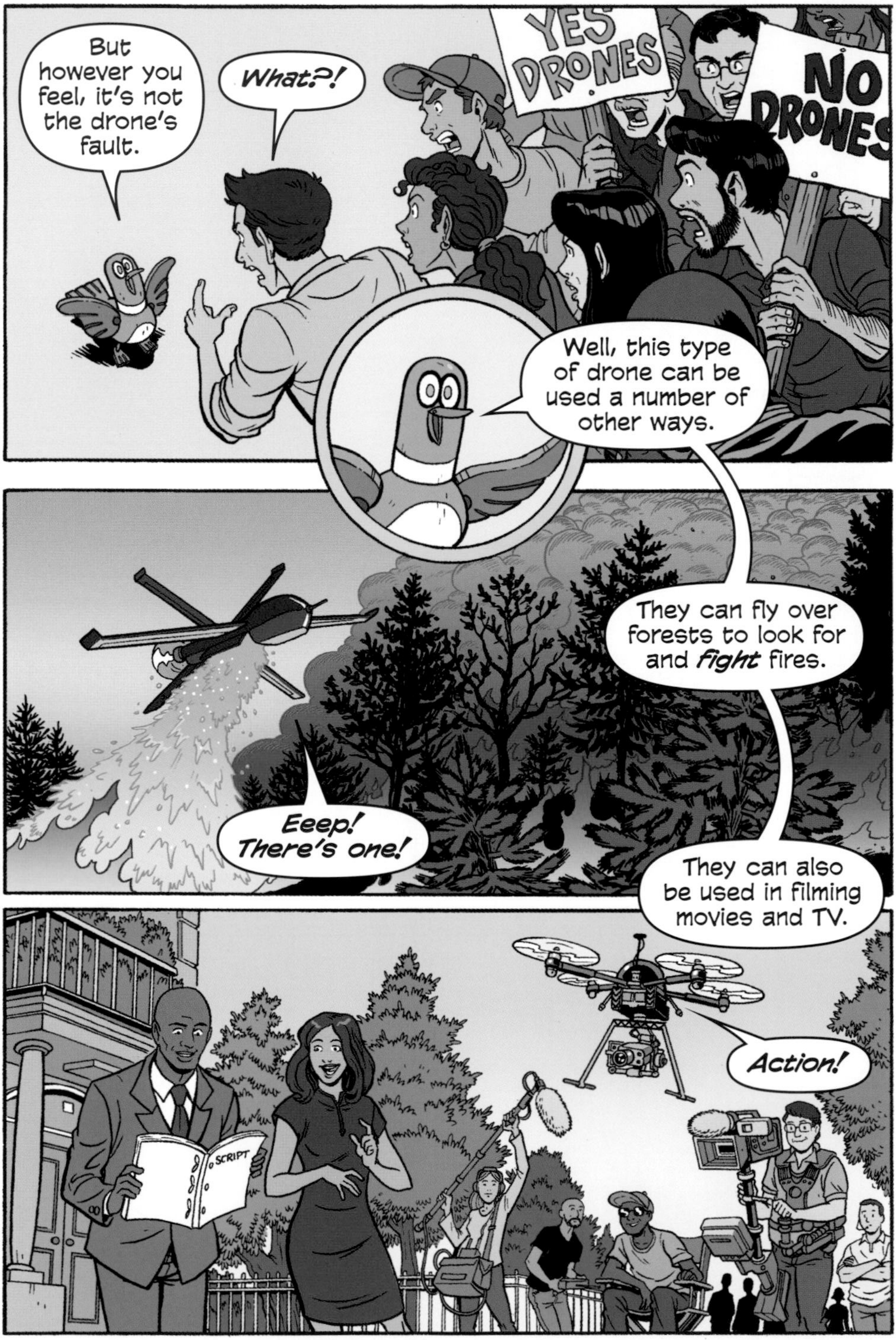
But however you feel, it's not the drone's fault.
What?!
YES DRONES
NO DRONES
Well, this type of drone can be used a number of other ways.
They can fly over forests to look for and *fight* fires.
Eeep! There's one!
They can also be used in filming movies and TV.
SCRIPT
Action!

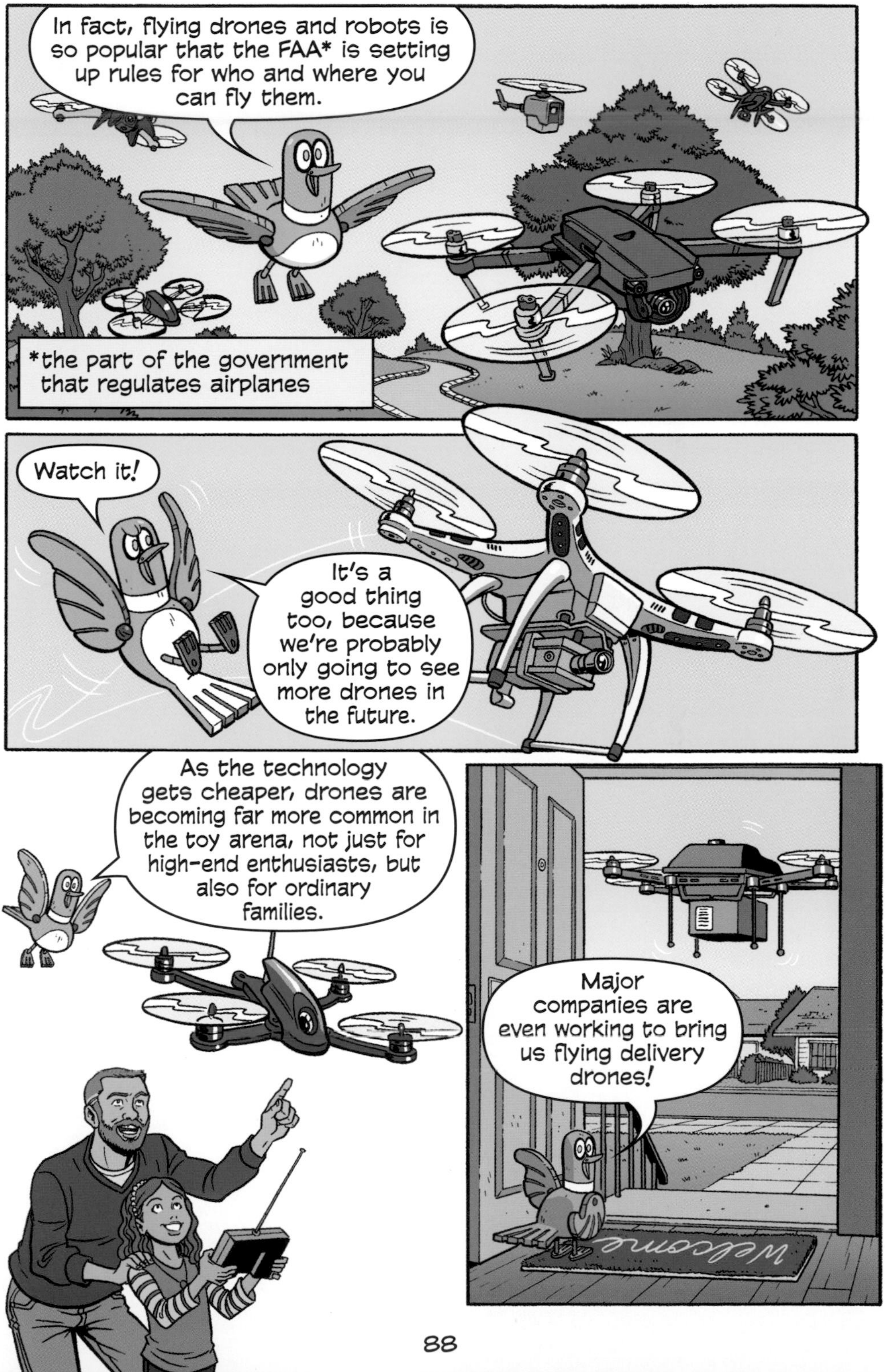
In fact, flying drones and robots is so popular that the FAA* is setting up rules for who and where you can fly them.
*the part of the government that regulates airplanes
Watch it!
It's a good thing too, because we're probably only going to see more drones in the future.
As the technology gets cheaper, drones are becoming far more common in the toy arena, not just for high-end enthusiasts, but also for ordinary families.
Major companies are even working to bring us flying delivery drones!
Welcome

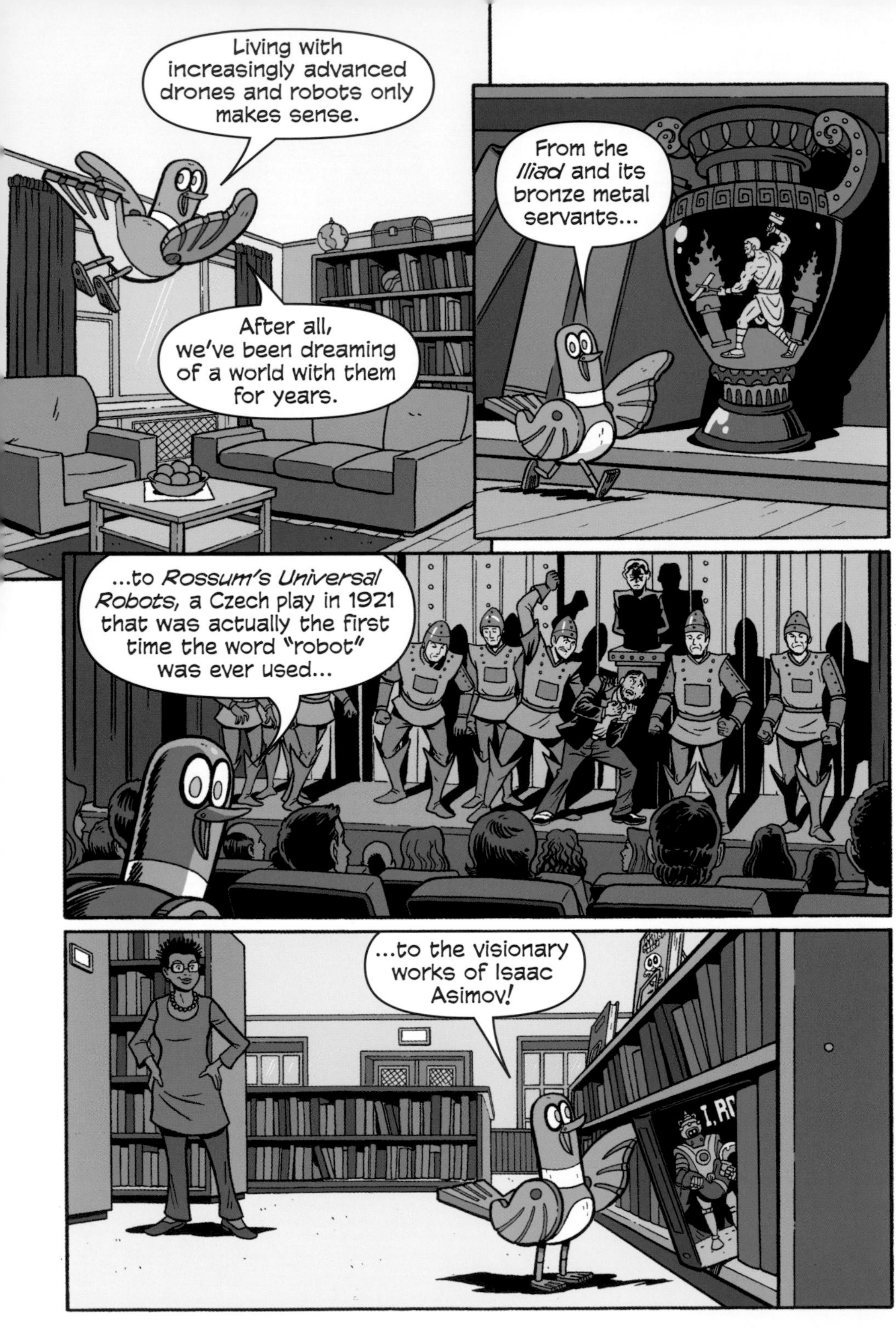
Living with increasingly advanced drones and robots only makes sense.
After all, we've been dreaming of a world with them for years.
From the *Iliad* and its bronze metal servants...
...to *Rossum's Universal Robots*, a Czech play in 1921 that was actually the first time the word "robot" was ever used...
...to the visionary works of Isaac Asimov!

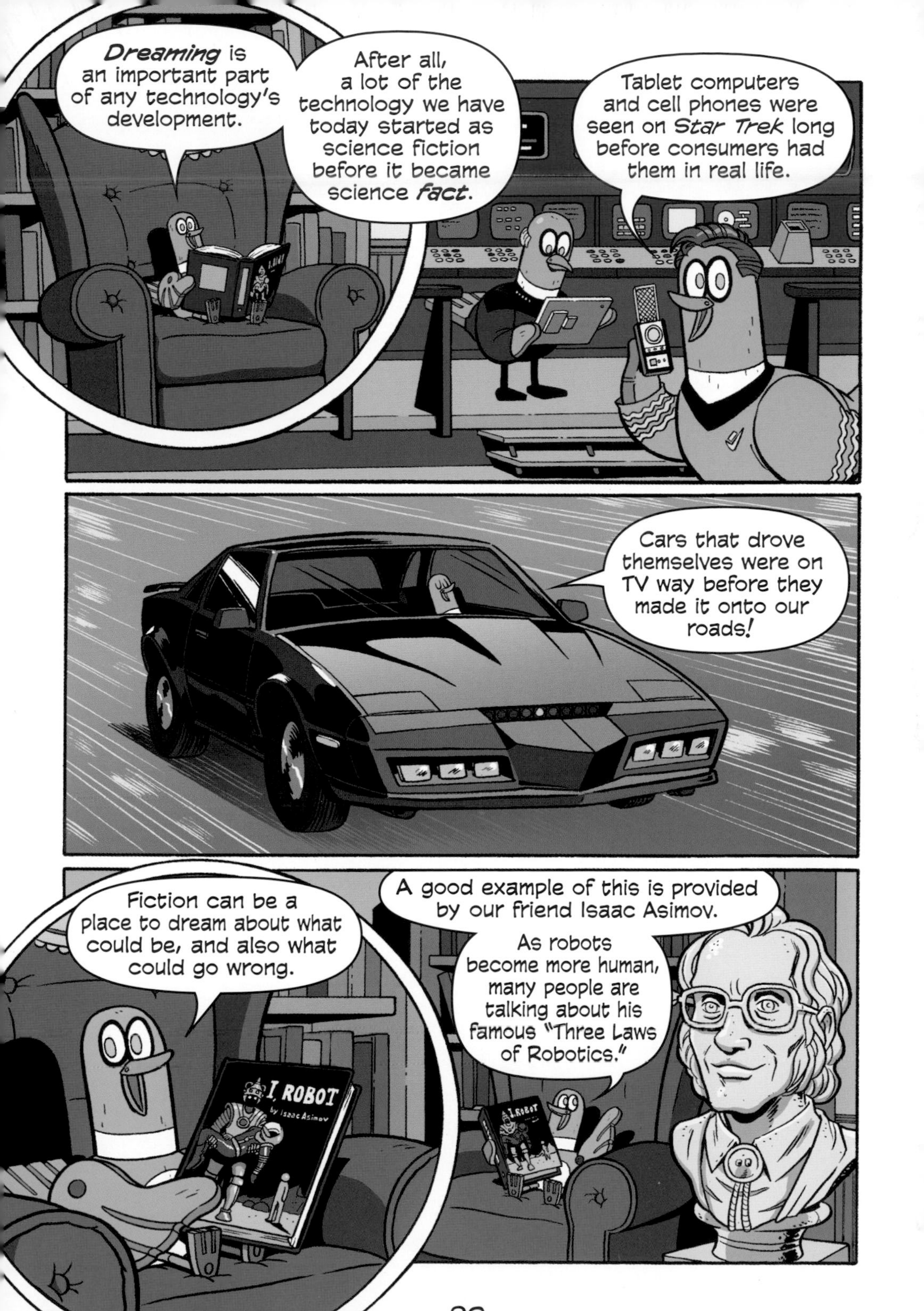
Dreaming is an important part of any technology's development.
After all, a lot of the technology we have today started as science fiction before it became science *fact*.
Tablet computers and cell phones were seen on *Star Trek* long before consumers had them in real life.
Cars that drove themselves were on TV way before they made it onto our roads!
Fiction can be a place to dream about what could be, and also what could go wrong.
I, ROBOT
by Isaac Asimov
A good example of this is provided by our friend Isaac Asimov.
As robots become more human, many people are talking about his famous "Three Laws of Robotics."

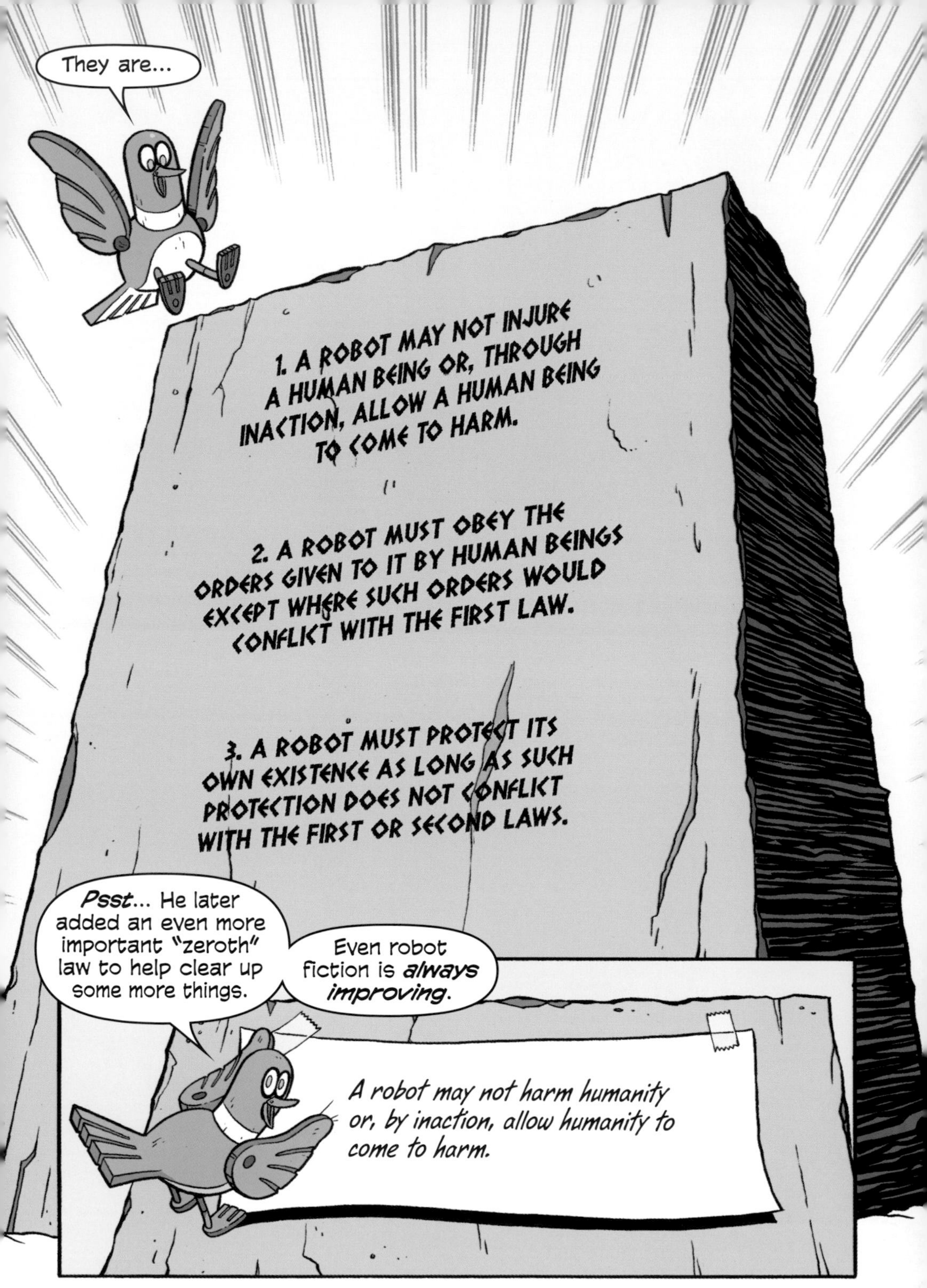
They are...
1. A ROBOT MAY NOT INJURE A HUMAN BEING OR, THROUGH INACTION, ALLOW A HUMAN BEING TO COME TO HARM.
2. A ROBOT MUST OBEY THE ORDERS GIVEN TO IT BY HUMAN BEINGS EXCEPT WHERE SUCH ORDERS WOULD CONFLICT WITH THE FIRST LAW.
3. A ROBOT MUST PROTECT ITS OWN EXISTENCE AS LONG AS SUCH PROTECTION DOES NOT CONFLICT WITH THE FIRST OR SECOND LAWS.
Psst... He later added an even more important "zeroth" law to help clear up some more things.
Even robot fiction is always improving.
A robot may not harm humanity or, by inaction, allow humanity to come to harm.

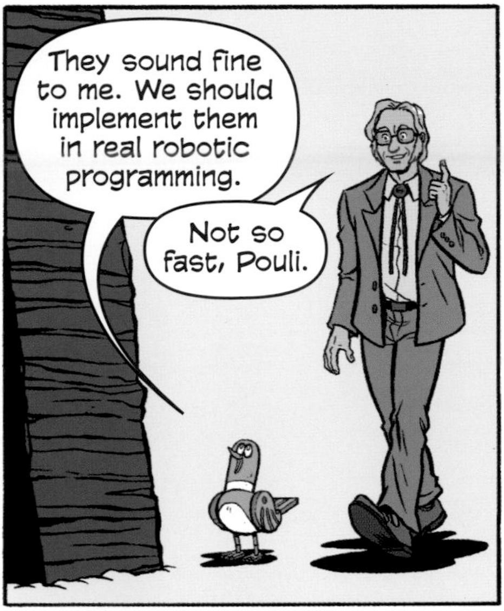
They sound fine to me. We should implement them in real robotic programming.
Not so fast, Pouli.

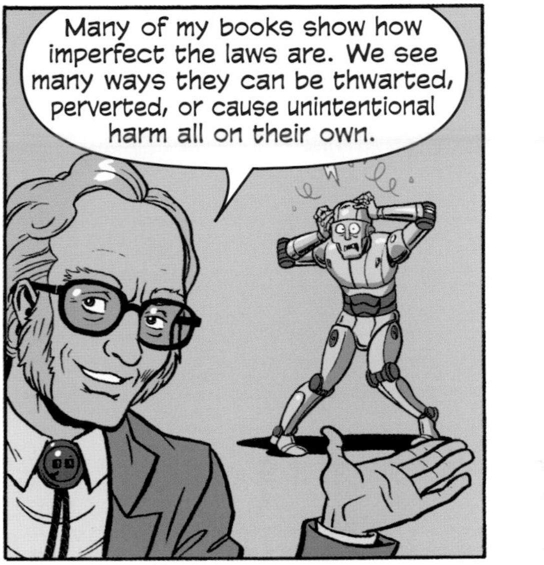
Many of my books show how imperfect the laws are. We see many ways they can be thwarted, perverted, or cause unintentional harm all on their own.

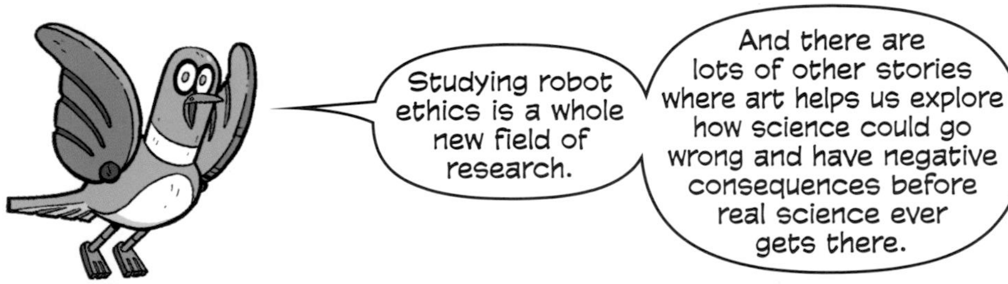
Studying robot ethics is a whole new field of research.
And there are lots of other stories where art helps us explore how science could go wrong and have negative consequences before real science ever gets there.

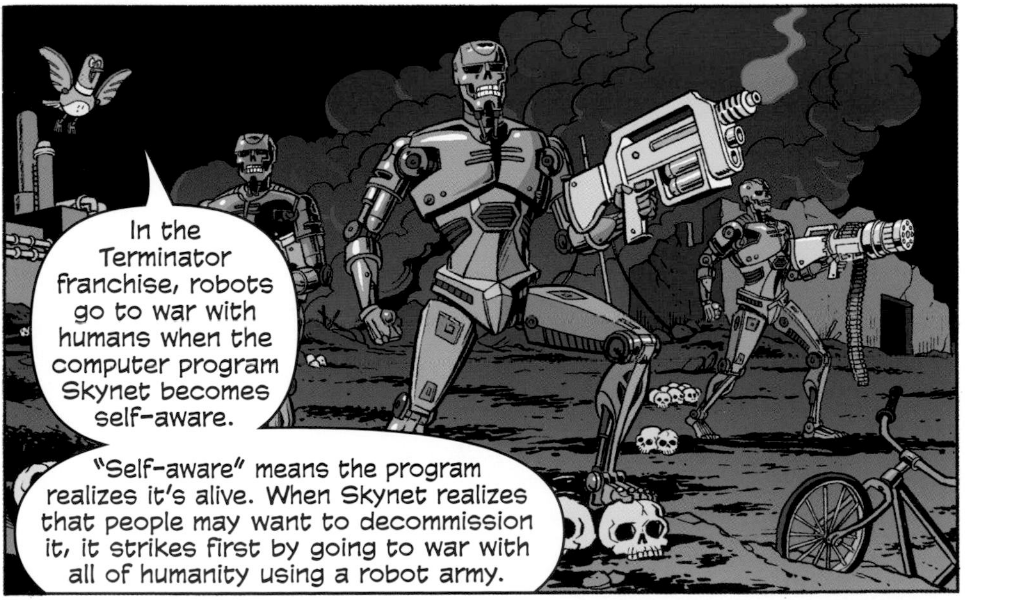
In the Terminator franchise, robots go to war with humans when the computer program Skynet becomes self-aware.
"Self-aware" means the program realizes it's alive. When Skynet realizes that people may want to decommission it, it strikes first by going to war with all of humanity using a robot army.

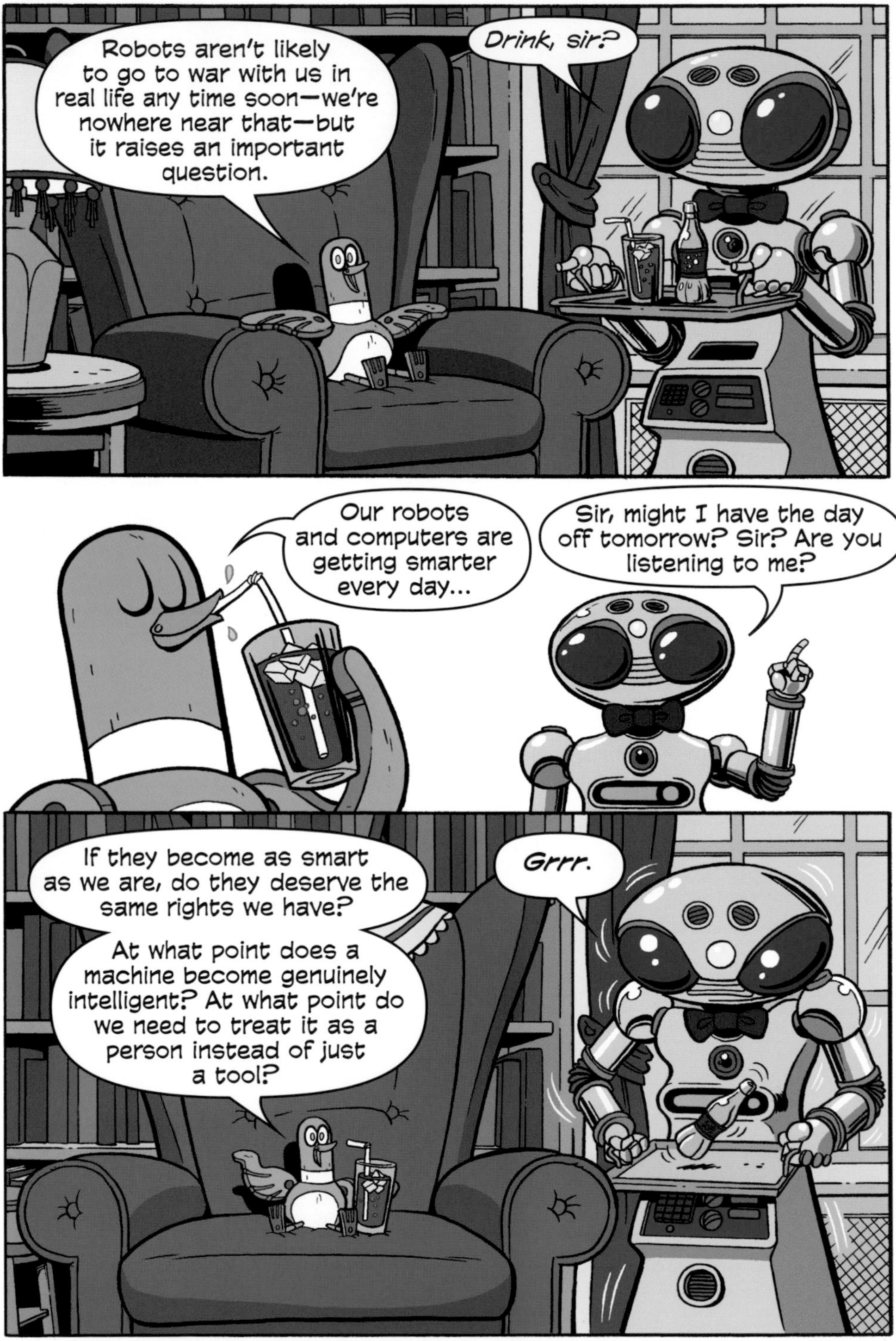
Robots aren't likely to go to war with us in real life any time soon—we're nowhere near that—but it raises an important question.
Drink, sir?
Our robots and computers are getting smarter every day...
Sir, might I have the day off tomorrow? Sir? Are you listening to me?
If they become as smart as we are, do they deserve the same rights we have?
At what point does a machine become genuinely intelligent? At what point do we need to treat it as a person instead of just a tool?
Grrr.

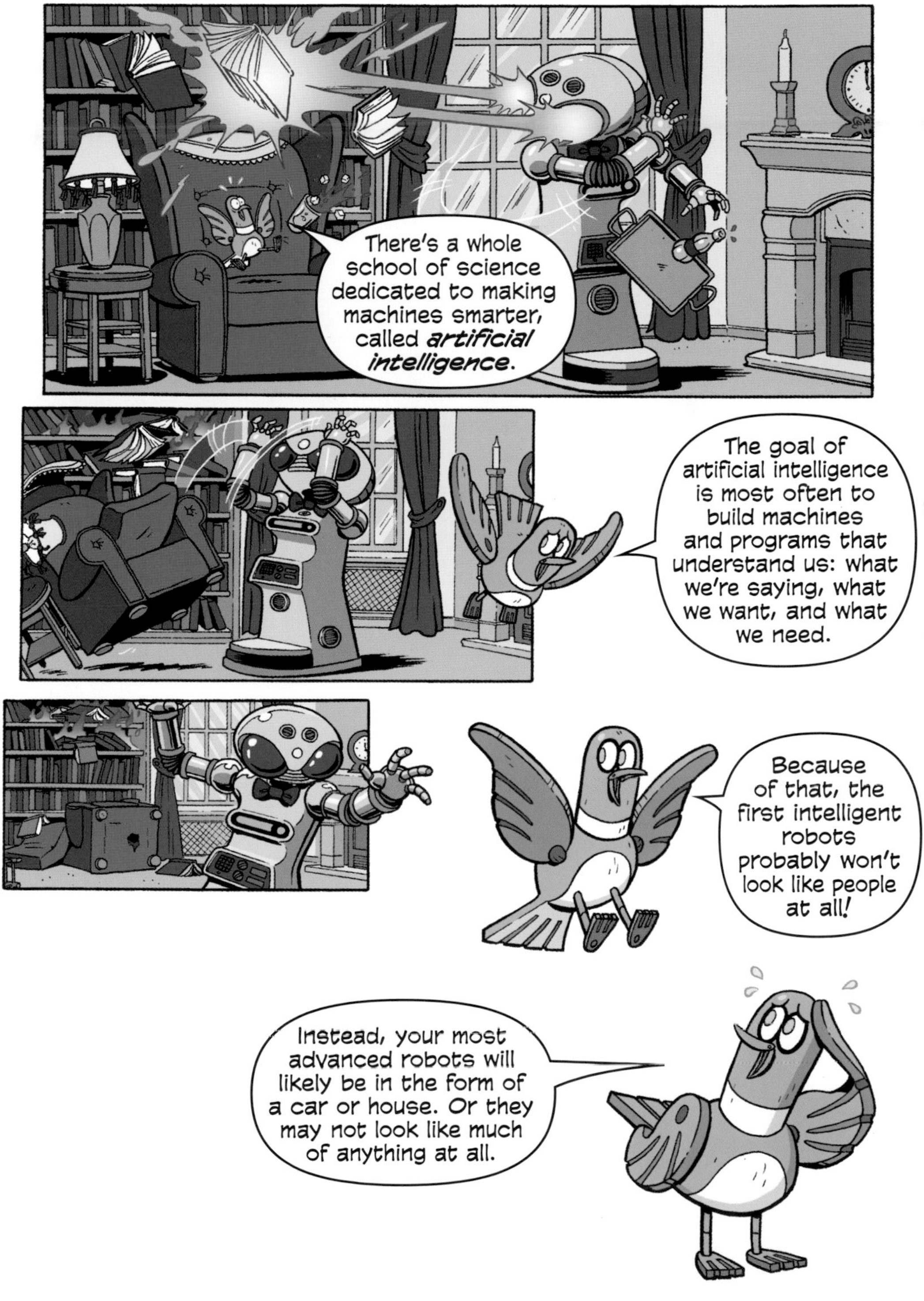
There's a whole school of science dedicated to making machines smarter, called *artificial intelligence*.
The goal of artificial intelligence is most often to build machines and programs that understand us: what we're saying, what we want, and what we need.
Because of that, the first intelligent robots probably won't look like people at all!
Instead, your most advanced robots will likely be in the form of a car or house. Or they may not look like much of anything at all.

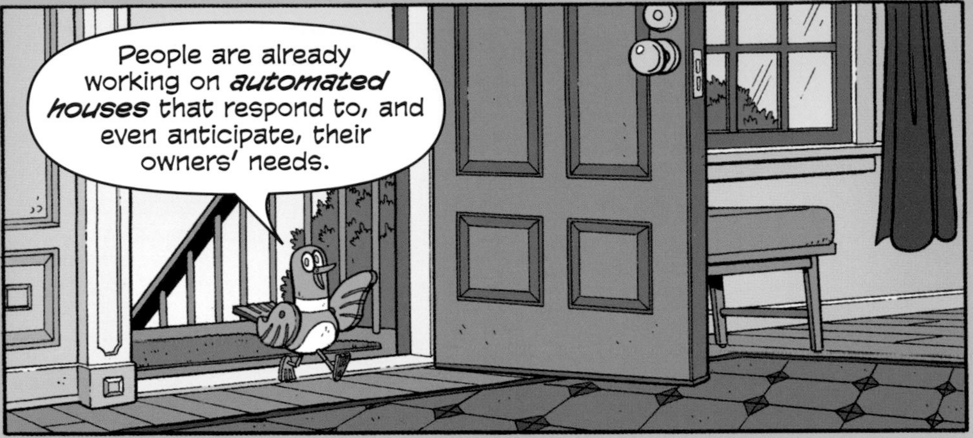
People are already working on ***automated houses*** that respond to, and even anticipate, their owners' needs.

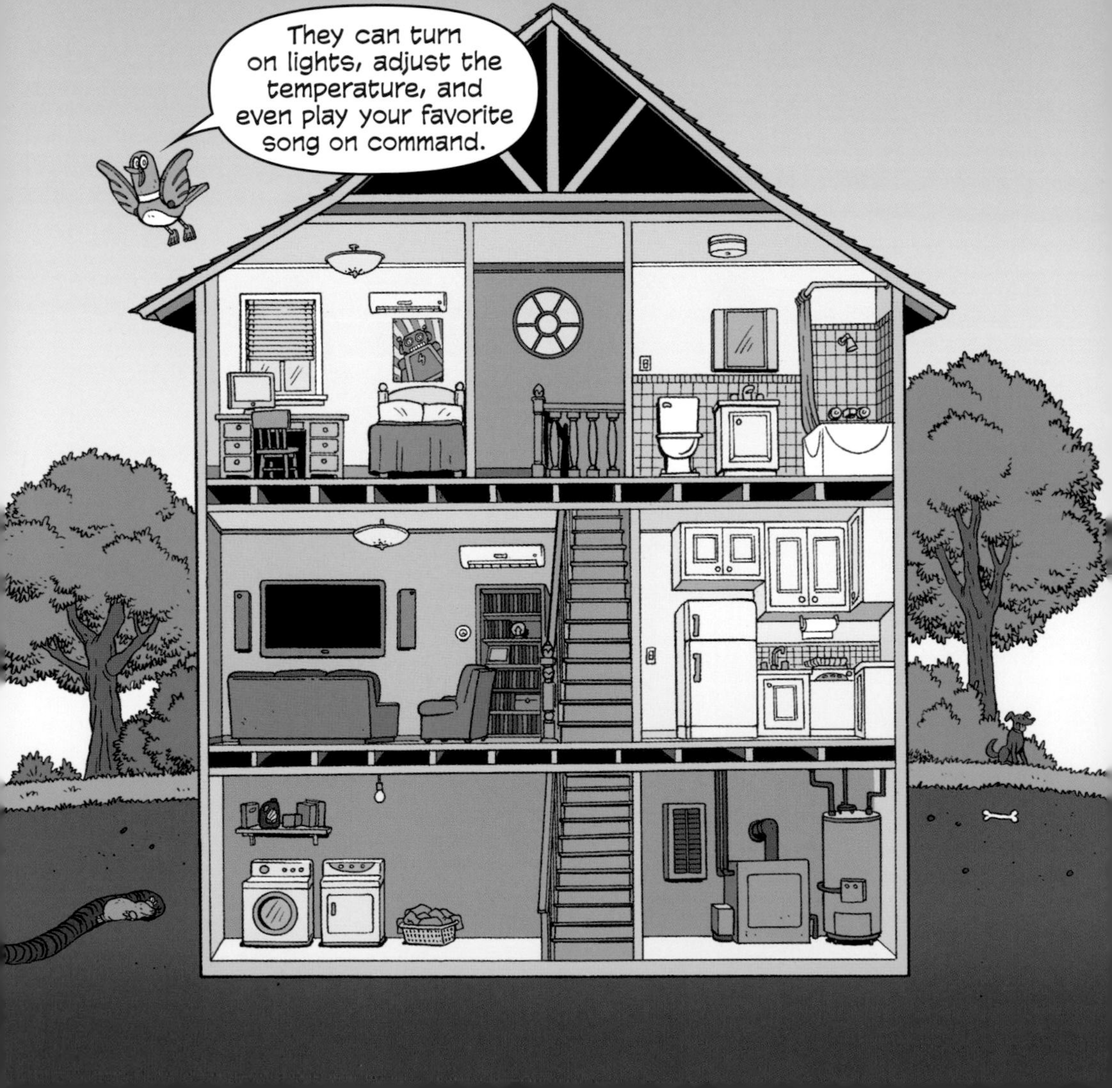
They can turn on lights, adjust the temperature, and even play your favorite song on command.

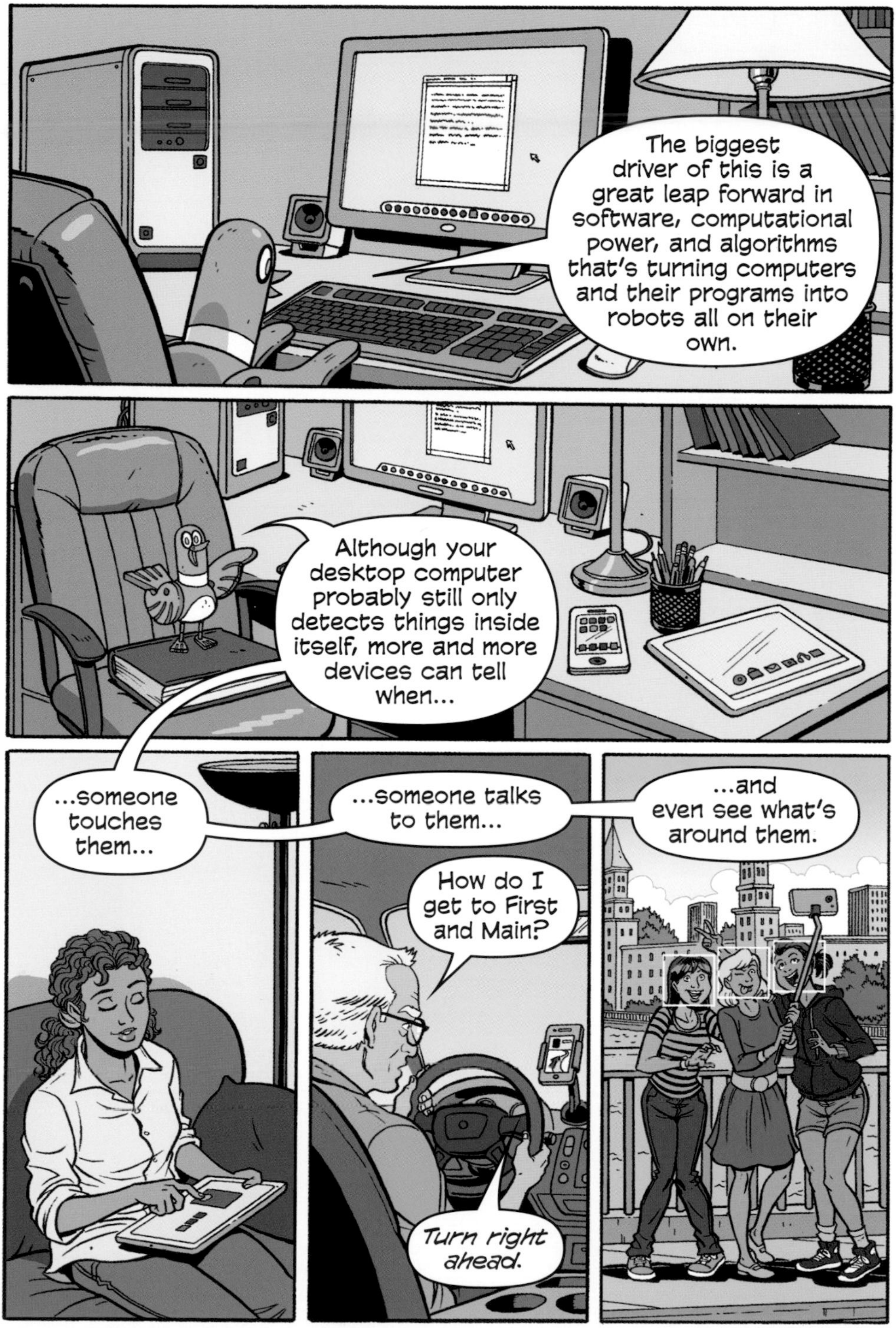

The biggest driver of this is a great leap forward in software, computational power, and algorithms that's turning computers and their programs into robots all on their own.
Although your desktop computer probably still only detects things inside itself, more and more devices can tell when...
...someone touches them...
...someone talks to them...
How do I get to First and Main?
Turn right ahead.
...and even see what's around them.

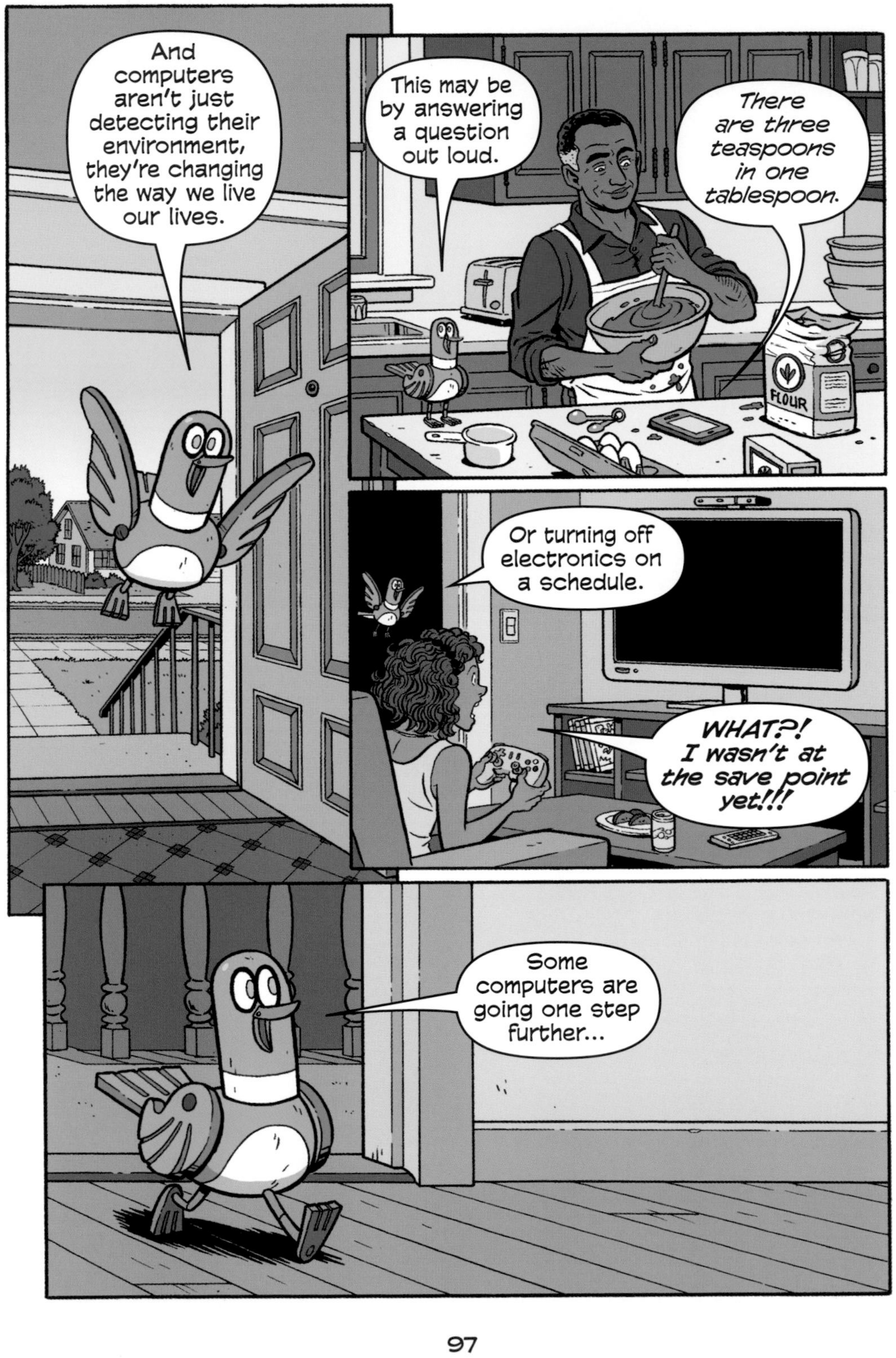
And computers aren't just detecting their environment, they're changing the way we live our lives.
This may be by answering a question out loud.
There are three teaspoons in one tablespoon.
FLOUR
Or turning off electronics on a schedule.
WHAT?! I wasn't at the save point yet!!!
Some computers are going one step further...

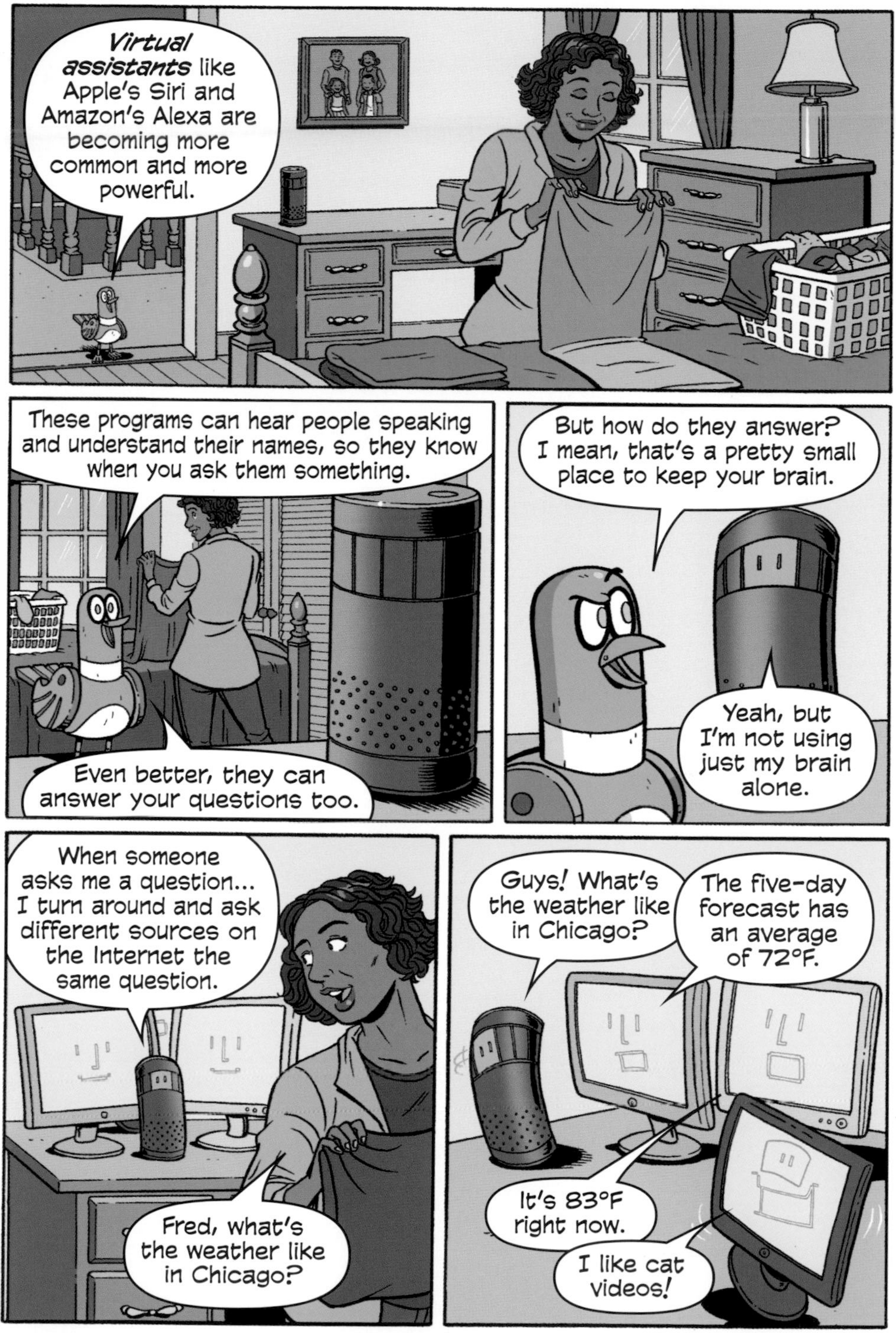
Virtual assistants like Apple's Siri and Amazon's Alexa are becoming more common and more powerful.
These programs can hear people speaking and understand their names, so they know when you ask them something.
Even better, they can answer your questions too.
But how do they answer? I mean, that's a pretty small place to keep your brain.
Yeah, but I'm not using just my brain alone.
When someone asks me a question... I turn around and ask different sources on the Internet the same question.
Fred, what's the weather like in Chicago?
Guys! What's the weather like in Chicago?
The five-day forecast has an average of 72°F.
It's 83°F right now.
I like cat videos!

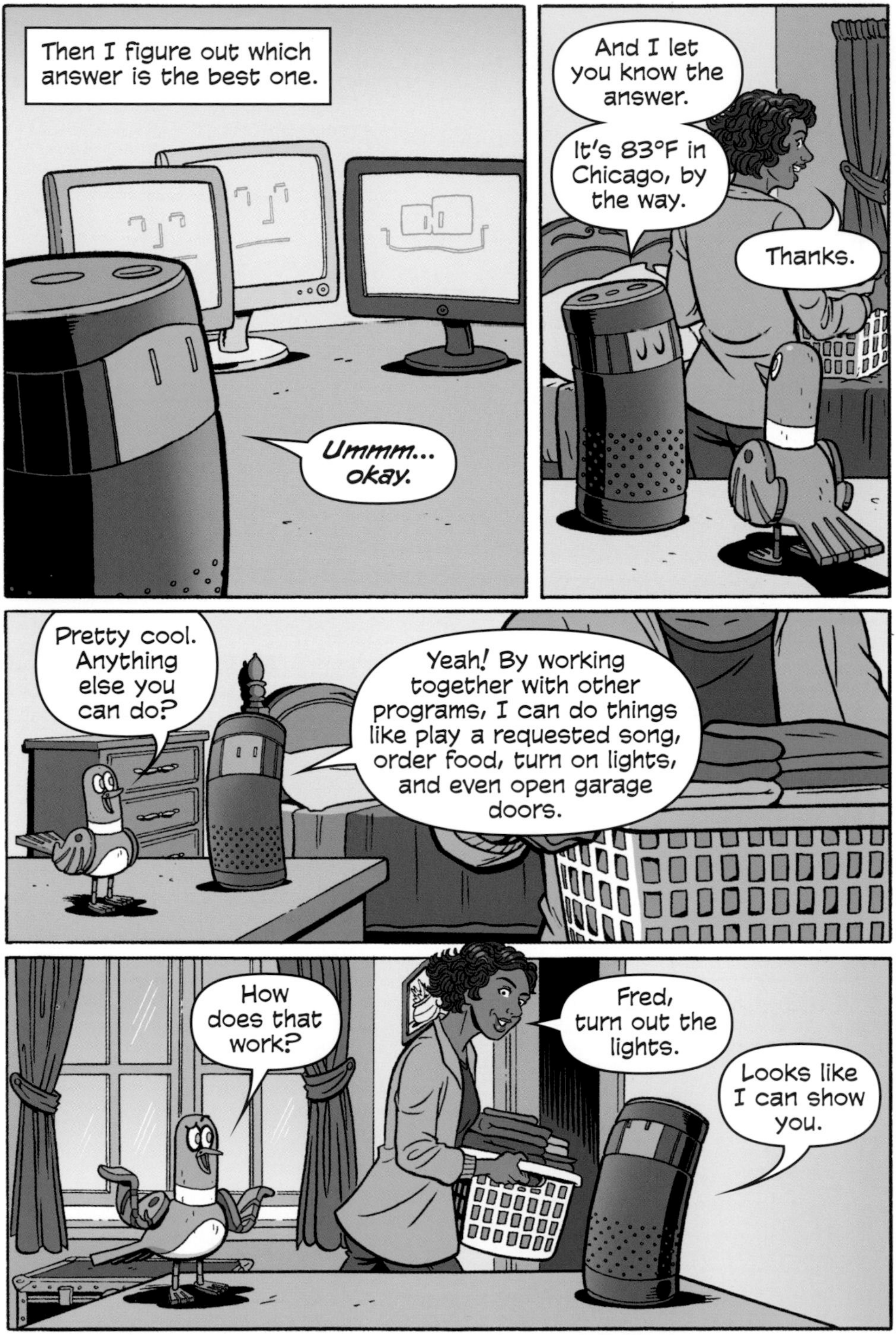
Then I figure out which answer is the best one.
Ummm... okay.
And I let you know the answer.
It's 83°F in Chicago, by the way.
Thanks.
Pretty cool. Anything else you can do?
Yeah! By working together with other programs, I can do things like play a requested song, order food, turn on lights, and even open garage doors.
How does that work?
Fred, turn out the lights.
Looks like I can show you.

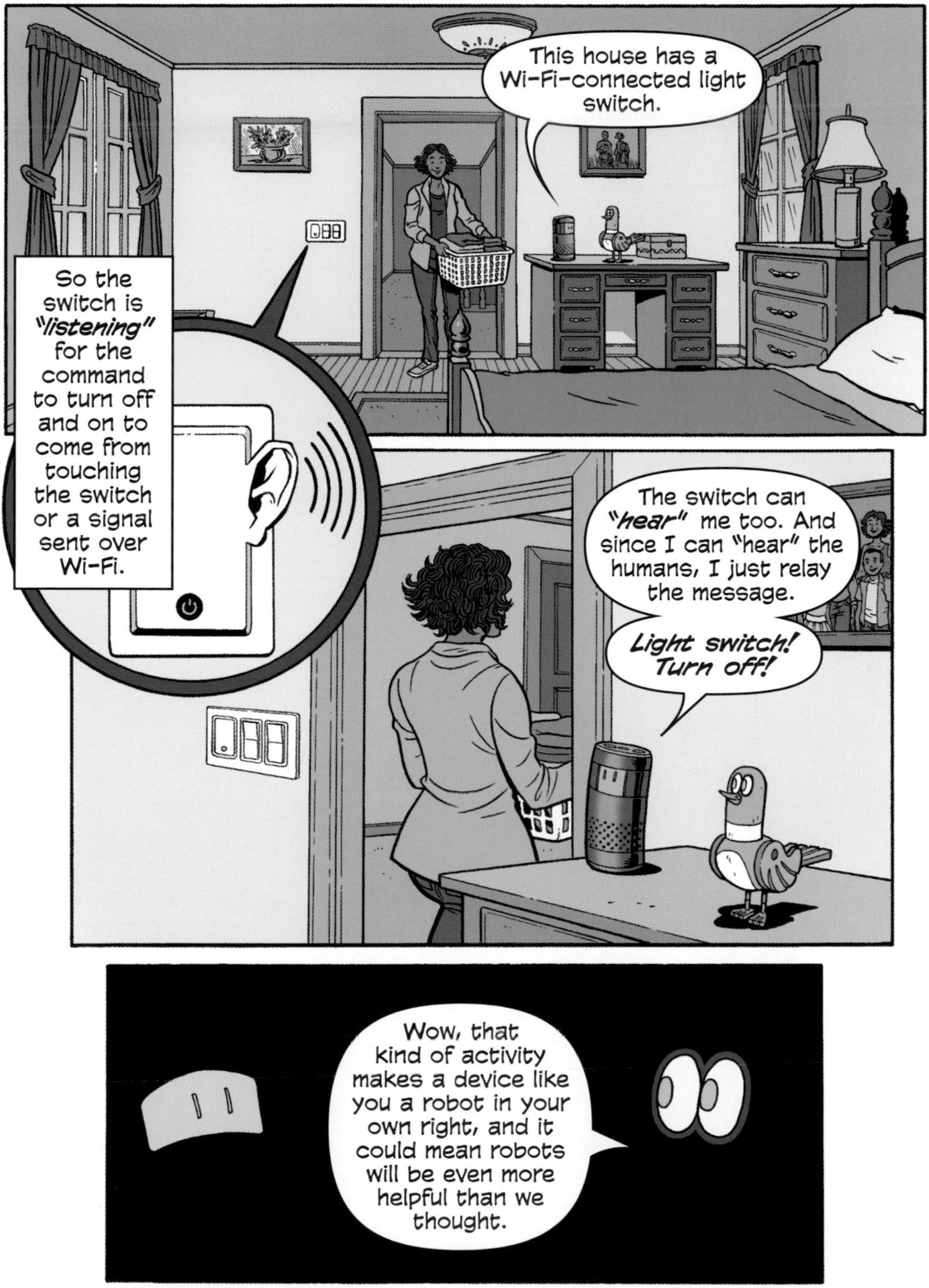
This house has a Wi-Fi-connected light switch.
So the switch is *"listening"* for the command to turn off and on to come from touching the switch or a signal sent over Wi-Fi.
The switch can *"hear"* me too. And since I can "hear" the humans, I just relay the message.
Light switch! Turn off!
Wow, that kind of activity makes a device like you a robot in your own right, and it could mean robots will be even more helpful than we thought.

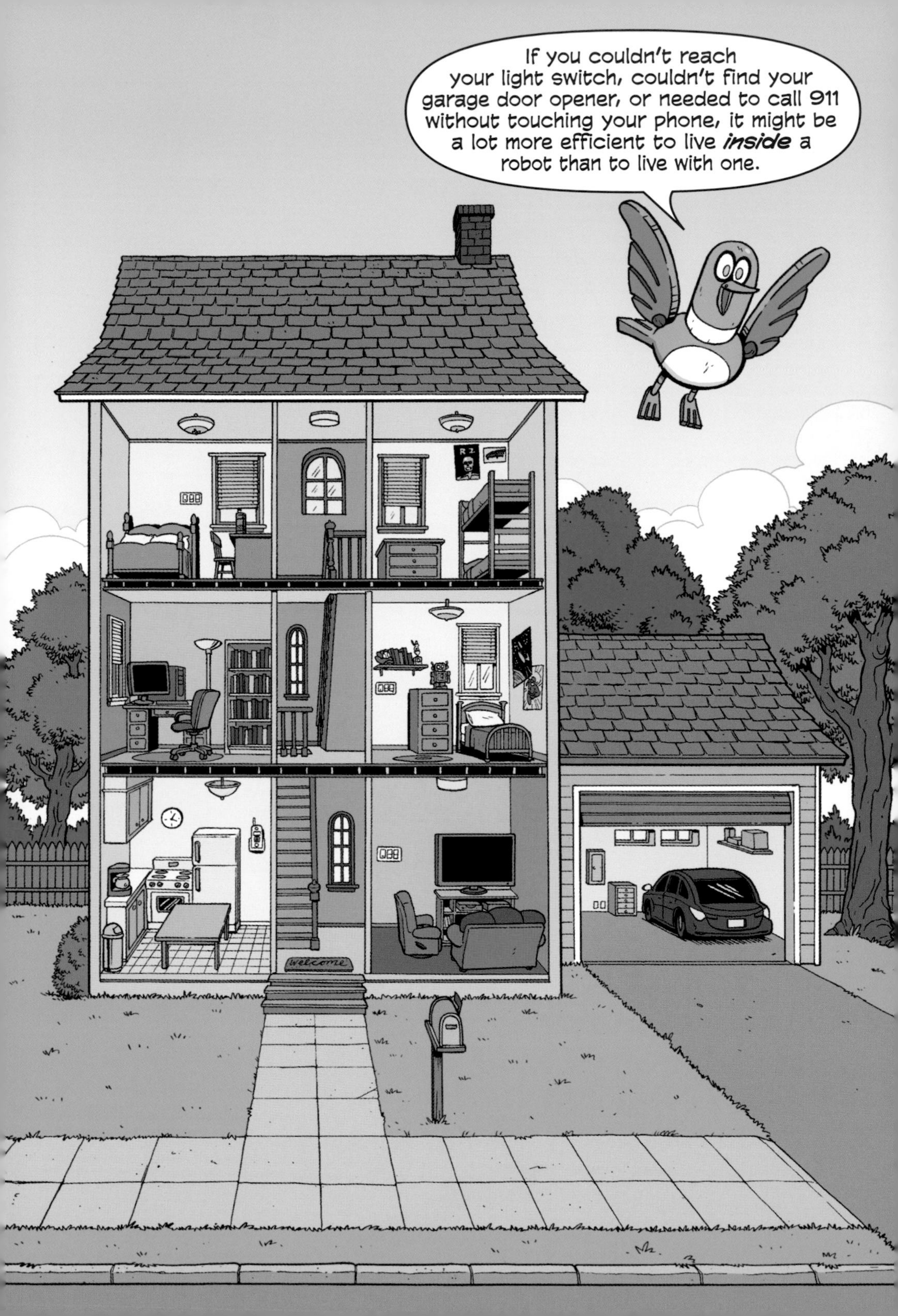
If you couldn't reach your light switch, couldn't find your garage door opener, or needed to call 911 without touching your phone, it might be a lot more efficient to live *inside* a robot than to live with one.
Welcome

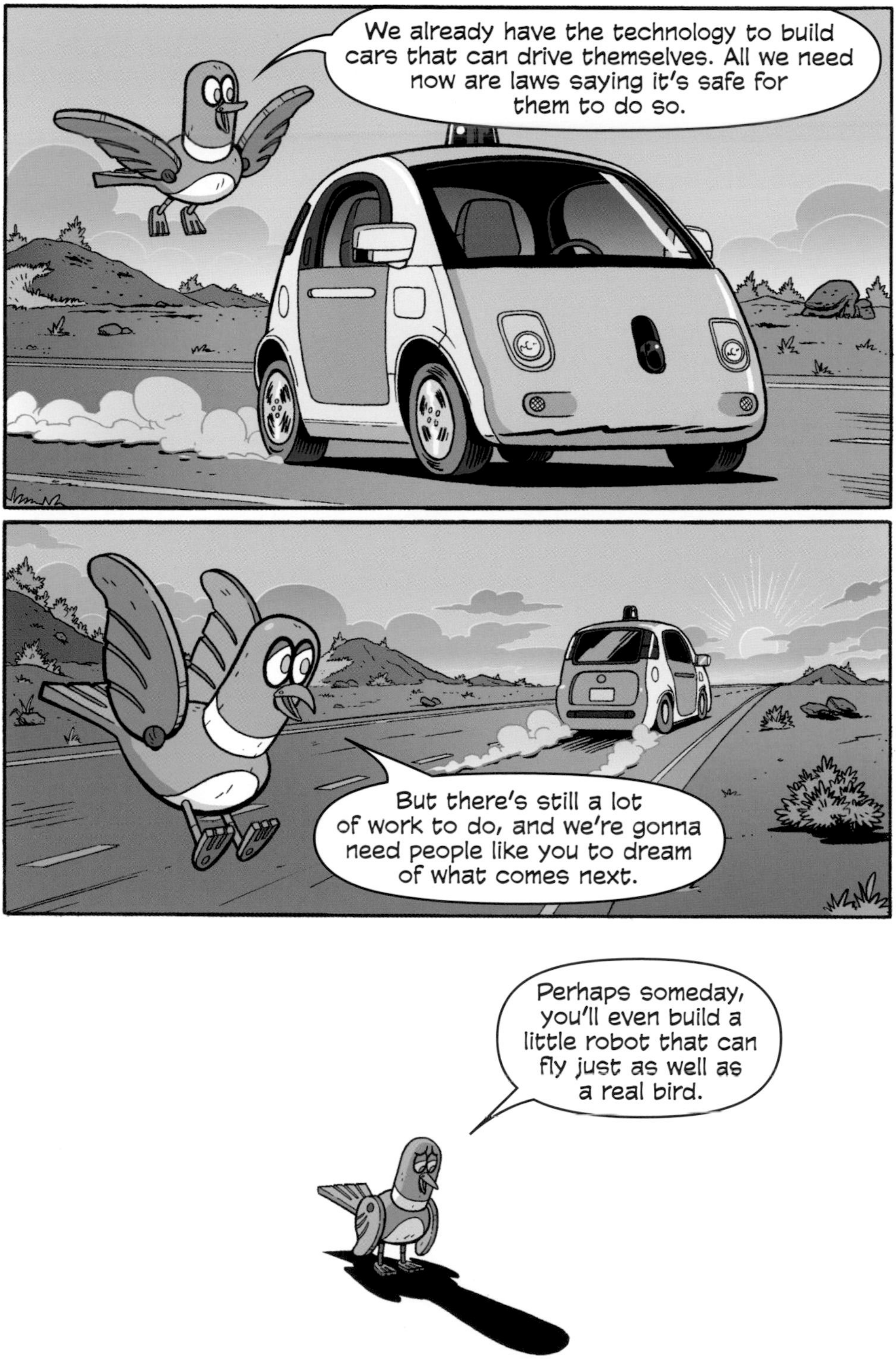
We already have the technology to build cars that can drive themselves. All we need now are laws saying it's safe for them to do so.
But there's still a lot of work to do, and we're gonna need people like you to dream of what comes next.
Perhaps someday, you'll even build a little robot that can fly just as well as a real bird.

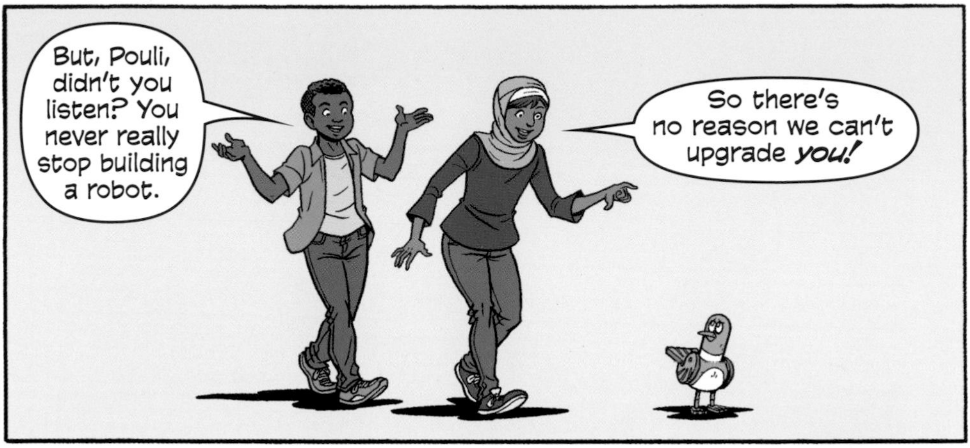
But, Pouli, didn't you listen? You never really stop building a robot.
So there's no reason we can't upgrade *you!*

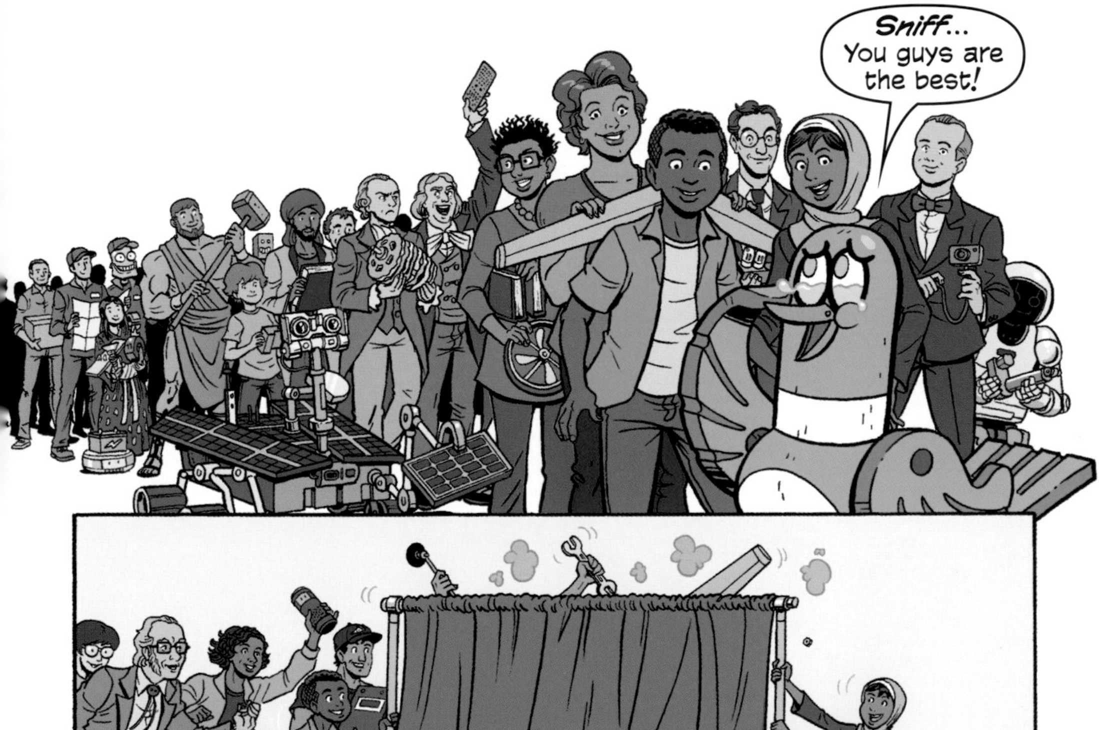
Sniff... You guys are the best!

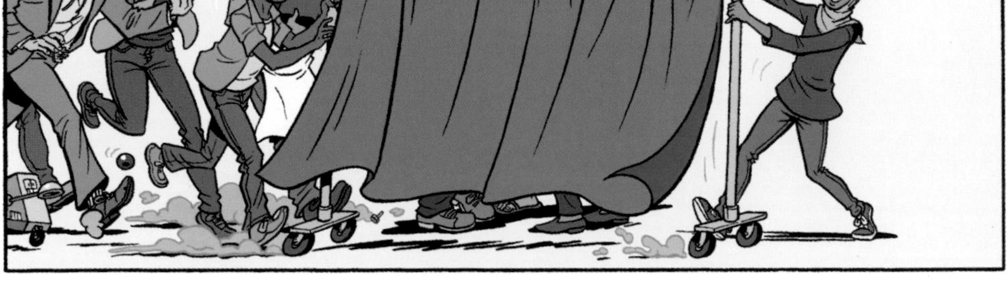

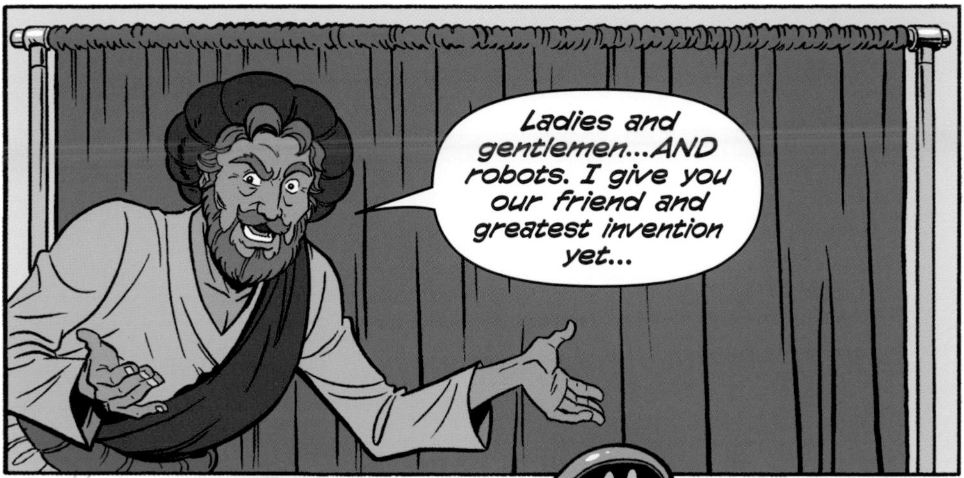
Ladies and gentlemen...AND robots. I give you our friend and greatest invention yet...

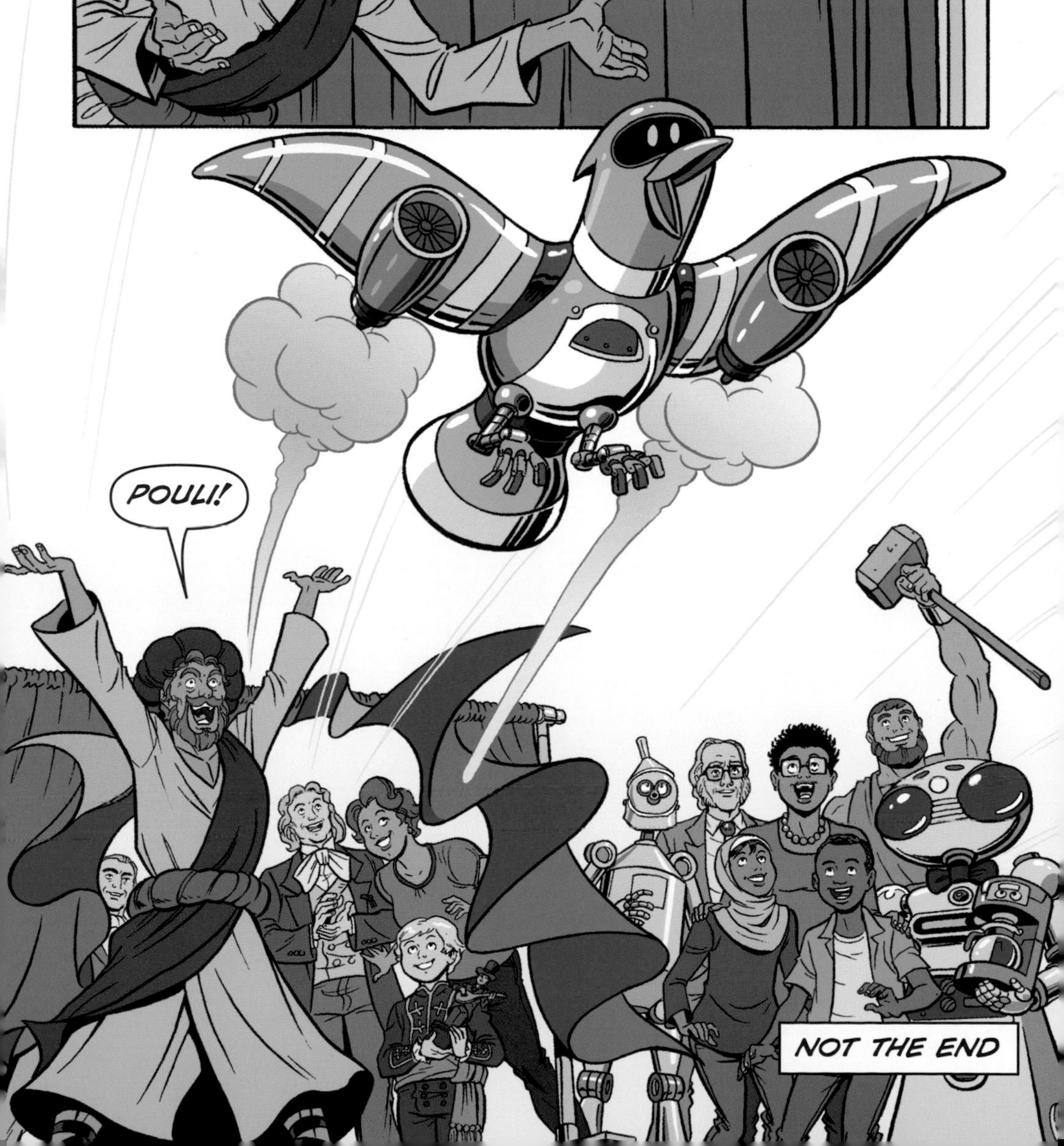
POULI!
NOT THE END

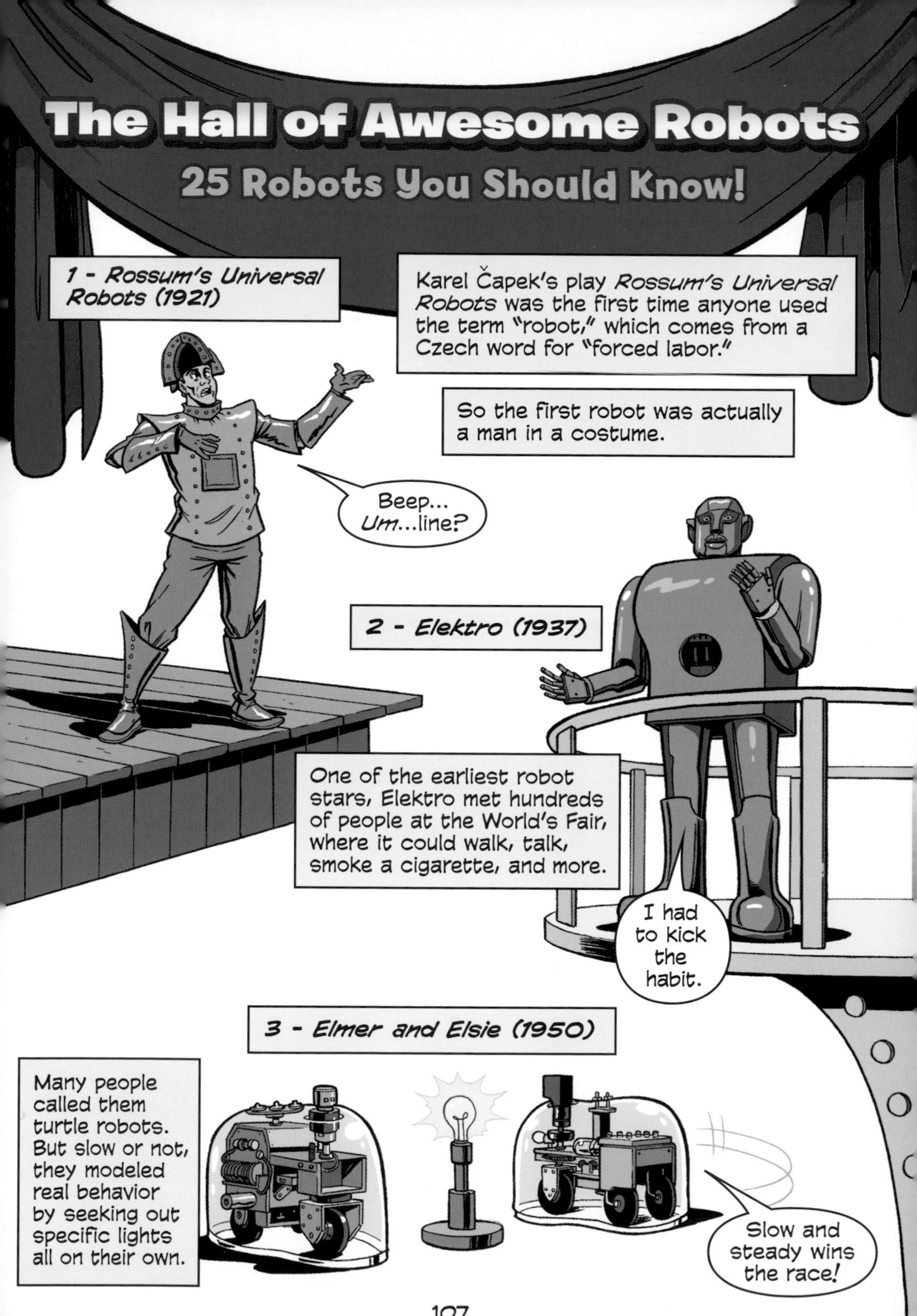

The Hall of Awesome Robots
25 Robots You Should Know!

1 - Rossum's Universal Robots (1921)

Karel Čapek's play *Rossum's Universal Robots* was the first time anyone used the term "robot," which comes from a Czech word for "forced labor."

So the first robot was actually a man in a costume.

Beep... Um...line?

2 - Elektro (1937)

One of the earliest robot stars, Elektro met hundreds of people at the World's Fair, where it could walk, talk, smoke a cigarette, and more.

I had to kick the habit.

3 - Elmer and Elsie (1950)

Many people called them turtle robots. But slow or not, they modeled real behavior by seeking out specific lights all on their own.

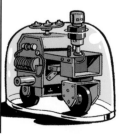 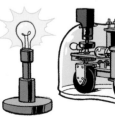 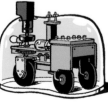

Slow and steady wins the race!

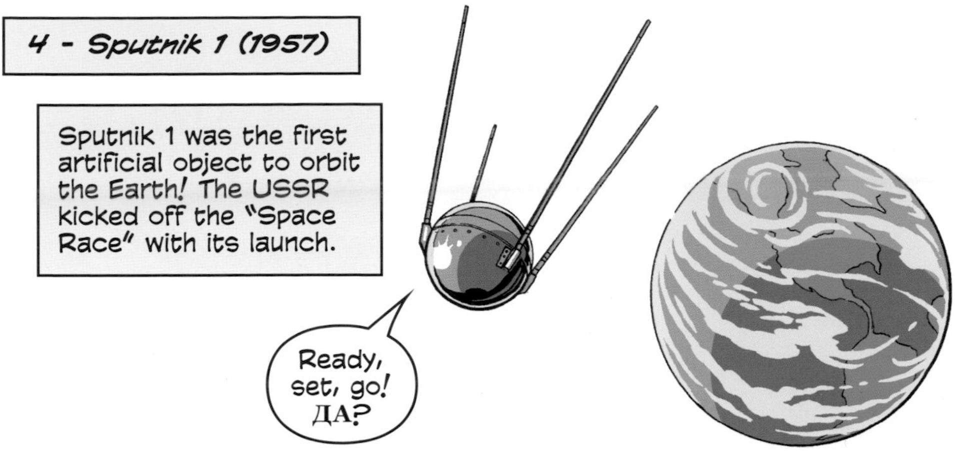
4 - Sputnik 1 (1957)
Sputnik 1 was the first artificial object to orbit the Earth! The USSR kicked off the "Space Race" with its launch.
Ready, set, go! ДА?

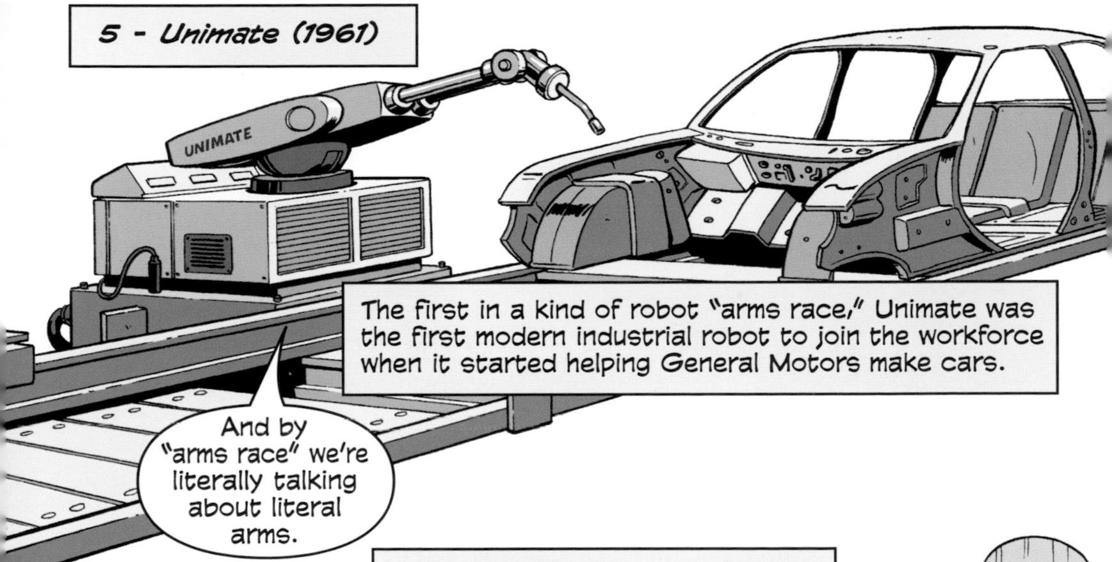
5 - Unimate (1961)
UNIMATE
The first in a kind of robot "arms race," Unimate was the first modern industrial robot to join the workforce when it started helping General Motors make cars.
And by "arms race" we're literally talking about literal arms.

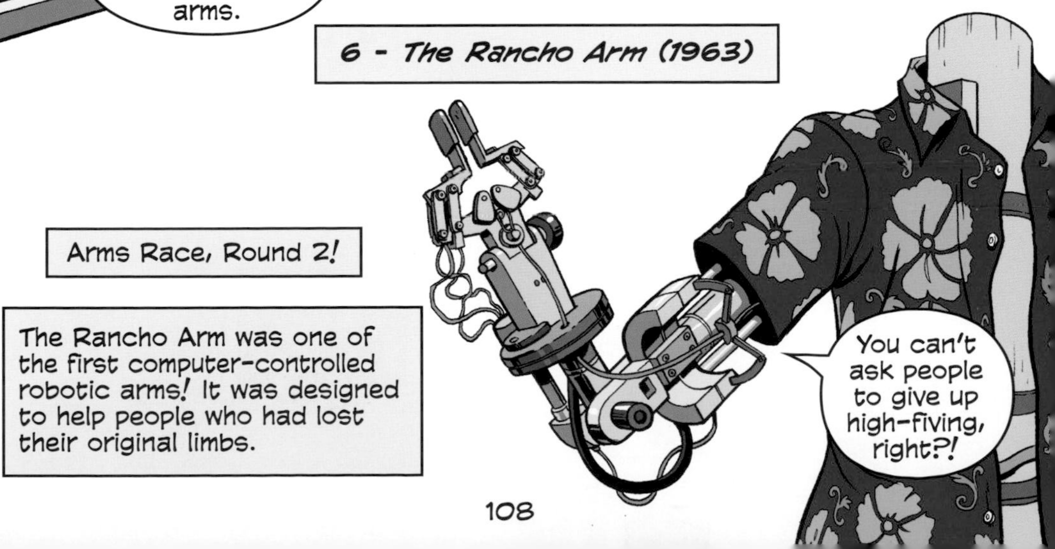
6 - The Rancho Arm (1963)
Arms Race, Round 2!
The Rancho Arm was one of the first computer-controlled robotic arms! It was designed to help people who had lost their original limbs.
You can't ask people to give up high-fiving, right?!

7 - Shakey (1966)

Shakey may be an odd name for a robot, but it was one of the first mobile robots with a visual system, meaning it could see and figure out where it was going.

...and maybe I wobbled a bit.

8 - Minsky Arm (1967)

Marvin Minsky took the arms race a step into the weird when he made the Minsky Arm, or the Tentacle Arm.

Well, I am designed after a crayfish claw. What did you expect?

9 - The Stanford Arm (1969)

The robotic arm got an upgrade! The Stanford Arm was electric and computer-controlled—the first of its kind.

A rather bright idea, don't you think?

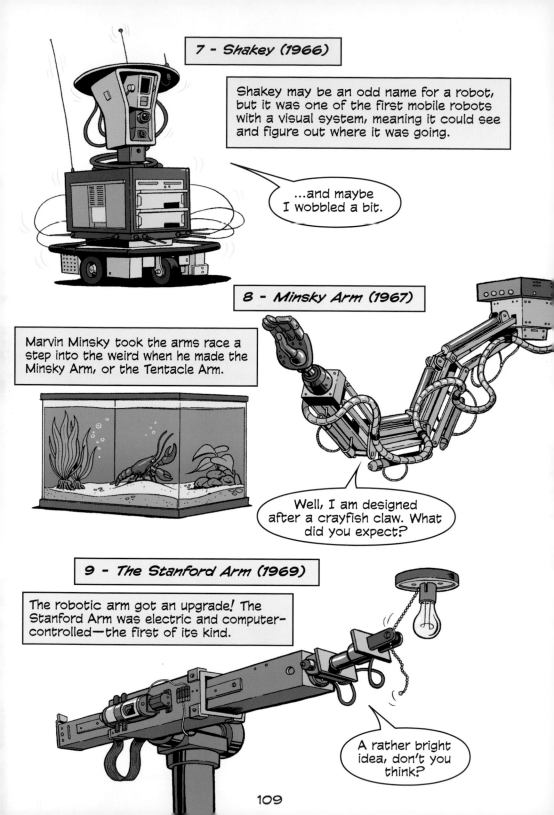

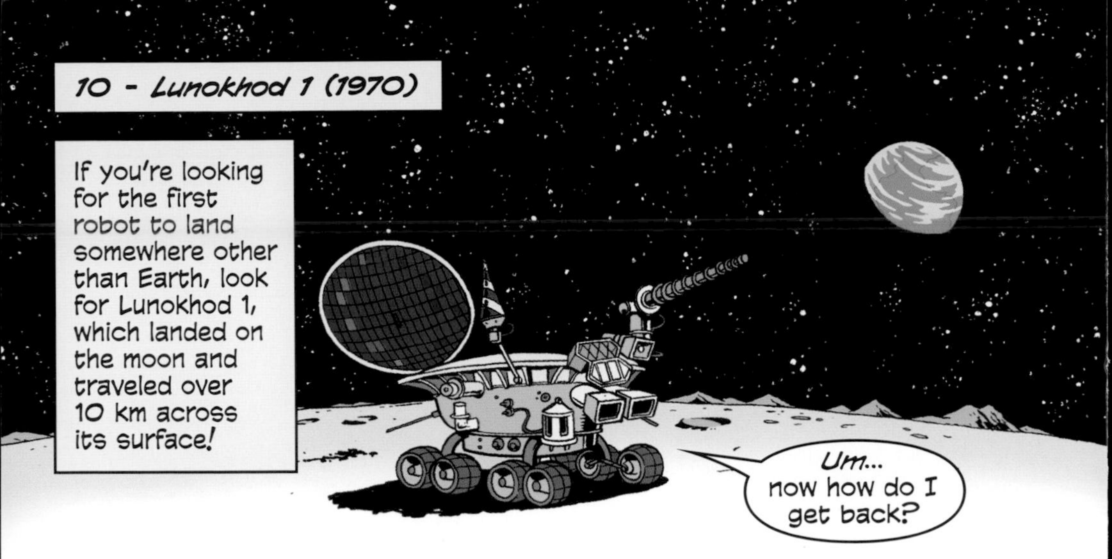
10 - Lunokhod 1 (1970)
If you're looking for the first robot to land somewhere other than Earth, look for Lunokhod 1, which landed on the moon and traveled over 10 km across its surface!
Um... now how do I get back?

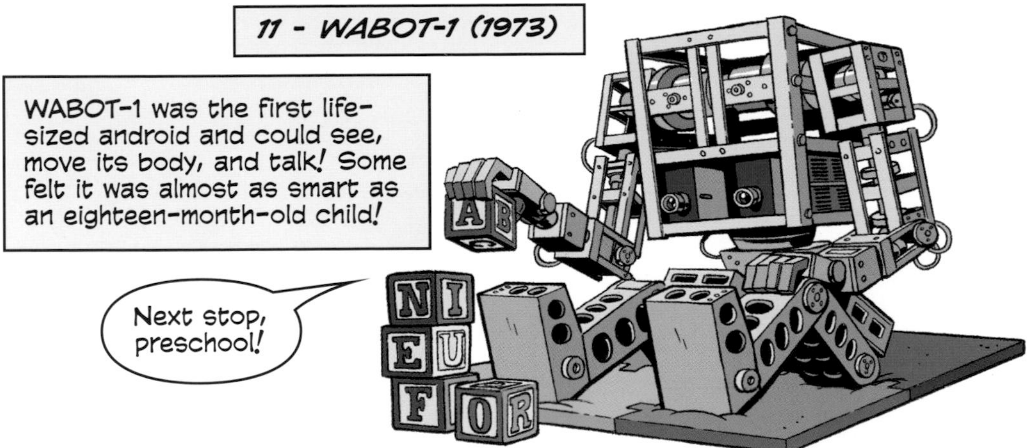
11 - WABOT-1 (1973)
WABOT-1 was the first life-sized android and could see, move its body, and talk! Some felt it was almost as smart as an eighteen-month-old child!
Next stop, preschool!
A
N I
E U
F O R

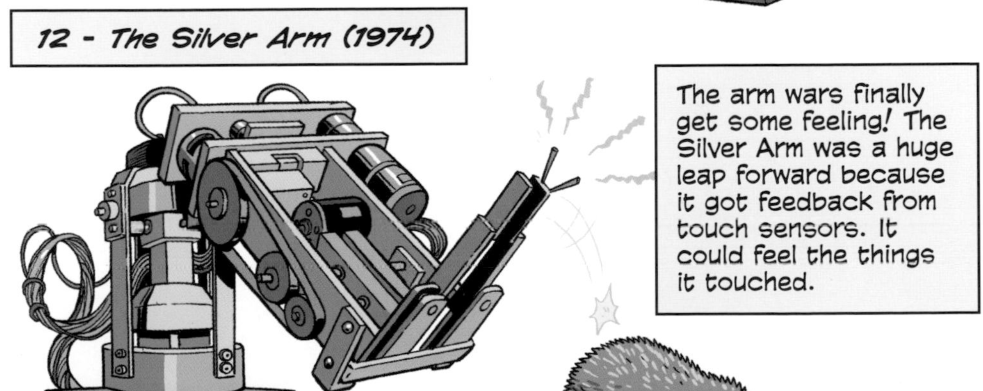
12 - The Silver Arm (1974)
The arm wars finally get some feeling! The Silver Arm was a huge leap forward because it got feedback from touch sensors. It could feel the things it touched.
Ouch!

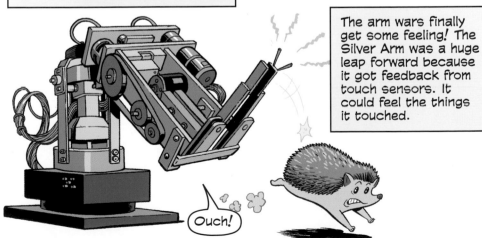

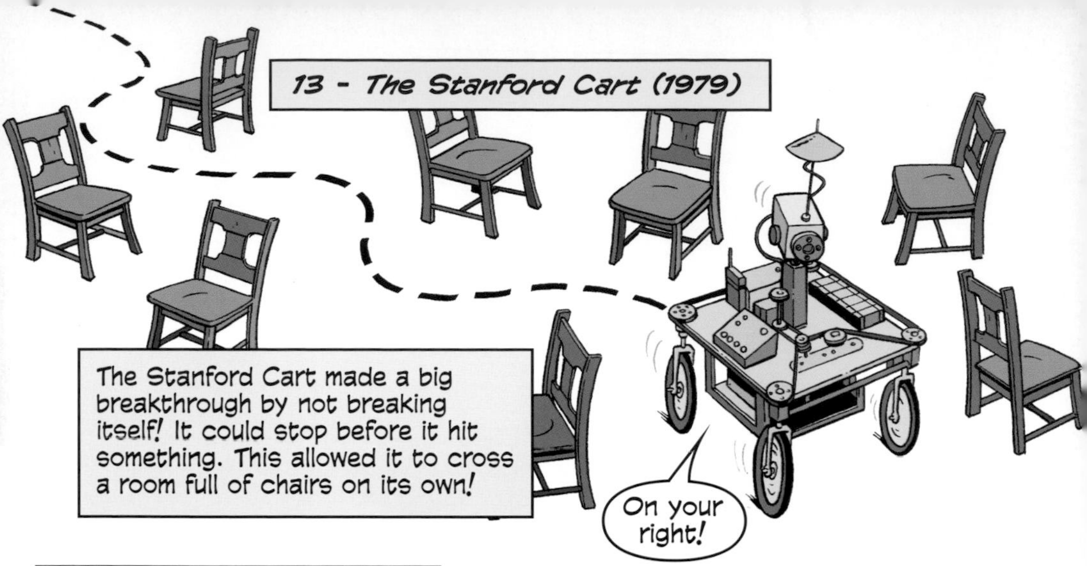
13 - The Stanford Cart (1979)
The Stanford Cart made a big breakthrough by not breaking itself! It could stop before it hit something. This allowed it to cross a room full of chairs on its own!
On your right!

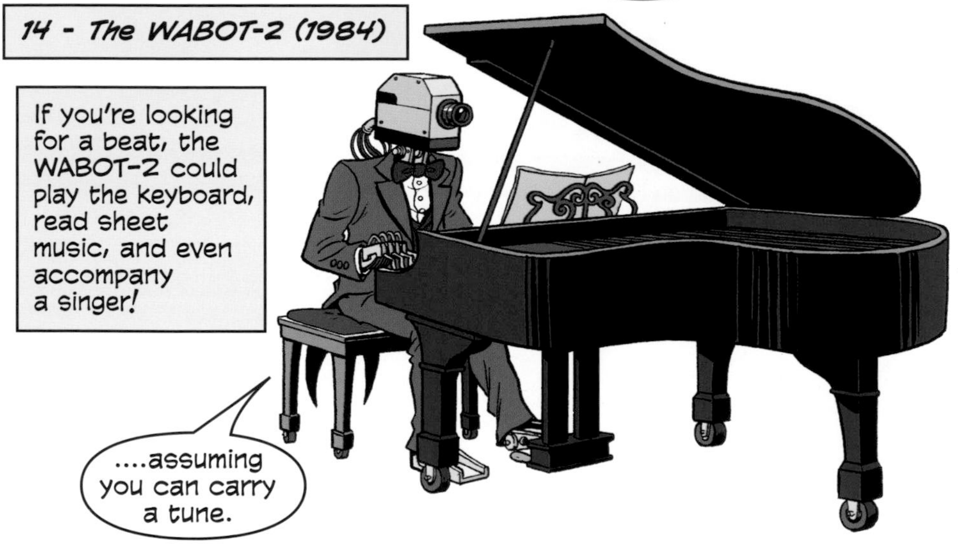
14 - The WABOT-2 (1984)
If you're looking for a beat, the WABOT-2 could play the keyboard, read sheet music, and even accompany a singer!
....assuming you can carry a tune.

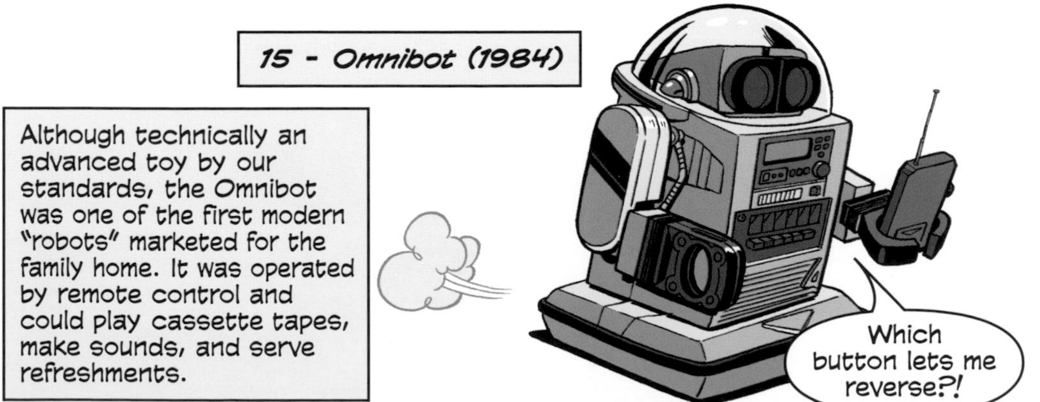
15 - Omnibot (1984)
Although technically an advanced toy by our standards, the Omnibot was one of the first modern "robots" marketed for the family home. It was operated by remote control and could play cassette tapes, make sounds, and serve refreshments.
Which button lets me reverse?!

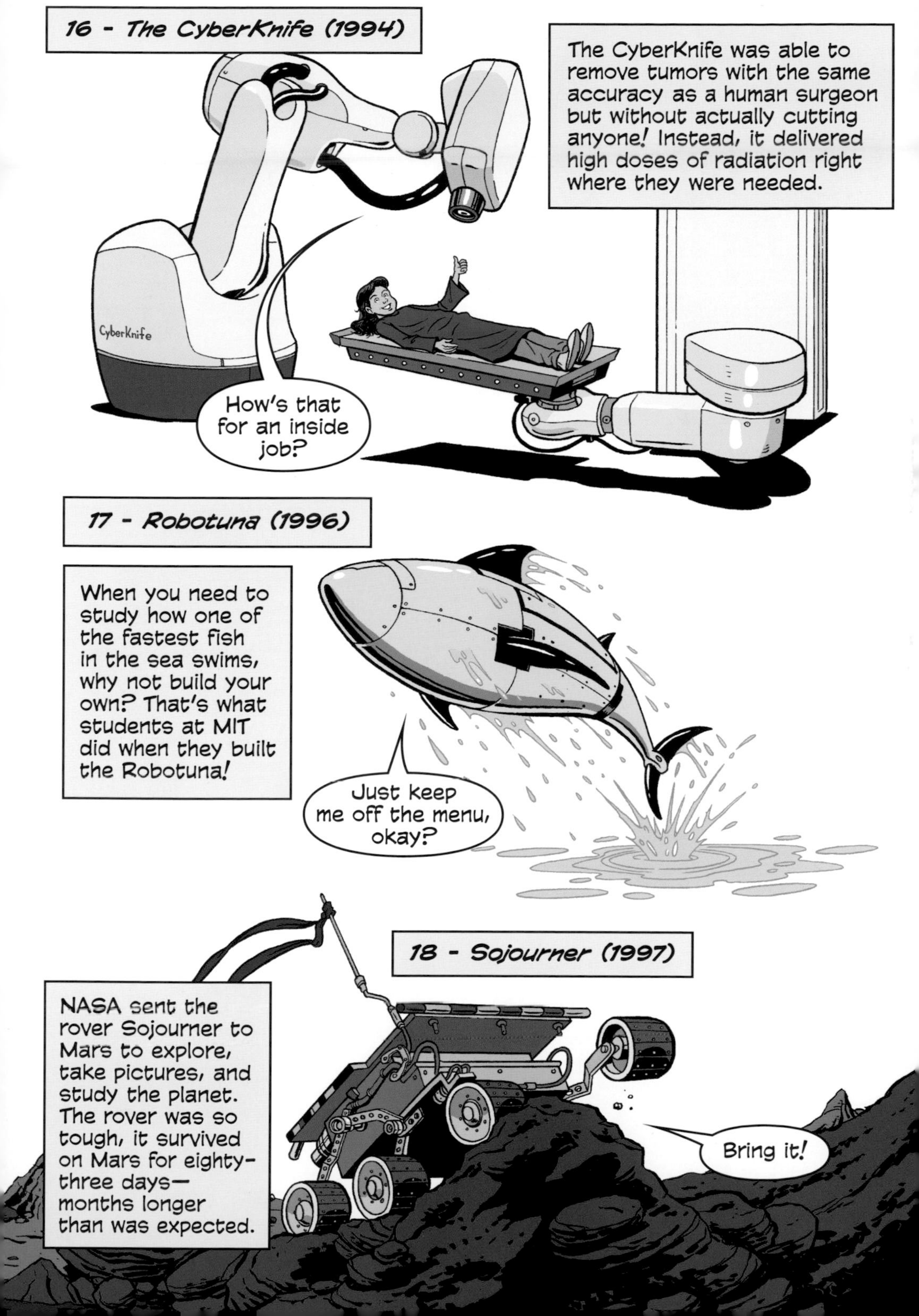
16 - The CyberKnife (1994)
The CyberKnife was able to remove tumors with the same accuracy as a human surgeon but without actually cutting anyone! Instead, it delivered high doses of radiation right where they were needed.
CyberKnife
How's that for an inside job?
17 - Robotuna (1996)
When you need to study how one of the fastest fish in the sea swims, why not build your own? That's what students at MIT did when they built the Robotuna!
Just keep me off the menu, okay?
18 - Sojourner (1997)
NASA sent the rover Sojourner to Mars to explore, take pictures, and study the planet. The rover was so tough, it survived on Mars for eighty-three days—months longer than was expected.
Bring it!

19 - AIBO (1999)

While it might not be the first robot animal, one of the first robot pets was a robot dog named AIBO. Designed by Sony, AIBO didn't just interact with its owners, it learned from them!

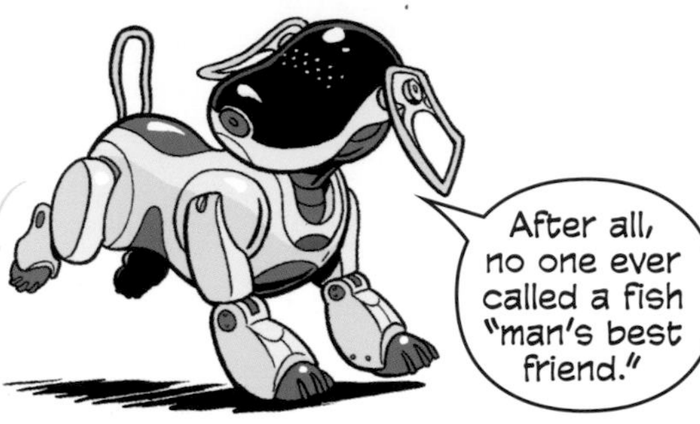
After all, no one ever called a fish "man's best friend."

20 - ASIMO (2000)

And the only thing better than a robot dog is a robot human. The robot ASIMO was invited to ring the opening bell at the NY stock exchange.

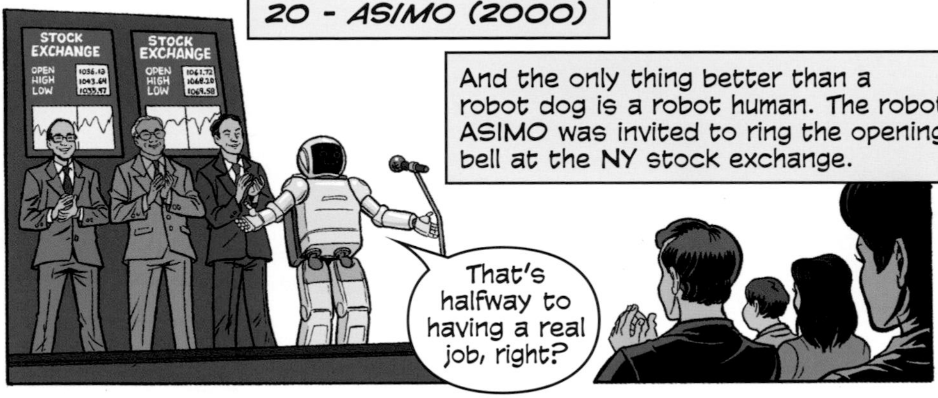
STOCK EXCHANGE
OPEN HIGH LOW
STOCK EXCHANGE
OPEN HIGH LOW
That's halfway to having a real job, right?

21 - Roomba (2002)

Although people have had robots in the form of appliances for years, the Roomba was one of the first household devices to be truly identified as a robot.

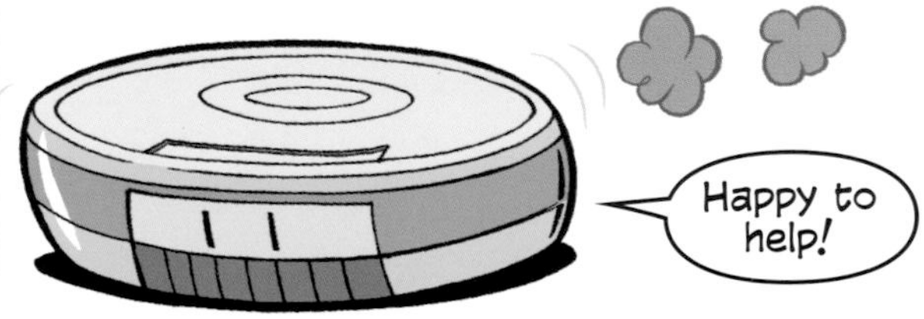
Happy to help!

22 - Spirit and Opportunity (2003)

Sojourner wasn't the only robot NASA sent to Mars. They sent both Spirit and Opportunity there as well! Like Sojourner, they've lasted much longer than people expected them to. When this was written, Opportunity was still going!

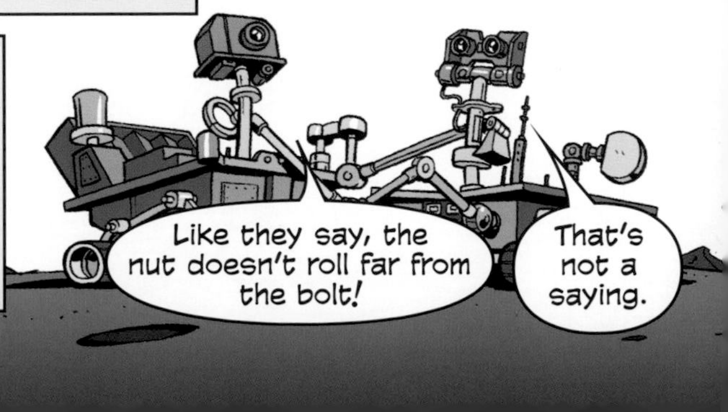
Like they say, the nut doesn't roll far from the bolt!
That's not a saying.

23 - Self-Replicating Robots (2005)

Cornell University made a huge leap forward by designing a robot that built copies of itself when given the right parts.

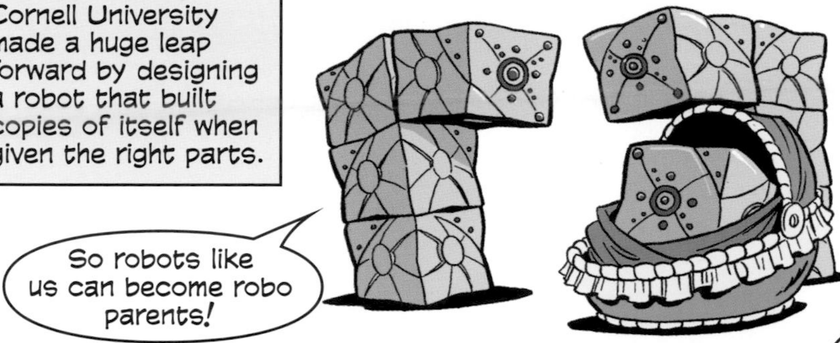
So robots like us can become robo parents!

24 - Stanley (2005)

Stanford University's self-driving car Stanley won the DARPA Grand Challenge! Stanley drove over a hundred miles in the desert without any human help!

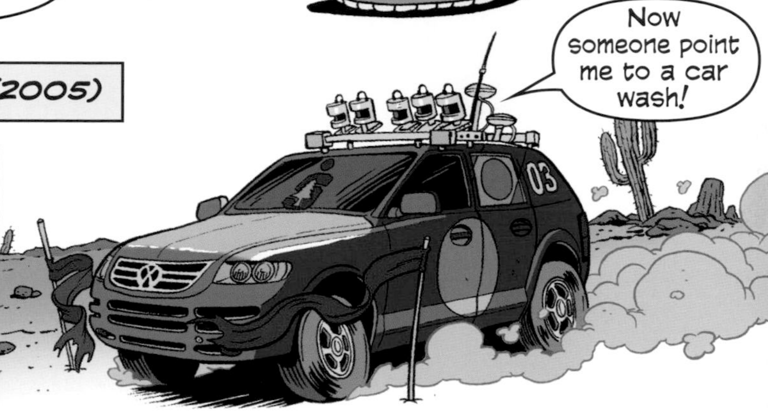
Now someone point me to a car wash!
03

25 - Jibo (in development)

Robots of the future will not only be useful tools, but also have unique personalities. Jibo is a social robot designed to help with day-to-day tasks as well as cracking jokes, make expressive gestures, and have facial features.

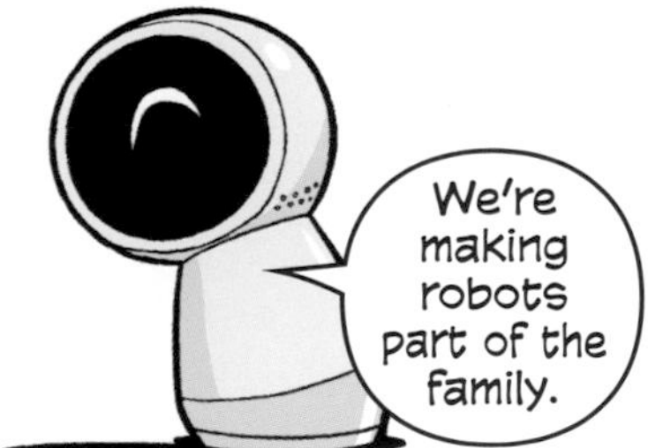
We're making robots part of the family.

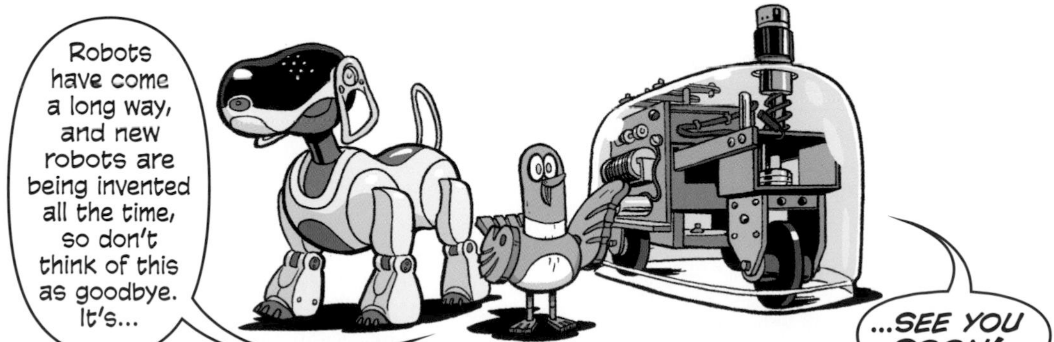
Robots have come a long way, and new robots are being invented all the time, so don't think of this as goodbye. It's...
...SEE YOU SOON!

Drones! Talking and Flying!

We've learned a lot about robots, but now let's take a closer look at drones. Every aerial drone (this type is called a quadcopter) is made up of two basic systems: one that talks and one that flies. Here's how they work:

The drone's battery holds its power.

The ESC (electronic speed controller) draws power from the battery and sends the right amount to the motors (and often other components).

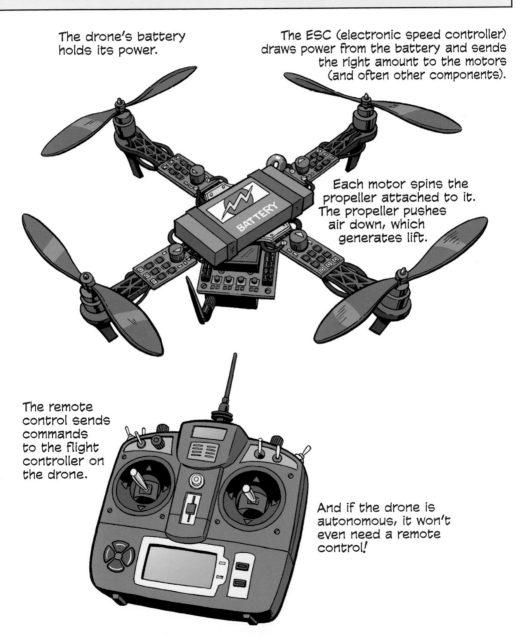

Each motor spins the propeller attached to it. The propeller pushes air down, which generates lift.

The remote control sends commands to the flight controller on the drone.

And if the drone is autonomous, it won't even need a remote control!

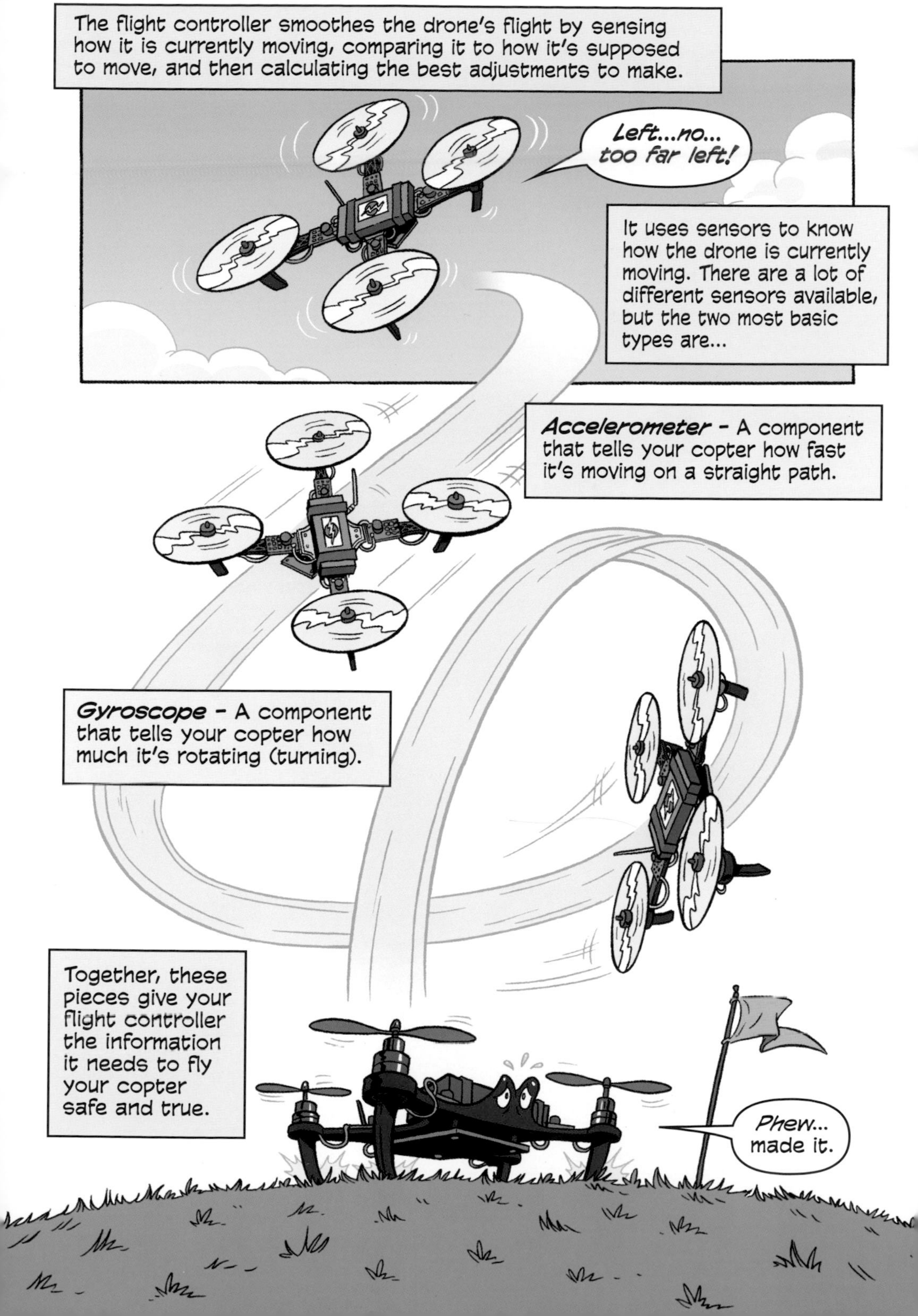
The flight controller smoothes the drone's flight by sensing how it is currently moving, comparing it to how it's supposed to move, and then calculating the best adjustments to make.
Left...no... too far left!
It uses sensors to know how the drone is currently moving. There are a lot of different sensors available, but the two most basic types are...
Accelerometer - A component that tells your copter how fast it's moving on a straight path.
Gyroscope - A component that tells your copter how much it's rotating (turning).
Together, these pieces give your flight controller the information it needs to fly your copter safe and true.
Phew... made it.

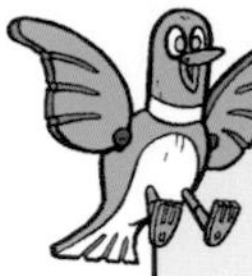

GLOSSARY

Actuator: A part that moves (or helps move) another part of a machine.

Antenna: A wire that sends and receives signals in the air. Antennas are used by remote-controlled machines to make sure the machine can "hear" the remote.

Archimedes' screw: A device that pulls water up higher when turned.

Artificial intelligence: The ability of a machine to display human-like intelligence.

Automatic/autonomous: When a machine can do something on its own, without a person helping.

Automaton/automata: A machine that could move and perform a complicated task automatically. The precursors to true robots.

Cam: A device that turns a circular motion into a back-and-forth motion or a back-and-forth motion into a circular one. Cams acted as programs for early robots.

Camera: A machine that captures and records images. Many cameras can see things human eyes can't, like heat or different kinds of light.

Circuit: The path electricity takes inside a machine.

Computer: A machine that can receive, store, display, and manipulate large amounts of information.

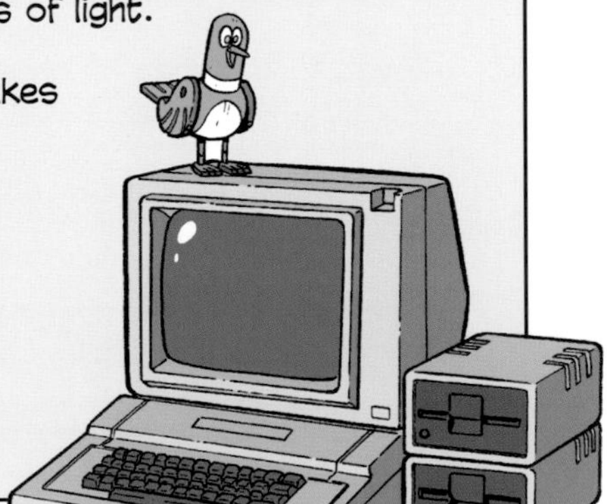

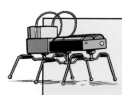

Conductor: A device that lets something easily move through it. In robots, it's usually a piece of metal that moves electricity from one point to another.

Controller/microcontroller: A term for the computer (or computers) inside a machine that gives the machine its instructions.

Converter: A device that changes one thing into another. In this book, converters change the type or amount of electrical current in a robot.

Current: The flow of electricity.

Drone: A machine that flies or swims without a person on board controlling it.

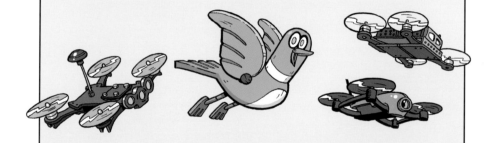

Engine: A machine that converts energy from fuel into motion.

Ethics: A branch of knowledge dedicated to behavior, morality, and what is considered good vs. bad.

Fastener: Something that attaches together at least two other things.

Frame: The structure in a machine that gives its other components support.

Hephaestus: Greek god of making things, the forge, and fire.

Hydraulic: When a machine uses a liquid (like water) to move or operate parts of itself by pushing and pulling that liquid.

Jacquard loom: A machine that uses instructions from punch cards to produce different designs in the fabric it makes.

Karakuri ningyo: A type of Japanese automaton that appears to be a person performing an activity, like serving tea.

Lever: A bar that tips back and forth on a single point.

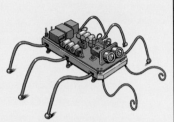

Machine: A thing made of smaller parts that does something only when you give it energy.

Mass spectrometer: A machine that tells you what elements make up a substance by measuring the mass of different particles in that substance.

Mobile: Being able to move freely.

Motor: Like an engine, it's a machine that converts energy from fuel into motion. Sometimes it means a smaller, more powerful engine.

NASA: The National Aeronautics and Space Administration. The part of the U.S. government that studies space and builds things that go to space.

Output: Anything that allows a robot to express itself to its environment. Components that light up, make noise, etc. are outputs.

Perimeter: The outer edge of an area.

Pneumatic: When a machine uses a gas (like air) to move or operate parts of itself by pushing and pulling that gas.

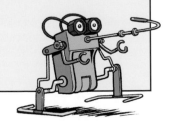

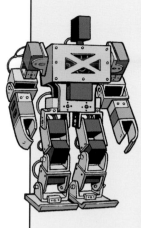

Preprogrammed robot: A robot that already has a set of instructions on what it should do once it's built.

Program: A set of instructions telling a machine, computer, or robot what to do.

Programmable: A machine, computer, or robot that can be given a set of instructions (a program) on what to do once it's built. Often, if something is programmable, you can also change the program to give it a new set of instructions later.

Pulley: A wheel (or wheels) with a rope, belt, or other kind of connector used to lift heavy things or change the direction of a force.

Punch card: A sturdy card with holes cut (i.e., "punched") into it that acts as a program for a machine.

Resistor: A device that limits the amount of electricity entering a circuit.

Robot: A machine that senses something in its environment, makes a choice about what it senses, and performs an action in response.

Screw: A simple machine that is made up of a tapered cylinder with a ribbon wrapped around it at an angle or cut into it at an angle.

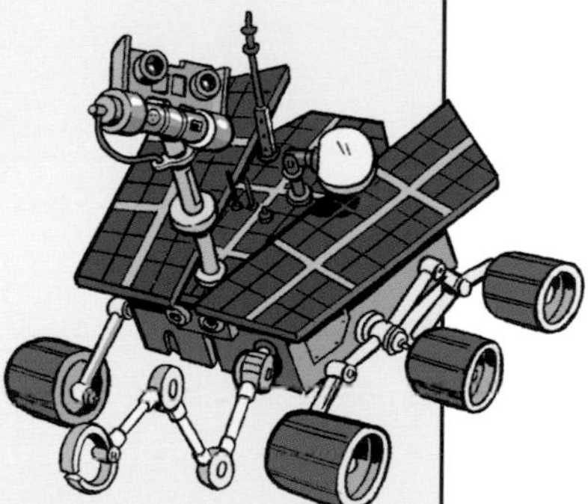

Sensor: Part of a machine that can detect something outside of itself. What it detects is often included in the sensor's name. For example, heat sensor, motion sensor, etc.

Simple machines: The most basic machines, like levers, pulleys, and screws, which all other machines (complex machines) are made from.

Solar panel: A device that creates electricity from sunlight.

USB: Universal Serial Bus. USB are cords and ports designed to connect machines to each other so they can share information.

Vacuum tubes: An electrical part that has very little air inside of it. (It was vacuumed out.) They were often used in older electronic devices.

Virtual assistant: A type of computer program designed to help people with many of their daily tasks (keeping track of meetings, getting directions, ordering things online, etc.).

Whisker sensor: A type of sensor with a thin wire attached to it. The sensor detects when the wire is bent, which means the "whisker" touched something.

Wi-Fi: A term that means a machine can talk to other machines wirelessly.

Wire: A long, thin piece of metal that electricity flows through. It's usually coated in plastic.

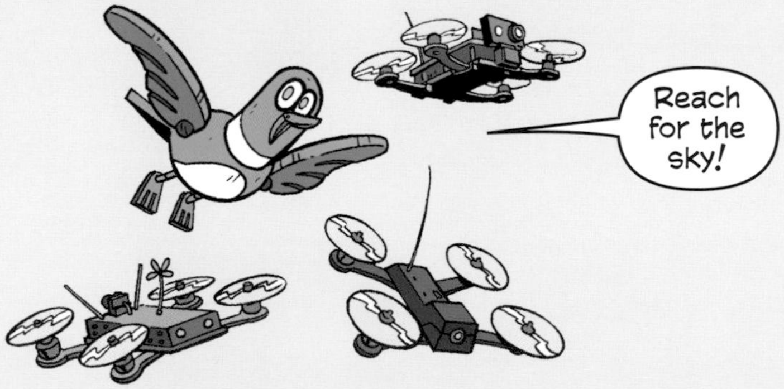
Reach for the sky!

GET TO KNOW YOUR UNIVERSE!

SCIENCE COMICS

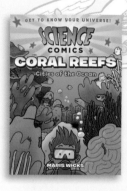

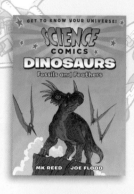

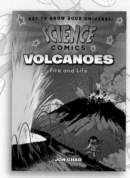

"Awesome!"
—*Popular Science*

"An excellent addition to school and classroom libraries."
—*School Library Journal*

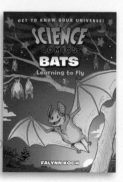

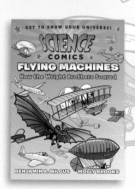

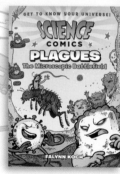

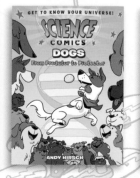

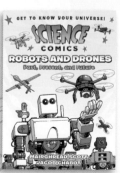

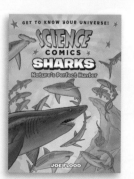

"Perfect for kids hungry for science."
—*Booklist*

...And more books coming soon!

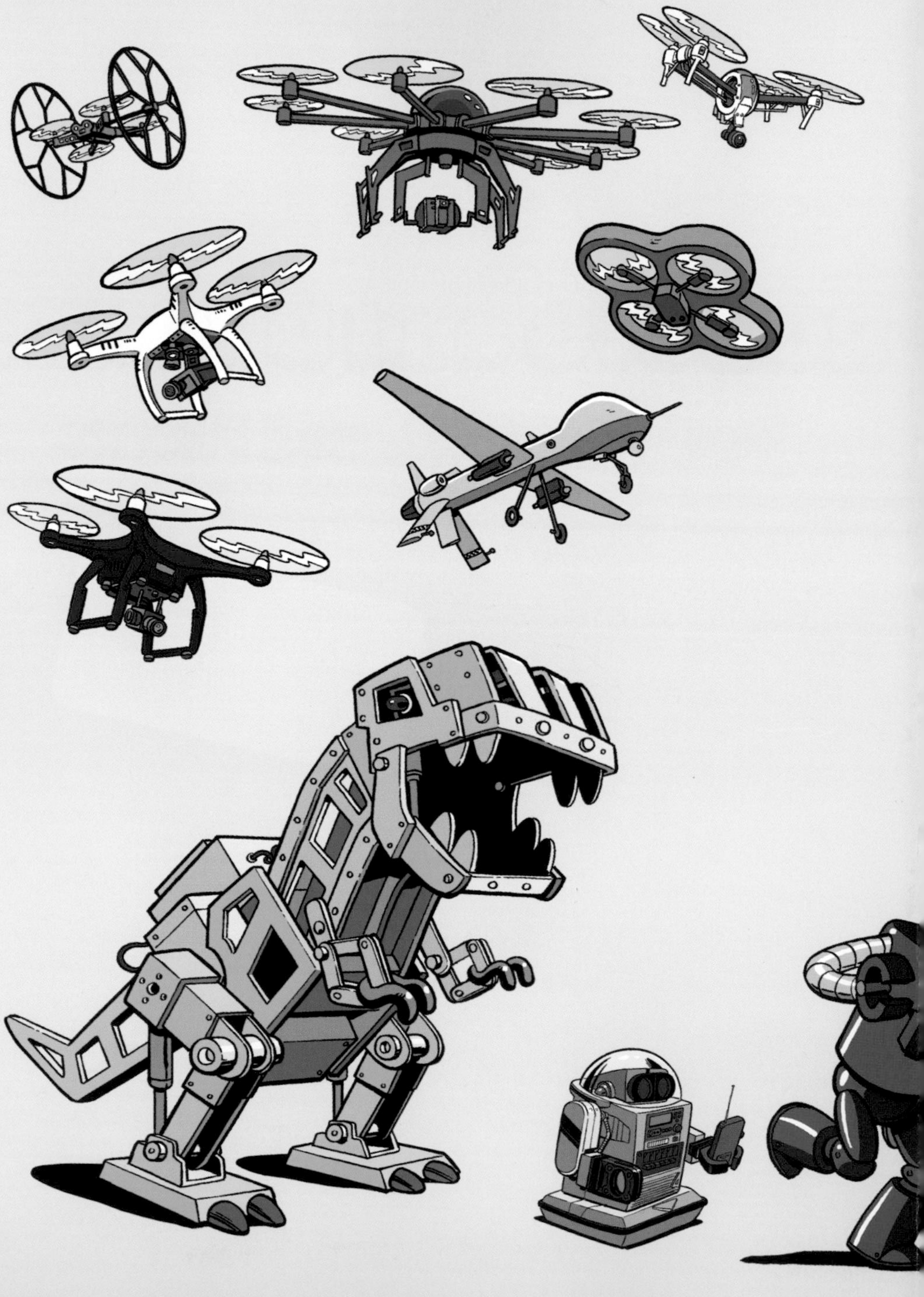

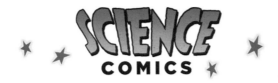

SCIENCE COMICS

ROBOTS and DRONES
Past, Present, and Future

T0018140